GO TO THE START

LIFE AS A
WORLD CUP SKI RACER

MICHAEL JANYK

 FriesenPress

One Printers Way
Altona, MB R0G 0B0
Canada

www.friesenpress.com

ISBN
978-1-03-915289-2 (Hardcover)
978-1-03-915288-5 (Paperback)
978-1-03-915290-8 (eBook)

1. BIOGRAPHY & AUTOBIOGRAPHY, SPORTS

Distributed to the trade by The Ingram Book Company

DISCLAIMER

Sport has had an overall positive impact on my life. I travelled the world, made wonderful and lifelong friends, competed on the world stage, made a living, and lived out my childhood dream, but I know this isn't the case for everyone who competes in sport. Even if all these highlights are present, there are many forms of maltreatment and abuse that can turn sport into a damaging experience with negative impacts on the lives of athletes who may have started out with the same innocent dream as me. Even within my story there are teammates, coaches, and others who may have experienced the opposite to me, and where maybe I was sheltered, they were not. The following events are from my perspective, written from memory, and I confirmed facts with friends, coaches, and teammates where possible. Specific events may be remembered differently by others.

I share my story because of all the amazing athletes, musicians, artists, and people who have shared theirs before me. These different stories resonated and inspired me throughout the chapters of my life, and it was in theirs that I found meaning and understanding in mine.

I hope you enjoy.

LAND ACKNOWLEDGEMENT

I grew up skiing on the shared and unceded territory of the **Sk̲wx̲u7mesh Úxumixw (Squamish) nation** and **Lílwat7úl (Lil'wat) nation** and on Whistler Mountain, originally known by them respectively as **Sk̲wik̲w (by the Squamish nation)** and **Cwítima/Kacwítima (by the Lil'wat nation).**

TABLE OF CONTENTS

FOREWORD

THE OLYMPICS ARE SPECIAL. On all levels, and in most sports, making an Olympic team and representing one's country on the world stage is the chance of a lifetime. The public enjoys glimpses into the lives of athletes, winter and summer, every two years on rotation. We are inspired by not just results but by the journey of these seemingly superhuman people doing magical things on ice and snow, water and solid ground. We come to know them by name and identify with them through the struggles and joys they share. They give themselves to a fleeting chance at glory and come away, no matter the result, with wisdom to share. The problem is, we rarely get to receive it. The media moves on and athletes continue or retire. The opportunity to learn from these athletes is often lost. Thankfully, some of them write books. Mike Janyk has not only allowed us to GO TO THE START with him, but he's also offered a story that is for everyone. A journey of a lifetime with so many twists and turns, and not just on the slopes.

Reading this book allowed me, someone with a whole lot of sport experience (winter and summer!), to be taken to a place I've never been and likely will never go. I felt like I was on the slopes with Mike, learning how to ski, jumping in headfirst into the wild world of alpine skiing, and the speed disciplines, of such an intensely dangerous and exhilarating sport. I can't imagine having the courage to execute the perfect race because quite frankly, skiing scares the crap out of me. Yet, Mike took me there. But it's not just about skiing. Mike's story is about struggle, growth and ultimately, acceptance. As much as I loved being taken into the travelling alpine ski circus through his stories, I enjoyed more the transformation of this fine person, Mike Janyk. Through his struggles and joys, and all the places and spaces in between, I witnessed someone learn who they are, find peace with who that person is and ultimately embrace changes and challenges in ways that allow for growth and development as a human being. This is why I love this book so much.

If you are an aspiring athlete, seasoned Olympian, coach, parent, teacher, or anyone looking to be inspired, this book is for you.

Clara Hughes O.C., O.M., OLY
6 x Olympic Medalist, speed skating and cycling
Mental Health Advocate

PROLOGUE

WHEN I STOOD IN THE start area, it suddenly felt empty. I looked around and saw Dave, who was in first; Ryan, who was in third; and a few others waiting to run, but they all seemed so far away. I would start in front of Dave and after Ryan, sandwiched into the top three after the first run, yet I felt alone, and an agonizing pain developed in my stomach. I'd experienced nerves before, but this was something new. My internal monologue consisted of: *Holy shit, I could win today. This could put me on the national team. I could be the best junior slalom skier in the country.*

All of the future's prospects smacked me in the face, and I soon felt it in my gut. Then came some new thoughts: *Why am I here? Why am I doing this? Why am I putting myself through such discomfort, such agony? For what? Why would I go to the start?*

Here I was, a few minutes from the start of a race that could be a stepping stone towards realizing my dream, and I felt awful. I could barely move my legs, let alone ski. I stood cemented in my boots, looking around at my competitors. No one seemed to be experiencing my paralysis. Soon though, in the silence created by my fears, another new voice came through:

Just go to the start.

What? I asked.

Just go to the start.

But I can't move.

Just go to the start.

Ok.

This seemed to be the only agreeable option to becoming unstuck. I inched forward with this voice repeatedly saying, *Go to the start.*

And so I went. I clicked into my skis, slid into position to the start gate, recalled my technical cues, took a few deep breaths, and put my poles over the timing wand. I still felt the stomach pain. I still had no answers.

"Racer ready." the starter called out.

In... Out... I paused for two last breaths, knowing I had only a short window to choose my own time to break the timing wand after the starter's final word. In... Out... There was nowhere to go but down.

"Go." the signal was given.

I pushed out to start the clock and was on course. By the time I reached the third and fourth gate, the pain in my stomach was gone.

I had my answers. *This is why I do it.*

I felt my skis right away; the front of the ski was picking up early in the turn, connecting me to the snow. My timing was in sync and flowing with the hill. I was dancing!

This is why I go through the pain and discomfort—for the feeling of being alive on course, I thought to myself while executing one great turn after another. Being connected to my actions, moving in partnership with the course and terrain, I was expressing everything I'd sensed inside for all these years.

I danced my way through the course, every turn an opportunity to build speed and showcase my abilities. When I crossed the finish line, I'd taken the lead, ecstatic, with only one racer to go.

When Dave, the leader from the first run, crossed with a total time behind mine, it hit me that I had won. In the celebration with teammates, coaches, and family that quickly followed, my nerves, the gut-twisting feelings from the start, and all the questions were easily forgotten.

Climbing on top of the podium between third place, Ryan, the best-ranked for our age in the country; and second place, Dave, a national team member, I also lost sight of the answers given to me on course. As I was handed the trophy, flowers, and a ceremonial cheque, my first-ever prize money, the feeling of dancing on my skis gently faded. With the medal around my neck, smiling for pictures while looking out over my teammates, friends, family, coaches, competitors, and colleagues, the thought came: *Maybe this is why I do it. Maybe this is why I go through the discomfort. Maybe this is why I go to the start.*

CHAPTER 1
THE EARLY YEARS

WHEN I WAS TEN YEARS old, I remember watching the Barcelona Olympic Summer Games and being taken over by them. In the middle of the summer, I glued myself to the one TV set in the lobby of Sandy Beach Lodge, a resort in the Okanagan where our family stayed for two weeks every year. From the opening ceremonies and through the events, I saw superheroes doing extraordinary things. I couldn't get enough, and I took in as much as my parents let me.

How does someone get there? What are their lives like? How is this even possible?

This was the spark I needed, and a fire was lit. I wanted to be an athlete and compete in the Olympic Games. I didn't have any of the answers or even know in which sport I'd compete, but something in me said this was it, this was my dream.

Growing up in between two sisters, there was already a natural level of sibling competition, or at least I was competitive trying to keep up with my older sister, Britt, and doing what I could to assert myself over my younger sister, Stephanie. Our parents had us in a range of sports from an early age, keeping us active, and as my mom would say, providing an outlet for my excessive energy. Soccer, baseball, field hockey, tennis, and gymnastics were the main ones, and my mom, Andrée, was sure to teach us the physical and spiritual benefits each of them offered. There was always an opportunity for a bigger lesson. In soccer it was the power of working as a team and involving everyone in the play. In gymnastics it was the benefits of getting to know the body and coordinating our movements, and for tennis it was the contrast between trying to beat an opponent and maintaining respect for their play while staying focussed on your own. Mom taught us to play with this mantra: "I accept this ball with love, and I return it with love." Of course we'd snicker and find this a little silly as kids, but throughout my career I often found myself whispering it to myself when the nerves got too high and the pressures of a big performance too great: "I accept this course with love and I ski it with love."

Both our parents were involved in our sports activities, either through coaching our teams or volunteering at events, though my dad, Bill, seemed happy to take a back seat to let Mom drive the athletic front. On this, she had two rules for participating: 1) When you decide to commit, you give your full effort, and 2) Play fair and with respect for your opponent. The results were secondary; primary was how we played the game and showed up as teammates. Not that we always lived up to this, but it offered a benchmark to come back to.

Mom also provided opportunities to grow our independence at a young age by giving us the freedom of choice. When Britt and I were in grades three and one, respectively, we rode our bikes the twenty five blocks to school for the first time alone. Mom's message to us was simple: "When you arrive at an intersection, look both ways before you cross the street. If you do, you live; if you don't, you die." With this to consider, we were off.

Out of all the sports, though, skiing was the family's main activity; it was in our blood. Each winter weekend, we made the trip from Vancouver to Whistler to ski as a family, with Mom leading the way. She had grown up on the North Shore of Vancouver with two younger brothers and played a range of sports, mostly on boys' teams since there weren't many organized programs for girls in the 1950s. Ski racing was one of their common sports, with all three joining the racing programs on Grouse Mountain, one of the three local hills near the city, and where Mom reached her heights of sport, joining camps with the national team and racing against the likes of Nancy Greene Raine.

My mom and uncles came to the sport honestly. Their father, my grandfather, Peter Vajda, was a skier and racer in his own time and was involved in the sport for most of his life. He immigrated to Canada from

Hungary via the US while competing in the States with The University of Zürich ski team sometime in the late 1930s. When World War Two broke out, he received word from his father to stay in North America, and with this landed in Banff and the Rocky Mountains. Over the next few years, he explored, skied these mountains, and forged a deep bond to the development of Canadian skiing. Eventually laying roots in Vancouver in the mid 1940s, he worked as an engineer, who, in part, designed the first chairlift on Grouse Mountain, one of the first double chairlifts in Canada at the time. Strengthening his connection to skiing, he was also the coach for the University of British Columbia ski team and led the post-war restart of ski racing in the region. He had a saying about the mountains that Mom passed on to us: "You can never conquer a mountain, it only tolerates you."

Of course, I knew very little about this history when my ten-year-old self had the dream to be in the Olympics, though clearly the stage was set for ski racing to be the sport of choice.

Mom was our first coach, and rightfully so. There were attempts to put us in ski school, but I quickly put an end to this at five years old. On that infamous day, my parents had plans to ski with friends—Mom just needed to drop me off with the instructor and she was on her way. I resisted. After some kicking and screaming, I had an idea.

I started the bargaining, of which she was all ears. "Mom, I'll make you a deal. You stay and watch the first run of the group, and if three kids out of the lot fall, I get to go skiing with you."

Mom pondered the details intently, always intrigued with a wager from a child. "Ok, Michael, you have a deal: if three of the group fall on the first run, you can come skiing with me."

We shook hands and the bet was on.

The instructor, Mom, and I stood at the top of the run and watched the group start off one by one. The first skier went down: crash number one. I shot a smug smile at my mom. The second and third made it clean, and she returned the smirking glance. But skiers four and five both went down before the halfway point, and on seeing this, I turned to the instructor with the same grin on my face, handed over my pinny, and said, "Have fun with these losers, I'm going to ski with my mom."

From this day forward and for the next five years, our days on hill were spent skiing as a family, exploring the trees, bowls, couloirs, groomers, jumps, and anything else Whistler/Blackcomb had to offer six- to twelve-year-old kids. This was my heaven, chasing Britt, trying to beat her in anything I could, watching Mom seemingly outski everyone on the mountain, Steph learning behind us, and Dad supporting the group.

In the fall after my little Olympic realization, Britt and I wanted to join the ski-racing program at the Whistler Mountain Ski Club. A few of our friends were already in the program and we were seeking a bit more competition. We went to Mom and Dad with the request to join.

"Are you sure? Do you really want to do this?" they responded.

We enthusiastically nodded our heads, and our parents looked at each other, realizing they would have a hard time saying no to it. As usual, though, when we asked for something, it came with a deal to hold up our end of the bargain.

"Ok, we can join the ski club..." Mom started with a clear voice, "but both of you have to keep your grades up, and if your averages dip, you get pulled out."

Britt and I looked at each other, our enthusiasm unwavering. We, of course, said yes.

That winter, when I was ten years old and Britt was twelve, we joined the programs. I loved the way our coaches pushed us, teaching 360s, cliff jumping, and getting us into race courses for the first time. It was not only the coaches who were amazing, but my peer group of friends as well. I was by no means the best in the group; there was a core of six of us who were all strong, and I felt each one was better than me at particular skills. It was exhilarating. I loved the competition, the energy the coaches brought, and the freedom to eat éclairs for lunch away from the parents. I couldn't wait to show up every weekend to see what they had in store for us.

Over the next couple of years, my skiing made big jumps of improvements. The club's main training run where the course got set up, (machine-groomed ski runs are also known as *pistes* in the world of skiing) ran with a couple of nice pitches for us to learn to ski steeps, three good breakovers to work on terrain changes, and a gradual flat section where the skill of generating speed was discovered—all of which was only halfway down to the chair lift. After leaving the training slope, we had a few different options to get down. One way was Goat's Gully, a steep run with cliffs, moguls, and jumps all over. Another route was picking our way through the trees, or we could run high speeds down the groomers, getting air off of rollers and side hits. We couldn't have asked for better grounds to nurture skills and develop as skiers.

By age twelve, I knew this was the sport for me. My on-hill success helped with this, most notably winning third place at the Provincial Championships for eleven- and twelve-year-olds. My two friends who came first and second were the ones I chased each run and felt were the best skiers ever! This was one of the first times I can remember really feeling like I belonged, that I had earned my place and was able to show everyone how good I could be. That's not to say I didn't have my insecurities growing up: I felt I was too small, that I couldn't control my energy/emotions, and that I was a late bloomer. But in these moments of great performances, I was enough. Ski racing was going to be my space to shine. This top-three result qualified me to represent my home province of BC at our home international juvenile race: the Whistler Cup. The dream of being an Olympic athlete was underway, with ski racing as the vehicle to get there.

CHAPTER 2
THE FORMATIVE YEARS

A FEW WEEKS BEFORE THE big international event, on my thirteenth birthday, I broke my leg. We had just finished racing a speed event, my first downhill ever, when during the ski out to the bottom of the mountain at the end of the day, I took a crash. Racers use significantly longer skis than normal in downhill, which are typically used only on the racecourse, but that day I had decided to ski out with mine. I was showing off to one of my friends how easily I could turn the long skis, and shortly after, having to dodge another skier, I hit a mogul the wrong way and went down. I fell in one direction with my body while my lower leg stayed behind, breaking the left tibia. This was March of 1995.

When I arrived at the Whistler ER, the doctor corrected the spiral fracture, returning the foot to its desirable position for his casting. The next day we had a follow-up visit with the specialist at Vancouver Children's Hospital, where he decided to replace it with the "Cadillac" of casts, as he put it, extending it all the way up to my groin. In this process, when the initial cast was removed, my left foot fell outward and remained this way until the new cast was put on. This is how the bone subsequently healed, twisted outward from the knee down.

As I was getting my cast off eight weeks later, the mini skill saw buzzed and cracked through the blue fibreglass, exposing my leg to the air again. I stared in disbelief, then turned to my mom and fell sobbing into her arms. It was like looking at someone else's leg and not the one I remembered. The muscle loss was the first shock, but when I took in the state of my ankle and saw my foot thirty degrees off to the outside, I thought my aspirations in sport had died before they really started.

When we got to the car, Mom sat me down and grabbed hold of my shoulders, tears running down her cheeks as well. "Michael, look at me. We're going to work through this and build you back up. I won't let you stay like this."

I wanted to believe her but mostly saw my dreams slipping away.

But my mother was prepared and educated, ready to help me through this challenge. True to her word, she found a great sports physiotherapist who took a keen interest in helping my rehab.

At some point during these physio sessions, my range of motion wasn't coming along super well, and there were talks about rebreaking the bone so it could be set correctly. A few months later, though, while rollerblading in the skate park, I went and did the rebreak for them. The same bone, the same leg, just a little higher.

When I returned to the Whistler ER the second time, it was the same doctor awaiting my arrival.

His greeting had tones of optimism. "Good, we get a second crack at this. We'll reset your bone and do our best to straighten this foot out for you. Ok, Michael?"

"Ok," I mumbled with a groan.

I was placed in a trauma room with a couple of nurses holding me down, my mom by my side, and the doctor at the foot of the bed, ready to twist my tibia back, as straight as possible. Between the drugs and screaming, I remember at least three good attempts.

"Michael, can you handle one more?" was asked between each one.

The doctor was able to bring the angle back a little, correcting around ten to fifteen degrees, but ultimately my foot still remained a little to the outside. This was how it would be.

In the months after the second broken leg, I was in bed, cast on, leg up, and agonizing about how far away I was from reaching my Olympic dream. "There's no way I can ever make it now. I'm never going to do it!"

I was missing the whole year. My friends were skiing, being active, improving, and here I was with another broken leg. I felt alone and lost.

With all this turmoil, in my moment of despair while lying in bed, I put a dare out to myself. "If I make it to the Olympics, if I can ski race for Canada on the World Cup circuit and reach the national team, this will prove anything is possible."

As soon as this thought came forward, I felt a surge of energy. The belief that anything is possible was simply this: a belief. I had read quotes from people expressing this, telling stories highlighting it, but I had no real proof in my own life. Lying in bed at that moment, my dream was the impossibility I needed to turn belief into knowing. Make the national team, race World Cup, compete in the Olympics for Canada, and prove anything is possible.

The fire was relit and the motivation set.

• • •

In the months after having the second cast removed, things looked a lot better, and my spirits improved. Walking and running were my first hurdles to face. Relearning how to foot strike, push off, and successfully recover my foot through to strike again were our main focus. In one of the physio sessions, they filmed me walking on a treadmill to analyze these parts of the stride, like analyzing a run of skiing, detecting and correcting as we went. It was hard to watch the video at first; I couldn't believe how awkward I looked on screen, but it helped a lot to see this new gait. On the physio's advice, I brought the film home and watched it from time to time. The camera we used was borrowed from the ski club, and when we returned it, the footage was still on the tape. Sure enough, the segment popped onto the screen in front of everyone during a weekend video session and with it, all the ammo a group of fourteen-year-olds needed to ridicule a friend. From this experience, I was given the creative new nickname "Club Foot." Feeling vulnerable and exposed, I used these emotions of insecurity as fuel.

"Oh yeah? I'll prove who's club footed and show you who can make it!"

Every time I'd hear the name, the anger became motivation and added to the "chip-on-my-shoulder" mentality that became a driving force for my return to the top of the group.

It wasn't easy coming back to sport after a year away, and any level of success I had previously found was slow to return. There were two main challenges with my leg, both in the short and long term. The first was that the bone had been set out of line, and the second was that being fully unweighted and in two casts over twelve weeks of a growth spurt had allowed the bone to grow without resistance, leaving my left leg 1.5 centimetres longer than my right.

Back on snow, I wasn't lighting it up with results the way I had hoped, and in the two seasons after coming back, I'd be lucky if I were in the top ten in a provincial race. To boot, we'd moved up in the age categories and were racing interprovincially, which didn't add to my confidence when finding my name on the result sheet. One stand-out poor performance was the Western Championships, racing against clubs from BC and Alberta, where I finished outside of the top thirty. Seeing teammates with whom I was once in touch way ahead and on the podium was a reality check to just how far I'd dropped off. With seemingly little control over my on-snow results, I put this frustration into my dryland training, which was less about skill and more about effort. I could control this.

Our ski club's director at the time was building a culture around dryland, and from him down through the coaches, an environment was set to foster a hard-working mentality and a solid physical foundation. This was my ticket. I was going to outwork everyone. If there was a team run, I would push to the front, if there was a challenge set for how many of this or how much of that could be done, I would fight for top. I loved the competitiveness with my friends, teammates, and older athletes of the club. I took any chance I could to prove myself in this arena.

Thankfully there were always others around who were better than me, setting benchmarks to strive for. Everything was motivation, and I even loved it when my teammates failed. It feels harsh to say this now, but it's true. In any competition, which was everything surrounding skiing, it didn't matter the reason for their failure: whether they were not in good-enough shape on the day, too tired, maybe not skilled enough for the task, or even because they were sick on the day and missed dryland all together, I took this as a win for me and a loss for them.

"You get out what you put in," I routinely told myself.

By the end of my time as a juvenile racer, at fifteen years old, my efforts in dryland were starting to show flashes of transferring into my skiing, highlighted by a thirteenth-place finish in the Whistler Cup slalom. This was my best finish of the season and best result for this major event. With competitors from the top ski-racing nations around the world like Austria, Norway, Sweden, Italy, Slovenia, USA, Japan, and Switzerland starting, I was thrilled with the result. Even with my own teammates winning and on the podium, it gave me a taste of what hard work paying off felt like and formed an arc for the rest of my return.

This drive to prove myself was only one side of the coin, though. On the top side, I held the deep feeling that I would make the national team, holding the energy that brought on this dream. But underneath, when the fear took over, there was a total scepticism that it would never come true. Both offered their own source of energy: one a running away from and the other a coming to. When stuck in scepticism, I luckily had my angels who saw through to the other side.

During a summer ski camp in Mount Hood, Oregon, in the off-season following my thirteenth place, we were on an afternoon hike for dryland, a routine post-ski activity. Our coach at the time, Maria, had been with our group for a few years and knew us well. She had come over from Sweden prior to working at the ski club, was full of the perfect mixture of wild energies, and knew how to push us to our best.

Prior to the day of the hike, I'd had some decently good days of skiing, and my times in the course were in relative touch with some of the best on the team. Feeling a little hopeful, I went searching for any bits of confirmation.

"Hey Maria, what do you think of Andrew, Mark, Joey, and Paul?" I opened the conversation with a question I answered before she could respond. "Andrew skis so smooth on such a good line, Mark skis so aggressively and fights hard, Joey has such a perfect touch for the snow and is so clean, and Paul's so consistent every run."

Maria kept looking forward. We were walking in the shade of the young pine and fir trees, little rays of light hitting us through the canopy. She was astute and waiting for me to get to my real question.

I arrived at my destination. "Out of all of them, who do you think is going to make it to the national team?"

"You will." She was direct and to the point, looking over at me without missing a stride.

"What? No, come on. Who do you think for real?" I said while laughing, trying to hide my desperate desire for this to be true.

She looked at me again. We were stopped now, and the dry pine filled the air.

"Michael. You work harder than anyone and you want it more. You're going to make the national team." There was a casualness to her words, yet a renowned, no-BS manner.

She returned to the hike.

I remained standing still.

Maria's belief shook my core. No one had said this so straightforwardly and with so much confidence in me before. Her words shocked me out of my head and away from the thoughts of scepticism and doubt, the feeling that *they* deserved it more than me.

From this, my own belief grew. *This dream is possible*, I thought to myself lying in bed that night. *I'M possible.*

This feeling carried me to sleep.

In the years to follow, I used this moment over and over again to come back after a bad result. If I got knocked down, I could accept it more because the feeling was still with me. "I can come back better tomorrow," I'd tell myself. "I'm the one who will make it and go far."

• • •

At fifteen years old I entered my first year of FIS (International Ski Federation). FIS is the level of racing when an athlete is no longer considered a juvenile racer because of having a ranking against the best and the rest of the world. The real world of ski racing starts in FIS. In it, athletes are trying to improve their world ranking through faster skiing in better-calibre races. In doing so, they aim to lower their FIS points. The number-one-ranked skier in the world has zero points, thirtieth in the world around ten points, seventieth in the world around twenty points, 150th in the world around thirty points and so on. In one way, going into the FIS is like turning pro; if you're fast enough, you can be on a national team, racing World Cup, and even becoming a world champion in a year or two, like the rise of Mikaela Shiffrin and others of her class. For most of us outside of this trajectory, it's a slower process of building skills and speed over a few years, hitting a variety of races, and working your way through the different stages of development: a provincial or regional team, onto a junior or development team, and then reaching a senior national team.

When I started FIS, the Whistler Mountain ski club hired two Swiss coaches, Thomas and Cedric, to head up this program. Thomas was my first coach in this new world of racing, and he electrified what it meant for me to be an athlete. He expanded the all-important scope of dryland, where challenges were presented to us rather than dictated, creating a continuous loop of self-checking-in.

"Hmm, can I do this? Do I want to do this?" I'd ask myself when Thomas had something new for us.

After some thought, I'd always come to, "Ok, I'll try this." An example of this was the juggling challenge. The goal was to learn how to juggle three balls continually for one minute.

Why would a ski racer need to learn how to juggle? was my first thought.

But just the simple challenge of something new was good enough to get me hooked, and being asked to learn these seemingly mundane skills was such a wild concept for me. Thomas pushed our linear train of thought with an approach akin to that of a curious child.

"Hey, try this over here; it might help and it's pretty fun," his tone would say.

Everyone who enters FIS starts out with 999 points, and most racers in the world reach a level of around one hundred to 150 points. For those with high performance aspirations, the aim is to land at least between fifty and seventy points after their first season or two to make a provincial or regional ski team. I started the year near the back of the pack, scoring over a hundred points in the majority of my races or not finishing and skiing out of the course. But I felt like my skiing was better than my results were showing, and a breakthrough had to happen soon.

A couple of weeks prior to the last races of the season, my sister Britt offered me a pair of hand-me-down skis, her old race set. Already on the national team and racing at the Nor-am and European Cup level, she held a good sponsorship from Salomon, which provided her with skis significantly better than I could ever get on my own. From World Cup and European Cup to a national level, and then everything else below, there are different tiers of skis. Even within the World Cup, a top-ten athlete can have a different setup than someone ranked twentieth or thirtieth. The faster you ski, the greater access you have to better equipment.

Knowing of this ski hierarchy, Thomas had a conversation with my mom to help with the decision. "Listen, Mom," he said in an endearing way. "Britt gets her skis straight from the factory in Europe; they have better material and are built with more care. They may not be the perfect skis for Michael, but they're better than what he's on now. We should make the switch." His guidance gave a clear choice.

I made the change and instantly felt the difference in my skiing. My confidence in the start gate shot up as well, which I took into the final races of the season. These races were so fun. I was skiing the way I'd known was possible for me for so many years. My results reached a critical benchmark, scoring points in the seventies, which was enough to get me an invitation to the BC Provincial Ski Team's summer camp the following off-season and an outside shot at making the team.

Thomas only coached us for one season. He moved back to Switzerland afterwards to work with their junior national team. Though his time with me was short lived, his energy and style of training left an invaluable mark on me. He paired play and work so effortlessly, had an infectiously positive spirit, and inspired me to push through this first year of FIS.

From lying in bed with my broken leg to an opportunity to ski with the BC team, I finally felt like I was back on my way, more committed and ready to keep going.

CHAPTER 3
GETTING SENT DOWN

I WAS FLYING HIGH AFTER this first season of FIS. My national rankings for my age improved significantly, and even though I didn't make the full BC team criteria, the summer ski-camp invitation gave me a hope at making it through my performance.

The BC team's head coach at the time was a Slovenian named Dusan who'd immigrated to Canada a few years prior for this role and had been running the team since. The team's reputation had quickly grown; it was all about putting in the most work, being the first to and last off the mountain, keeping the athletes on a need-to-know basis, and set in a hypercompetitive environment. Mostly, though, Dusan's philosophy was anchored in volume, volume, volume; if we could train more than any other team, work harder in dryland, and ski through all conditions, then success would come.

For this camp, we headed back to Mount Hood, Oregon. Hood, as it's better known in the ski community, is a volcano that makes up part of the Cascade Volcanic Arc and is a major summer ski destination for Canadian and American ski and snowboard teams. The Blackcomb glacier in Whistler and Mount Hood are the only two places that offer year-round skiing in North America, but as Hood offers significantly longer training terrain and is only a six-hour drive from Vancouver, it was Dusan's go-to off-season ski venue.

I felt nervous coming into this new provincial team environment. Being a late bloomer and one of the smallest in the group, I was moving onto a team of men when I was still a boy. The stories I'd heard about the daily workload, training intensity, and even hazing didn't do much to ease these feelings. I did have good friends around, which helped, as we were a tight group that had moved up together and could lean on each other for support. With about twenty young guys and girls, spanning across sixteen to nineteen years old, a mixture of provincial team veterans, rookies, and invitees, the camp turned out well. The rhythm of early-morning warmup routines, fifteen runs in the course per day, and afternoon dryland sessions started to feel somewhat normal. It turned out that I thrived with the inherent competition built into every activity. The more opportunities I had to win at something, the more I felt like I came into existence. I lived for it.

Most of our days on snow consisted of timing in the gates. Prior to this, our coaches would rarely use timing as a tool during training, but Dusan and the coaches were keeping a pulse on where everyone was and using the data to help form their decisions. I was in the mix on most days but ultimately not fast enough to make the cut, and while my friends all ended up being selected off their results from the previous season, I was sent back down.

In our post-camp debrief, Dusan was straight and honest with me. "Mike, you are close. You showed a lot in these last ten days, but taking in your results from last season being just short, we won't name you to the team," he said in his deep-voiced Slovenian accent, combining multiple words into one.

I slumped in my chair, even though I'd known this was the likely outcome coming down here.

Dus continued. "Take your time, go back with the club, and when you're skiing fast enough, there will be opportunities to come with us for some bigger races." Knowing I was hungry, he was giving me a pathway to make it back.

Dusan was right. I wasn't ready for that environment, but I was still upset about being left behind, knowing the work I had put in.

Coming back to the Whistler ski club, though, I landed in a great situation. We had two enthused and experienced coaches, Jordan Williams and Igor Dostal, leading a strong group of athletes, two of whom, first-year

FIS athletes Ben Thornhill and Ashleigh McIvor, were the fastest juvenile racers in the world and provided a strong push. There were also some veterans, fourth-year FIS athletes who acted as our mentors, and a mixture of racers of all abilities in between. Our head coach, Jordan, had coached with the national team and was coming off three years working as an assistant for Dusan on the provincial ski team. He knew Dusan's program well and what it took to reach the next level. Igor, on the other hand, our assistant, had recently finished his racing career and offered the perfect mixture of knowledge and youthful energy to partner with Jordan's vision. To them it was simple math; the BC team had fifty-five days planned for their pre-season on snow, so we scheduled fifty-six. This was the most I'd ever skied in the off-season, and the coaches continued to push in dryland, and did their part to keep it fun. There was always time to spin a few donuts with the van in an empty parking lot full of fresh snow.

Getting sent back also fuelled my chip-on-the-shoulder mentality, and when I got into the start gate for the first race of the year, it was a major part of my motivation. I wanted to show I could be the fastest in the province, and in the opening December race series in Panorama, BC, the same hill I'd ended the last season on, I started where I'd left off. I finished with my two best point scores and was doing exactly what Dusan told me to do: "ski fast and get called up."

True to his word, Dusan invited me to the team's European leg of the season, joining four other BC team members to race over two and a half weeks across four countries. Outside of the excitement I had for my level of skiing, this was also my first trip to Europe, the birthplace of ski racing and the place that had been part of many of my mom's stories from her formative years. I was going to race in these towns, see the same mountains she'd seen, and be in the same valleys she'd explored.

With a send-off from my parents and grandmother at the Vancouver airport, I was the newest sixteen-year-old enroute to Europe, ready to take it in with four good friends and teammates: Scott Hume, Scott Anderson, Munroe Hunsicker, and Morgan Maguire. We landed in Zürich, and after Dusan made it through the van rental process, we were on our twelve-hour drive to his home country for the first race in Maribor, Slovenia. Seeing all the different road signs as we wound through the mountain roads and open highways, we asked Dusan a thousand questions, like "what is this?" and "what is that?"

"Dus, how big is the town of Ausfahrt?"

"Where is the autobahn?"

"What's the exchange rate between a Swiss franc, Slovenian tolar, and Italian lira?"

Just the fact that Dusan knew these roads so well, like where to stop for food and what town was coming up next, blew me away. I wondered if my grandfather had done these routes and seen these same peaks in his time. Though I tried to keep my eyes open as much as possible, the seductive pull of jet lag eventually took its toll on all of us, and we fell asleep, much to Dusan's relief, I'm sure.

In Maribor, on one of the first mornings of training, Dusan went up and set a training course for us. As we started running it, not finishing many runs, it didn't take long for us to jump on the complaining train, and soon we were after him about his course set.

Munroe started nagging. "Dus, how do you expect us to get a good feeling to prepare for the races?"

"Dus, it's way too turny! We're basically hiking across the hill," Morgan piled on.

Run after run we complained about this turn or that gate or that the snow conditions weren't good enough for his set.

Eventually he had had enough. "Fine! If you morons think you can do better, here's the drill: there are the gates, go set your own course!" Dus handed over his Dewalt drill with the big twenty-inch-long aluminium drill bit coming out of it. This was the standard coaching tool used to get the gates in snow. "I'll be over there having a coffee. Come get me when you're done!" And with this, he picked up his skis, turned his back, and walked off to the café.

"Well, you really pissed him off now, didn't you?" Scott Anderson piped in with a laugh, placing the blame squarely on the rest of us. He was none too fussed with the turn of events, though.

While I was thinking that we'd maybe just continue to run the course that was set and make the best of it, Anderson had something else in mind. "Guys, new plan. We're not training anymore, we can't let Dusan win."

He had our attention.

"I saw on the mountain map, this place is pretty big. Let's take off, go free skiing, and see what's out there." The others were in agreement, and since they'd spent more time with Dus and knew this dance better than I did, I followed suit.

Maribor is a long resort that extends along a ridge with two main stations at either end. You can work your way across by skiing down and across to the next lift, bumping back to a new peak, and then going back down and across again. It was a beautiful sunny day in January with mild temperatures, and by the halfway point of our journey, this seemed like the better way to spend the day for a group of sixteen- and seventeen-year-old, first-time European travellers. Adding to our enjoyment, we laughed and joked as if we'd pulled a fast one over on Dus.

When we reached the other end of the resort, we were greeted by a nice restaurant with a relaxing deck to soak in the afternoon sun. It was now Morgan's turn to add his stroke of genius to the plan. When the server came to take our order, he cut in first and ordered five beers for the table. We looked as though we were in a little shock, but no questions were asked. When the beers arrived, we cheered and continued to laugh at our success. It seemed to us like we'd gotten the best of Dus, and in a world full of structure, our little day of independence felt like complete freedom.

Races are held all over Europe in the winter months, and if someone is keen enough and thrives on a lot of driving, you can find a new race every few days. Luckily for us, this was Dusan. He had the European contacts, knowledge of the areas, and a strong affinity for the autobahns and mountain roads. Our itinerary started in Maribor, then up the road six hours to Garmisch-Partenkirchen, Germany; three hours of driving back east to Altenmarkt, in Austria; returning to Slovenia for a series of three races; and then finishing the trip with a nine-hour drive west to Grindelwald, Switzerland, for our last series. It was a total of 2,600 kilometres, nine races, and a handful of training and off days mixed in. This became the normal rhythm of our lives as ski racers, moving every few days from one destination to another, hitting up races and training venues throughout the winter, never fully unpacked, and always ready to change plans at a moment's notice.

We were pushed during this trip, and it elevated our understanding of racing.

"Guys, there's nothing to lose in these races, go out in full attack, take risks, push to the end," Dus encouraged us every chance he got. "This trip is about learning, not about results." He wanted us to keep fighting each run and see what speed we could bring.

I only finished two of nine races, but true to Dusan's mantra, my successes were more than the results. We gained exposure to how deep the world-wide competitive field really was. For example, in a race at home with a combined two-run time of two minutes, the top ten finishers would be separated by three seconds. Over here in Europe, this three-second time difference would hold the top thirty finishers. The bigger goal was revealed. In addition to this, we also got to see that there was real speed in our group. Scott Hume closed the trip out with a solid, top-ten result, and the best point score of his career to date. This left us feeling like we could hang with our European cohorts and survive the rigours of life on the road.

• • •

Alpine skiing has four main disciplines: slalom, giant slalom (GS), super G, and downhill. Slalom and GS are the technical disciplines, while super G and downhill are the speed events. Each one has its own rules and regulations for how the courses are set. Slalom gates are set the closest, around ten metres apart, with speeds around fifty km/h. GS gates are set around twenty-eight metres apart, with speeds around seventy km/h. Super G gates are forty metres-plus, with speeds touching ninety to a hundred km/h, and downhill is stretched way out, more or less following the terrain of the mountain with athletes averaging speeds of 115km/h, topping out around 150km/h.

Speed events are one-run races while technical events are a combination of two runs, each run with a new course set. The start order is flipped for the second run, based off the first run results. If you finished first, you start thirtieth, and if you finished thirtieth, you start first. Everyone else after the thirtieth starts in the order they finished, except in World Cup, where if you finish outside of the top thirty, you don't get a second run. Both have their psychological challenges for performance; Downhillers face more speed, forces, and risk of serious injury while tech skiers have to perform twice for one result. This contrast seems to attract two different personality types; speed skiers tend to be more laid back while tech skiers may be a little more high-energy or twitchy as some would say.

Our first race series back on home soil was at Sunshine Mountain resort in Alberta, and I was back with my club team. The field was a strong mixture of racers from western Canada, which got me excited. I was feeling so good on my skis that I wanted to put it to the test. The morning of the first slalom race, it had snowed close to a metre overnight, which was potentially too much new snow to run the race. Ski racers generally want a hard snow surface because the conditions stay relatively fair for the whole field of eighty-plus racers and the skis perform better. Race organisers do everything they can to prepare the hill to this effect with side slipping, shovelling and raking to push snow to the side, boot packing, and using water, salt, or chemicals, all with the hopes of firming it up. If the conditions are cold and clear enough, they'll inject the hills with water the days before to ice it up. On this day, though, the conditions were more typical for the coastal mountains of BC, and after a series of side slipping and boot packing by the coaches, things weren't perfect, but good enough to race.

The first run course set had two tough sections: one was a flush, which is a quick combination of three gates, and the second was a delay, two gates set close together to create one long turn across the hill. Both are used as a course-setting strategy to change up the rhythm of a course. The flush was set at the bottom of the steeps, in a transition that ran onto the flats, which meant we'd be carrying a lot of speed into it. Plus, two gates later was the delay, swinging us back across to the closing gates, not an easy set of combinations given the conditions.

Jordan's message to us during inspection was simple: ski it smart, make it through this section. "Michael, in these conditions, the course will be rutted up by the time you go. Take the little rounder line, work with the ruts, and carry your speed onto the flats. You don't have to do anything fancy here."

I had something totally different in mind. "I don't know, Jordan, I think I can run it straighter into the flush, be inside the ruts, and make it through faster than anyone. I think it can be done."

He cautioned me again. "Mike, with the soft conditions, there will be shelves of snow at the gates, especially through the flush. You won't be able to get close enough with your feet for your line to work."

I just nodded and said ok, but I was still looking past him at the course. I was too curious to see if my line could actually work out.

I came out of the gate with a huge push, took a fiery attack and energy to the opening gates, and built a ton of speed onto the steeps. Coming into the flush, I was showing no signs of slowing down. Jordan covered his face with his hands, looking between the fingers of his gloves, and in a cloud of snow, I went down. I had gone into the flush too straight, not adjusting for my speed, and with the snow piled at the gates like the side of a pyramid, my skis slipped out, hitting one off the other, catching my tip square on the front of the next gate and sending me flying face first into a plume of snow.

Jordan's thoughts, naturally, were on my disappointment. *Shit, Mike's going to be so bummed he missed out on a great opportunity for a result.*

When the snow cloud settled, though, there I was with my head lifted, a smile on my face, and laughing away. Jordan slid down to meet me on the side of the course.

"That was so fun, did you see how I almost pulled it off?" I exclaimed before he could come to a stop.

"Yup, Mike, you almost did," he responded, shaking his head with a smile of his own. He was relieved I hadn't shared his same thoughts.

I didn't pull it off that day, but it didn't matter. I was so stoked to finally perform on my skis in real life, the way I'd always felt I was capable of in my mind. I had started the season with inconsistencies, not finishing eleven out of seventeen races, but after the Sunshine races I found a rhythm, closing the year finishing fifteen out of twenty races, and lowering my points along the way. This qualified me well within the BC Team criteria for the next season and gave me a chance to find my own place in this group.

Getting sent back down to my club team had given me time to discover who I wanted to be as an athlete and the space to explore it. Jordan and Igor's team environment nurtured self-discovery, showcased the value of a diverse group, and humbled me to the process of development.

In the moment, though, I was just excited to tap into my potential and push for it in every run.

CHAPTER 4
THE DEVELOPMENT YEARS

THE SUMMER ON THE BC Team was one of the biggest development periods of my career. Where before I was mostly wiry and light, I was now putting on size and started to feel like an athlete who could compete with the adults. Our team was made up of some of my best friends, four from the Whistler Mountain Ski Club and a selection of other eclectic characters from around the province. We travelled to Hood five times over the course of the summer and fall, each in ten-day blocks of skiing. If it was a stretch of good weather, we'd do all ten days in a row or just ski until we were fried.

In the summer months, Mount Hood and its base town of Government Camp is North America's bustling centre for ski racing, with teams coming from all over the continent, including the US and Canadian national teams. It was the ski racing scene, with lots of energy that made it easy to push day in and day out. In the fall, though, on the fourth and fifth trip of the year, it became a dull and lonely place. With only us and a few other local teams, motivation moved up and down with the energy of the group and a lot of the drive had to come from within. This was the first time I remember thinking, *Oh, so this is the "real work" athletes speak of*—being able to push with no one else around.

Dusan remained as head coach with his assistant Matt Kerr, and his coaching philosophies continued: first to and last off the hill, maximum volume, keep athletes on a need-to-know basis, and create a competitive environment in everything.

The Hood camps embodied these philosophies, with 5:00 a.m. morning runs for warm-up, four to five hours of on-hill training, mandatory fifteen runs in the course, and intense afternoon dryland sessions. Woven into our regular routine, there was also the strategically placed thirty-minute, winner-take-all sprint to the top of the Ski Bowl, Government Camp's little ski hill in the middle of town. We dubbed this the "hell run."

At the start of each camp, Dusan would let us know how many times we would have to do the hell run over the ten days, but he'd never tell us which days they'd be. It was usually between two and four times per camp. All day on hill we'd debate the likelihood of *this* being the day for one of the runs and whether we should be saving our energy or keep pushing with the hopes that dryland would be a game of soccer. But even in the games, there were consequences for lacklustre performances. Most of the time this meant the losing team would carry the next day's equipment to and from the hill. Dusan always had his ways to keep the intensity up, and I thrived in this environment.

In addition to Dusan's philosophy on maximum volume, we were also trained to ski through every condition and in all weather. In the early mornings, while still in bed, when the weather turned and the sound of rain pattered outside our windows, part of us always hoped for the pre-alarm knock on the door to let us know that the day was cancelled. This rarely was the case because if the mountain was open, we were going up. On one of these questionable training days, we went up into a thick fog with only a gate or two of visibility ahead of us, and Dus was pushing the obligatory fifteen runs.

While waiting at the top of the course after run number two, Dusan skied up to the group of us. His larger-than-life presence felt like it would eclipse the sun, if it were out. "Guys, you're skiing like shit." He stood tall on his skis, wearing his baseball hat, sunglasses, and a big coaching rain poncho that was blowing in the wind. "We have to learn to ski in every-thing." A little smile was held gently against his cleanly shaven and dark-tanned face. You could tell he was enjoying this teachable moment.

He spoke directly and to the point. "This could be what you get at a World Cup or in any other races this season. If the organizers say the race is on, they will still give out the medals." His deep voice penetrated through the mist and the fog, a lieutenant in the Slovenian army addressing his platoon.

The speech had its desired effect and raised morale until about run number seven.

"Guys, this is brutal!" Anderson had hit his limit and started venting to three of us while riding the chairlift. "We can't see more than a gate ahead of us, and I'm hitting ruts without even seeing them. We gotta stop this!" He was adamant, since the grooves in the snow we'd been creating over the course of the day were now more like bomb holes.

While all four of us shared the feeling of fatigue and annoyance, we searched for a plan that could end the day's training.

Ben grew a smile and threw out an idea. "Someone has to fake an injury. Pretend like you hurt yourself on one of the ruts and then go complain to the coaches. It's the only way!"

Scott added to Ben's thought train. "Yes! But you know Dus won't stop training with only one injury. He could say that it was pilot error and not the conditions. Two of us need to fake them if we want out of today."

It was now my turn to add to the plan. "And make sure you do it just above Matt so he can see, and with any luck, he'll radio Dus with *his* safety concerns. This way, ending training is their idea, not ours."

Ben and I drew the short straws to play out the hatched pot over the two other Scotts on the chairlift. We were probably the best candidates for it anyway, as our complaining skills were seasoned and ready to go.

Pushing out of the gate on the next run, I scanned ahead, looking for Matt along the course. I spotted him halfway down, took my chance, ran the gate above him too straight, and sharply hit the rut, popping me out of the course. I gave a yelp, clutching my back, and slid over to him, yelling on the approach. "This is awful! We can't see anything! Ruts are turning into holes and we're hitting them dead on. I don't even know where the right line is," I ranted, hunching over and falling to the ground at his feet. "What are we trying to get out of today? What are we trying to prove?" It was loud and believable. I was really selling it.

Before Matt could answer, Ben was on his way and we turned uphill just in time to see him hit the same rut as me, ski out, and slide over to us, holding one foot in the air. A similar charade had been performed but with stronger convictions.

Matt took in our grievances with little reaction, paused for a moment, and clicked the button on his radio. "Hey Dus, Mike and Ben are with me, both just tweaked themselves on one of the holes halfway down. The visibility is pretty low in my section. Think we can call it a day?"

A long moment of silence ensued on the other end. Then, from the bottom of the course, in broken Slovenian English, where all the Vs are pronounced as Ws, we heard the glory call to the rest of the team in the start: "Ok guys, I *beliewo* [believe] training is done for the day. The *wisibility* is not good enough to continue. Grab your bags, go down and we meet at the *wans*." Dus was calling it a day.

Some days athletes do have the better judgement, but in the brief moments after our successful mission, it was more about pulling one over on the coaches. We took Dusan's coaching philosophy of "competition in everything" to play that day, even if it was between athletes and coaches, and with it, victory was ours.

• • •

When I recovered from my broken leg, I was told by a doctor that the leg length discrepancy would eventually cause back pain because of how my hips now sat unevenly when I was standing. These words sounded like a death sentence at the time, and I wanted to escape the room as fast as possible. I resisted the diagnosis. *No way! You're an idiot! You have no idea what my life will be like!* I wanted to call, but I kept these thoughts to myself.

Coming into this race season at the age of eighteen, though, I experienced my first case of it. After a normal day of training on hill, my lower back started to tighten, and soon I was having trouble putting pressure on my leg, doing squats, or even standing up straight. The provincial team at the time didn't have an extensive sport medical support team like a national team would, so we were left to make the sidelining calls between ourselves as athletes and the coaches. It was shocking to have a seemingly invisible injury, something less tangible than a broken bone or torn ACL, be so debilitating and to not able to ski. We were a couple of weeks away from the first races in Panorama, everyone was ramping up their preparations, and I was slowing down, going into town for physiotherapy.

This opening series was a BC/Alberta cup, two GS and two slalom races held over four days. To boost the quality of the race, the organizers had brought in some US collegiate athletes with low FIS points to compete. Ski racing calibrates their races similar to horse racing: the better the athletes in the field, the greater potential for a low race penalty, which gives everyone a chance of scoring better point results. These college athletes were those who had missed qualifications for their own national teams and turned to the US NCAA circuit to finish out their careers or to use it as a secondary springboard back to the World Cup. This was the perfect race situation for our team and where we all were in our careers.

My teammates had been training with the invitees throughout the days leading up to the races, with a few getting close in times and even winning some runs. The energy was buzzing around our dinner table as we got closer to competition.

Paul opened the floor, looking for race-winning predictions. "Who do you think's got it?" Then he continued with his own. "Ben and Scott have been skiing really fast, and Jeff's thrown down some fast times too. I think one of them could win the slalom for sure." He was holding court, elaborating on his analysis.

Naturally, I was left out of the predictions since I hadn't skied in over a week, but the snub still triggered me, and the angrier I got, the more fuel I had to prove their guesses wrong. A day before the races, I finally got back on my skis and spared little time getting up to speed, quickly pushing through any lasting pain. Not exactly the most recommended return-to-the-snow process from an injury, but I needed to show everyone that I deserved consideration for the win!

With all the down time I had while my teammates were on hill, I'd started using visualization to practice mentally what they were doing physically. To stoke the fire, I watched more video than normal, made notes about my technical cues, and used self-talk to keep my focus off the pain of missing out. These training runs felt surprisingly good, like I hadn't missed much, and when I eventually got to stand in the start gate, there was little negative thought of "what ifs" because there were no expectations. I wasn't even in the conversation and therefore had nothing to lose. It was just me and my skis.

Seemingly out of nowhere, even a bit to me, I ended up winning back-to-back slaloms and scored the two best results of my career to that date by a long shot: twenty-eight and twenty-nine FIS points—down from fifty-two. It felt incredible being on top of the podium and overhearing the college racers say to each other, "Who's Mike Janyk? Where did he come from?"

I was amazed at how fast I skied without training in the weeks leading up to the race. These were my first insights into the realm of performance, that it differs from training and how much of it plays out in the mind. It was validating, and I wanted more.

Within our team, there were five of us were close with speed in slalom and GS, while the rest of the team were performing better in downhill and super G. This grew a natural programming split, leading us in the "tech group" to head over to Europe for a different series of races. On this, my second trip to Europe, Dusan was taking us on a shorter, twelve-day stint with nine races squeezed in between Slovenia, Northern Italy, and Austria. We were a way stronger group than the year before, and Dusan's message shifted: now we were there for results, not just an experience.

"Don't be scared of them, you guys belong here," he'd repeat in his *ohm*-like voice.

I took this into an Austrian junior event where we were up against some of the best-ranked juniors in the world. I finished third, my best international result ever, and could barely believe it.

Dus is right, we are good enough to have results here, I thought to myself, now really letting his words sink in.

While standing on this podium, in ski racing's powerhouse nation of Austria, a defining mentality grew: *Dus knows what I'm capable of. If he says I can do it, then I can do it.*

By the end of the season, I felt better than ever on my skis and I was building confidence on a national level. The Canadian Championships were being held in Sun Peaks, BC, and in lieu of any speed events because of conditions, the organizers decided to run two of each tech race, two slalom, and two GS. Only one of each would be considered the National

Championships, but they would both have similar fields of athletes and caliber of racing.

The coach of the national development team at the time, Urban, also a Slovenian, and a friend of Dusan's, was talking to Dus about how his guys were skiing and engaging in the usual ski-racing water cooler talk. As the conversation continued, Dusan was gaining more and more confidence about how his guys, us, were skiing, and he put up a wager. He bet Urban that one of his BC team racers would be the slalom champ for the year. Word got out amongst the athletes, and hearing this lifted me up.

If Dus had this kind of confidence in our skiing, then I had it too, I thought. His confidence was my confidence.

The day of the National Championship race, though, it was Urban who won the bet. Our teammate Scott Hume was the closest, in third, and I was sixth, scoring our best results of the season in the process. It was a strong showing by our group, but I felt like we hadn't lived up to the benchmark that was set for us. I took aim at the second slalom in a few days' time.

In my best performances, I feel connected to the snow, from the tip of my ski right to the tail, as if every inch of the edge can be used in any given moment to gain more speed. These were my senses in the warmup runs on the morning of this second slalom race. I looked around at the competition with an internal nod, thinking, *I got these guys.*

First run went well; I came out of the start, felt strong through the first gates, skied consistently the whole way down, and ended up finishing second on the run. This meant I would start twenty-ninth in the second run.

For a tech skier, the gap between runs is a challenging balance between maintaining the intensity required to focus while relaxing enough to have energy for a second leg. The time period is usually around two and half to three and a half hours, depending on the race, where the organizers and coaches have to tear down the first course, set the second course, prepare the snow on the new track, and get the timing re-tested and ready to go. As racers, we'll use the time to decompress after first run, have some food, watch first-run video, talk with coaches, inspect the second-run course, maybe do a free run or two, and then shift our mindset forward and ramp back up for run number two.

On this day, my routine was fairly normal: a mixture of time talking with the team in the lodge and focussing on my own run. I headed out to the top of the course, aiming to arrive at the start, with fifteen racers to go before my number, giving me roughly fifteen minutes to warm up, visualize, check my skis, get a course report, and click into my bindings. This is where my *Go to the Start* moment first came to be.

When the nerves became overwhelming and seized my body, I repeated this mantra back to myself: "Just go to the start. Just go to the start."

Slowly the blood diverted back to my extremities, and I could move again.

"Just go to the start. Go to the start."

I soon found myself in the start gate. I had made it to my destination, and the rest came back to me naturally. All my training, the good thoughts, focus, and feelings started to come back. I took my deep breaths, and when it was time to go, I pushed out and onto the course. The feeling of connection came first, then the rhythm, and finally the enthused sensation of outwardly expressing what you know to be so true inside.

The answers came to me on course.

This feeling of the dance is why I go through the discomfort, I thought to myself.

But then I crossed the finish line and won the race.

I had a newer revelation. *No. It's the feeling of winning, this is why I go through the worry and self-doubt.*

But then I stood on the podium.

My head was now full of ideas. *Or is it the recognition from friends, coaches, and family? The prize money and status. This has to be why I go through the nerves and nauseous pain.*

Wherever the truth lay, to my eighteen-year-old self, they were all good reasons to push through and *Go to the Start.*

CHAPTER 5
REACHING THE NATIONAL TEAM

ALPINE CANADA ALPIN IS THE sport's national organization and governing body. The team structure for Alpine can change from year to year depending in large part on funding, who's at the helm, and what philosophy they subscribe to. Traditionally, a well-funded, full national team of athletes can have up to twelve separate groups within the greater team. Each gender has its World Cup, "A" and "B" group, a continental cup, a "C" team, and a development or junior "D" team, and within each of these, two subsequent groups for technical and speed skiers. The year 2000 was my first year qualifying for the Canadian National Ski Team... well, technically only the development team, but in my eyes, it was the same thing at the time.

The team's athletic director of the day, Joze Sparovic, believed in a junior team program, and he had the funding to back it. Bridging the gap between a provincial and senior national team, this level can be a big strength to a nation's development system. Four of us from the BC team, Scott Hume, Scott Anderson, Ben Thornhill, and myself, plus two graduating Alberta team members, Cameron Barnes and Danny MacEachren, formed the men's side of the junior team. Just above us on the "C" team were Erik Guay, Ryan Semple, Julien (Cousi) Cousineau, and Jan Hudec, all of whom were part of the group that would become the next generation of Canadian ski racers. For now, though, I was eighteen years old, newly graduated from high school, had just made the national team with my best friends, and was on my way to Calgary for summer dryland training. This was the start of the dream and felt totally liberating.

Most of the senior ski team athletes centralized in Calgary for their summer training, but we on the junior team were only called in for two weeks at a time. Britt was one of these senior athletes there at the time, and both Scotts also had older brothers on the team and living in town, who helped familiarize us with the program, guiding us around the curricular and extracurricular activities. Outside of general team orientation and dryland training, this camp's main purpose was fitness testing, which took place on days one and two.

All our lab testing ran through the University of Calgary's Kinesiology Department. It was my first trip to a university, and walking through it felt exciting, like I was graduating into something bigger. The halls were quiet; only a few people were in them, seemingly either for summer school or maintenance of some kind. Our footsteps echoed off the walls, making the hallways seem like they went on forever. The walls to my left turned to windows, and I could see down into the multiple volleyball and basketball courts with bleachers all around: home of the Dinos. People were gathering around a basket of equipment; it looked like a summer kids' program. Opposite the windows, on the other side of the hall, were the cases holding the school's plaques and trophies, showcasing the individual and team athletic accomplishments. I wondered if I would ever go to a university and what it would be like mixing with athletes from across so many different sports. I let my mind wander, thinking about going to race for a school in the States, playing out another dream.

I continued my walk in a bit of a daze but soon the natural light coming from an atrium up ahead drew my attention back to reality. Making my way underneath it, I stood looking in all directions. Three hallways all merged into this one gathering space, which held rows and levels of avant-garde seating with some ferns and greenery placed throughout. I enjoyed this little oasis for a moment longer and then turned left towards the testing labs. As the ceiling lowered back down above me and the natural light was swapped for fluorescent, I passed through the first series of double doors into a dark space with sensors and cameras all around, empty of people with a distant noise of cheering and physical exertion coming from the single door across the room.

My nerves grew the closer I got to the noise; this was it, there was no turning back now. I took a deep breath, not really sure what to expect, and walked through. When I finally came into the testing area, I saw the skiers I'd looked up to and watched on TV, like Edi Podivinsky, Thomas Grandi, and Allison Forsyth, dripping with sweat as they ran through their own bike tests or lying on the floor having just spent their maximum effort.

I was in awe. It was like having a backstage pass to my favourite concert, only I also had to perform, and therefore I tried to play it cool like I belonged.

These Calgary trips became a routine for us throughout the off season, and in the fall, it was finally time to get the team gear and uniforms for the season. This ritual changes a little from year to year, and after a while the shine can wear off, but this being our group's first one, we showed up with sunglasses on. At a Holiday Inn hotel in the northwest part of Calgary, we walked down a hall lined with hardened carpets, muted wallpaper, and photos on the walls of wild horses and cowboys sitting on ridges in the sunset. Yet as generic as this place was, the hairs on my arms started to stand up the closer we came to the gear room. An ordinary meeting room that held no apparent value was transformed into a site of ceremony and affirmation simply by the contents it possessed.

The six of us walked into the room together, grinning from ear to ear, to be welcomed by duffle bags lined up with our names on them. This was the feeling of *making it*, I was sure. After being given our bags by the equipment manager, we went next door to the changing room, going through the bags item by item, seeing if the kit fit. There was banter and snickers and laughs as we modelled every item for each other—no piece was left untouched. This was Christmas in November as we put on our national team jackets for the first time.

Changing teams also meant changing coaches. I was moving on from Dusan, which came with an excitement about growing and a nervousness about leaving someone who'd brought me to this next level. Sean Langmuir was the team's new head coach, and the core of his season's plan was to race a lot and in all four disciplines. This was not too dissimilar from the strategy of other junior team coaches, as it gave us the variety and amount of starts needed to really learn how to race. In total we had over sixty race starts planned, a mixture of regular-level FIS races, NorAm cups, and National and World Junior Championships. I raced a total of fifty-seven of them, the most I would ever race in a single season throughout my whole career.

We started in Colorado, went on to Lake Louise, and then over to Switzerland and France for the bulk of the winter. On this latter leg, it was my first chance to race on one of the iconic World Cup tracks in Wengen. Located in the middle of Switzerland, Wengen sits on a high plateau, nestled gently halfway up a mountainside, looking like so many other seemingly impossible villages around the country. The mountains continue up and up beyond the town to such iconic peaks as the Eiger and Jungfrau, hovering over the town like an ever-present parent waiting to chastise a child's wrong action.

Wengen is a town of only electric-cart-like vehicles and foot traffic. All regular cars must be parked in the valley, and a thirty-minute train ride takes residents and tourists up into town. With little chalets, big hotels, a school, and a community centre awaiting atop, the Jungfraubahn clicks and clacks through its gear system, snaking back and forth, climbing and cutting its way up the mountain. It's a unique ski experience because to reach the top of the hills where the skiing happens, you continue up with the train like a morning commuter on the subway, only this one is packed with ski gear instead of briefcases.

Each year a World Cup winning runs tape is released, highlighting the fastest runs from both genders in all disciplines from the previous season. We would watch this tape over and over again on the BC team, talking about who our favourite racers were and arguing about which hills were the best and why. Kitzbühel, Cortina, Alta Badia, and Adelboden were always in the mix, but Wengen routinely topped the list, and for good reason. The Lauberhorn, as its downhill track is called, is one of the most iconic of the circuit, being the longest course at 4.5 kilometres, which takes a skier around two and a half minutes to descend. It boasts some of the highest speeds of up to 160 km/h; the coolest jump on circuit called the *hundschopf*, which falls off a cliff; and the most unexpected downhill turn called the Kernen-S, which snakes through a chicane[1] and onto a banked turn and then under the train bridge. The slalom also keeps a place in the race hill Hall of Fame for its drastic and ever-changing terrain, with the steepest six or seven gates on tour.

In my first course inspection down the slalom hill, there wasn't all the hype of a World Cup surrounding it as I was just racing a regular FIS race, but the slope spoke loudly enough. When I looked from the top of the course, it didn't seem too difficult, until I got closer. The start is a little corridor with a ton of micro-terrain features of sharp bumps, sidehills, and basketball-esque humps that fall away as you try and turn around them. The course then leads onto a relatively flat bench, a little reprieve before sharply dropping into the abyss of the pitch.

When I reached the bench, a few gates from the breakover, I could only see sky, and the closer I got to the edge, the mountain continued to fall away. I'd never seen such a sharp breakover on a groomed run, let alone with a course set on it. I slid to the edge and forced my eyes up to assess the rest of the course, which from this vantage point I could see all the way to the finish. After the steeps and only halfway down, the hill's next biggest feature comes into play.

Since this is Switzerland and the land is used for grazing in the summer, a little farm shed naturally lives right in the middle of the piste, with the first run set on the right side and second on the left. Both directions offer their equal amounts of challenges, and though you feel like the finish line is close, the extreme terrain changes, and compressions and banked and fall-away turns can easily tack extra seconds onto your time from one gate to the next. When I finished my inspection, looking back up at the run, I stood physically as a racer, but mentally I felt way more like a fan. It was so cool!

In the start gate, I was my usual mixture of nerves and excitement, fired up to race on this hill while trying to focus on the task at hand. I pushed out and instantly could feel the challenges in the terrain. My skis didn't have much snow contact, and I flailed around trying to keep them connected.

---

1   A series of tight turns

As I came onto the bench before the breakover, though, I started to feel them a bit better under my feet—like I was in the driver's seat again.

"Bite the tip, push into the ski, release, recentre," I told myself, making up for lost time. "Make speed, make speed, make speed," I said over and over.

It was working. I was making speed, but I got too caught up in my turns, enjoying the good feelings that had evaded me at the start of the course. Losing focus on what was coming up next, I completely forgot to make a move to adjust for the sixty-degree-angle change of the breakover, and as the hill dropped away, my hips stayed back and behind my feet. I naturally lost contact with the snow, and with it my ability to turn the skis. Though I tried to salvage my run, at this point, staying in the course was more of a wish than reality. When I touched back down, well below my desired line, I fell inside, sliding down the rest of the pitch on my hip, missing every gate along the way.

This was my first attempt down the legendary Wengen track, and I had pulled the classic rookie mistake.

One of the veterans came over to me in the finish area to teach a lesson. "World Cup hills are different than the junior ones you're used to racing. On Europa Cup and NorAm hills, you can get away with a lazy position and no thought. On World Cup pistes, you have to look ahead and work over the terrain or they'll eat you alive," he said with a smile, finishing the lecture of the day with a little laugh at my misfortunes.

Both a bit pissed off and grateful, this stuck with me, and once I under-stood it, I felt more comfortable on these challenging hills. If I was smart about it and willing to take risks in the right spots, there were advantages to be had on them.

• • •

Athletes have to requalify for the team every year based on their last sea-son's performances. Criteria varies based on age and is usually centred around head-to-head results or world rankings. After forty-plus starts and nearing the end of the season, my results hadn't yet qualified me for the "C" team, and the runway of opportunities was shortening. My mind was starting to fill with "what if" scenarios about not making the team. I'd likely be ok to make the development team again, but with the team-fee price tag of $18,000, I wasn't sure our family could afford this for a second season. I had to be realistic, so I started to explore the NCAA path, where I would go to school, get a formal education, and still continue my ski-racing dreams. It wasn't the optimal route to find your way back to the World Cup, but it was possible, and I started talking to coaches. Coming into the National Championships, I began preparing myself for the possibility of disappointment from a bad race series.

It's ok, school is a good option. My parents always wanted me to go to university, maybe this is the best thing for me. Exploring the possibility that maybe my dream of being a World Cup racer and Olympic skier wouldn't happen.

It took until the last day of nationals in Mt. Orford, Quebec, for me to see the truth. We were racing slalom, as it's traditionally held last out of the four disciplines in big events. The slalom hill was steep at the top and transitioned onto a long flat section, all the way to the finish. Nothing too tricky terrain wise, and the snow surface was icy, a challenging factor that I liked. This year's field consisted of our country's best at the time and current "A" and "B" team athletes, Thomas Grandi and JP Roy. Just inspecting beside them felt special. I had a great first run and sat in second place between JP and Thomas.

I liked the hill, had grip with my skis, and standing in the start area before second run, I felt like I had nothing to lose.

If things don't work out, I'll just go to school. No big deal. Just go for it, I told myself, hoping these words sounded believable enough to free up a great performance.

But as I got closer to my turn in the gate, the cracks of this mantra started to show.

Wait. This is my chance to podium at the National Championships. I can save my season here. I let myself see the potential that stood before me.

As much as I tried to convince myself that I was ok with an alternative outcome, standing in the gate, watching Thomas ski down in front of me, I realized I wanted the original dream more than anything.

I skied with some tightness in my turns as I didn't want to ski out, but even with these second run apprehensions, I held it together and finished third fastest of the day.

This was my first National Champs podium! JP won, Thomas was second, and standing beside them on the podium was a dream in itself. An extra surprise was that this result also gave me a second-place finish in the combined event, which takes an athlete's downhill race and adds it with their slalom for a total three-run-combined, timed event.

I walked away from the nationals third place in slalom and second in combined. With these two podiums, I qualified for next year's national "C" team, and my dream of World Cup and Olympics was still alive and well.

In the days after, reflecting on how I'd considered the possibility of going the NCAA route and had told myself that I was ok with this, I was able to see through this lie.

Who am I trying to fool? I don't want a secondary route and to potentially give up on my dream.

I was waking up to the strength of my desire.

If I hadn't qualified for the team, I would have been devastated. The acceptance I'd expressed before the race was fake, just a brace from the inevitable sadness I would have felt from the loss. In this, though, I gained deeper insight into my goals. I not only wanted to race in the World Cup, but I wanted to be one of the best in the world.

I wanted to win.

CHAPTER 6
NOT THE NOR AM CIRCUIT ANYMORE

PART OF THE EXCITEMENT OF the ski-racer lifestyle is travelling the world and getting to know different cultures. The competitive winter months are spent mostly in central Europe, while the summer off season is often in the Southern Hemisphere, chasing the winter snow of Chile, Argentina, New Zealand, or Australia.

In 2001, our group formed into a true development team, with a mixture of last season's members and a couple of newbies. Scott Hume, Ben Thornhill, Cam Barnes, Ryan Semple, Julien Cousineau, and I were the returning group while Paul Stutz and Brad Spence, graduates from the Alberta team, made up the new additions. Leading us as head coach was Marc Gagnon, a stockily built, fiery Quebecois with short-cut, salt and pepper hair, who'd been coaching for years and had run the Continental Cup team the year before.

Marc was a player's coach. As a previous athlete himself, racing on the USA and Japanese pro tour, his style was more of a partnership than dictatorship. In his racing days, he had held the unofficial record of most broken poles in a single season, somewhere in the thirties, so he clearly understood the frustrations felt by an athlete in the throes of performance. As a coach on a hill, he was calm, hard-working, and super knowledgeable, but when travel went a little sideways, a van broke down, or a computer, video camera, or on-hill timing system had technical issues, the fire would come out. We'd have front row seats to the wrath, usually much to our comic relief.

In the assistant role was our former BC team assistant, Matt Kerr, and rounding out the staff was a multi-mark, half-coach, half-ski technician, Tom Penny. Skis have to be tuned every day to handle the on-hill demands, sharpening the edges and waxing the bases, like a mechanic tuning a car after a race. Up until this point we'd worked on our own skis, so having a ski tech helping out was a major milestone. We still helped with some aspects of the job like waxing and scraping, but Tom did the vast majority of the work. As a skier moves up in the rankings, the ski tech or service man, as the role is also called, typically looks after two to four athletes; though, if you're the best in the world like Marcel Hirscher or Lindsey Vonn, you may have two ski techs for just one athlete. Altogether, the staff had a youthful vibe to match with the young and competitive energy of the athletes.

Marc booked our big summer training camp in Bariloche, Argentina, which was my first trip to the Southern Hemisphere and everyone on the team's first time to Argentina. The travel to Bariloche had a one-day layover in Buenos Aires to change airports and catch a short-haul flight southwest to the mountain resort town. Coming out of the clouds above Argentina's capital city, I was struck by its enormity. I saw a mixture of office buildings, residential areas, roads, and traffic—there were people and homes as far as I could see, but it was the shanty towns that drew my eyes the most. I'd never seen poverty in person like this before and was glued to the window without thought, just staring, unsure of what to think.

Ski teams don't travel light, and as a racer you get comfortable with the packing, unpacking, loading, and unloading lifestyle. We typically bring two ski bags with six to eight pairs of skis in each, three pairs of poles, two duffle bags full of ski gear and personal clothing, plus a carry-on backpack with ski boots in hand. Ski boots are always carry-on, because if your luggage gets lost you can borrow the rest of the gear, and a day of training in jeans is better than no skiing at all. The coaches would have their own personal gear plus a dozen other pieces, consisting of gates, boxes of ski-tuning gear, drills, bits, radios, video equipment, and timing systems. Altogether, our team of eight athletes and three staff travelled with forty-two pieces of checked luggage, and if we had been a World Cup team, it would have been up to sixty pieces.

As ski team budgets go, the World Cup teams have the biggest ones, spending roughly $100,000 a year per athlete, and with each step down the budgets shrink, eventually making their way to a development team athlete, whose costs are around $75,000 per athlete per year. These sums can run out quickly if coaches aren't careful in building and executing their programs, adding to the pressures of their roles. The transport and layover hotel that Marc arranged was in accordance with the "save where you can" philosophy, especially after just spending thousands on overweight charges. With the fast-paced energy of Buenos Aires, a significant amount of luggage, multiple logistical challenges, and the fear of over-spending, the stage was set for a classic Gagnon freakout.

Pushing our carts out of the terminal, each one stacked higher than the next, jetlagged and sleep-deprived, we took a pause.

"Yo, Buenos Aires guy!" Semple said while jabbing Cousi in the ribs with a side smile, for which Ryan received an arm punch in return.

The rest of us laughed and stood there with looks of relief on our faces.

"Hey *amigos,* come this way! Come, come over here," a short, stocky Argentinian man called our way in broken English, snapping us from our tourist fog.

With the few more Spanish words that followed, we understood that he was gesturing to the mid-size bus behind him.

"I think that's our ride," Scott said, trying to translate.

Cam added his doubts to the situation. "No way! That's not nearly big enough. How are we all going to fit in there?"

In a murmur of French and English curses, Marc came speeding up from behind us, making quick and short strides. "Eh, come on, boys. Let's go, this is us. Start loading up." The agitation was building in his voice as he walked through us towards the driver.

What had started out as just us and the bus driver moving the gear quickly multiplied and there were soon half a dozen other Argentinians helping Tetris our gear into the cargo and passenger areas of the bus.

"*Amigos.* Team inside the bus now—we pack around," the driver said in his mixture of Spanish and English.

They eventually had success loading everything in, with bags underneath seats and all around us to the roof. We were enclosed. Marc came in last, sitting at the front of the bus, covered in sweat. He already looked at the end of his rope before the driver came to him with one last request.

"Come on! Come on!" We could hear Marc heating up. "We didn't ask for help! *Câlice!* You gotta be kidding me." His hands waved back and forth, palms facing up with his shoulders rolled back as if waiting for God to deliver a different answer.

The driver just stood there until Marc handed over a few US twenty-dollar bills, his precious budget heading out the door, to which the driver passed on to our newly made and short-lived helping friends.

"Tabarnak!" Marc shouted, taking his frustrations out on the back of his seat, us laughing in the back.

On the trip into the city, I noticed some different driving habits. I didn't know two lanes of traffic could accommodate three vehicles across or that stop signs were merely suggestions.

I looked at Cam, and his eyes were as wide as mine. He mouthed something like, "What the hell?"

Turning off the highway, the bus eventually came to a stop on the right-hand side of a narrow, two/three lane, one-way street. The driver turned back and pointed across, to the left side of the street. "Holiday Inn, Holiday Inn."

This was our hotel for the night. It was great that we'd made it to our destination, but the situation now required us to get the gear off the bus and stored in the hotel for the night.

Standing outside on the street and assessing the challenge, we discussed how getting each piece across this busy street through unyielding traffic and delivering it safely inside the hotel lobby was even possible. We looked at each other to see if anyone would take the lead, but before we could decide, our driver cracked open the luggage compartment and started handing out bags.

"I guess this is happening," Ben said with shock.

Barely a few hours inside one of the biggest cities of the world, we were shuttling gates, skis, boxes, and bags through honking horns and waving fingers, trying to get the cars to slow down long enough for us to pass. Out of breath and dripping with sweat, we all eventually made it through to the safety of the hotel lobby.

Marc remained outside on the sidewalk talking to the driver. "Come on! You're kidding me!" he said over and over as the driver told him he couldn't park the bus next to the hotel and we'd have to re-shuttle everything back in the morning.

But this was a future team problem, and before then we were off to explore a free night in Buenos Aires, imitating Marc's reactions and laughing to no end along the way.

The next morning, Marc had a plan. "Ok guys, we're going to have Matt and the driver on the other side of the street, loading the bus. I'll be on this side with the bags, and five of you will shuttle the gear across." It was a more organized attack for the repacking. "Mike and Cam, you stay back in the lobby and watch all of our carry-on gear—make sure nothing gets stolen."

With this, everyone took off their backpacks and shoulder bags, packed with passports, money, and computers, put them in a pile against the wall beside the check-in desk, and took off to their jobs. Cam and I positioned ourselves on the couch directly across, about eight feet away from the pile, taking up our post.

The hotel's first floor was a squeezed rectangular room with way more length than width, the check-in desk was near the front just inside the front doors, and beyond this were the elevators with a little lobby bar/restaurant at the back that wafted air full of cigarette smoke towards us. The only light for the whole space came in from the two glass doors at the front, which were opening onto the street.

Shortly after our shift began, a couple of girls walked into the lobby and started a conversation with the front desk attendant. Our eyes followed them, watched for a minute or so, and soon returned onto our crew's bags. The girls eventually left, and Cam and I continued to talk and watch. No fewer than five minutes later, a man came hurrying in off the street carrying three computer bags and looking visibly upset and a little angry. He marched right up to the clerk, speaking loudly and pointing at us, our pile of backpacks, and back to us again. He placed the three bags on our pile and went to the restaurant at the back of the room. Stunned and very confused, we eventually realized that these were our bags that the man had dropped. We were baffled.

The clerk came around from behind the desk and over to us. "That man," he said, pointing to the back of the lobby, "saved your friends' computers from being stolen."

We still looked confused, and he continued. "When the two girls came in and talked to me, there was another person who walked into the lobby behind them and grabbed your backpacks. This gentleman was back there having breakfast," he pointed over to him again, "saw this happening, rushed out after the person, and recovered your bags."

We couldn't believe it. How was this possible?

"Please keep a better watch on your belongings; the thieves can be very tricky here with tourists."

The clerk returned to his post and we went to ours.

How could the bags, resting just steps away from us, have been taken right out from under our noses? We hadn't even seen the man from the lobby restaurant pass in front of us as he ran out of the hotel to reclaim our gear.

Cam turned to acknowledge our lack of big-city smarts. "We're not in Canmore anymore."

It wasn't until we were safely on the bus that we shared the close call with the team.

"WHAT?!" they screamed in unison.

Cousi vented his frustrations, now punching me in the ribs. "I would have killed you two. How do you even let this happen?"

No one was impressed except for Marc, who turned around from the front of the bus with a smile. He watched, amused, as the ribbing continued. Finally, the joke was on us.

• • •

In the 2001/02 race season, this was the year that I got to start my first World Cup. Before this, though, Semple and I went with Marc for a ten-day, pre-Christmas trip in Northern Italy and Süd Tirol, Austria, where we would get our first taste of Europa Cup racing, the circuit just below the World Cup. Just one race into our trip, Marc got a call from the World

Cup head coach saying that there was a spot for one of us to race the next World Cup slalom in Madonna di Campiglio, Italy.

"Are we getting called up?" I asked Ryan, trying to decipher what was coming through the other end of the phone.

At the time, Canada only had three World Cup slalom spots. Thomas Grandi and JP Roy held the first two, leaving one extra for us. After the coaches deliberated, Ryan was given the spot, but we could both come, and I could take part in the course inspection and pre-race free ski on the race hill and then watch from inside the athlete zone in the finish area.

Madonna is a classic stop on the slalom circuit, a race always held at night, and it ranks up there with some of the best hills on tour. With great terrain features out of the start to keep you on your toes, it levels out a bit halfway down, letting the racers regroup briefly before taking a hard left turn, breaking over onto a steep pitch, and gradually flattening with terrain features all the way into the finish. It's an exciting hill to race because the whole way down it dares you to release your skis and let them run, but if you're not careful, it spits you out quickly, leading to some exciting crashes and setting the stage for anything to happen. Adding to its character, the hill ends in the middle of town, surrounded by hotels, houses, and buildings, which naturally shapes the finish area into a horseshoe inside of them. A true slalom hill through and through.

Being a night event, the first- and second-run start times were 6:00 p.m. and 9:00 p.m., which meant our official time for the pre-race free ski was 3:00 p.m. This free ski is an opportunity for the athletes to get on the race hill without any gates set, to feel out the snow surface, make any necessary adjustments to their equipment, and ski out some last-minute jitters in any rhythm they'd like. Joining the World Cup team for the day, we were now under the leadership of head coach, Thierry Meynet, a soft-spoken and friendly Frenchman, who'd been with the Canadian group for a couple of years. Thierry was always so encouraging, had an astute eye for technique, and did his best to support athletes through the struggles of development.

The plan was to leave the hotel at 2:30 p.m. and drive to the start to make it in time for the free ski. It was 2:15 p.m. and Ryan and I were still milling about in our rooms, organizing our gear, packing our backpacks,

and wondering what we needed for the day. I was nervous from just anticipating the warmup free ski, but this was Ryan's first World Cup, so the
jitters for sure were fogging his brain too. It was 2:35 p.m. when we got
outside, and the van's engine was already on, fresh diesel burning fumes
from the exhaust. At five minutes late, we rookies were making everyone
wait. Jumping in the open door, I was already sweating when Thierry
turned around from the driver's seat and addressed both of us: "Eh, this
isn't the NorAm circuit anymore! Be here on time or don't come at all."
There was no leeway in his voice.

It took a lot to push Thierry past his usual warm and supportive nature,
so this clearly was not ok. A few jokes were cracked by Thomas and JP on
the way up the road, dissolving the tension, but Thierry's message stuck.
Be professional and come prepared to support the group. Even if we race
as individuals, this is a team sport.

At this venue, you can drive up a mountain pass road right to the start
area. When we reached the top, I grabbed my skis, backpack, and poles
from the van and followed behind Thomas like a puppy. My eyes gradually
lifted from the heels of his boots and soon caught hold of the spectacle.
There were huge TV trucks, race organizers running between tents and
the hill, fans intermingling getting autographs from their favourite racers,
equipment reps managing their gear, ski technicians organizing their athletes' skis, coaches grouping up at the hill, and then there were the athletes.

There's the Norwegians, Aamodt, Kjus, the Austrians, Raich, Pranger, Matt,
the Americans, Miller, Schlopy, Puckett. I recited all the names I knew in my
head. My attention was drawn to all of them.

Thomas called over to the American, Eric Schlopy, and started talking
to him about windsurfing.

Dumbfounded, I thought, He knows these guys!

I was seeing everything through the eyes of my ten-year-old self and
learning that all my favourite superheroes were also humans.

Marc found Ryan and me near the snow and brought us back to the task
at hand. "Ok, you two. They've sectioned off a little corridor on skier's left
of the 'ill for the free ski lane. It only goes 'alfway down to the corner, so
come to a stop when you 'it the end, traverse over to the skier's right side,
and side slip the rest of the way down. I'll be positioned 'alfway if you want

to stop and talk." His Quebecois accent allowed the H's to stay silent and we nodded in agreement.

A few minutes to 3:00 p.m., the whole field of seventy-five starting athletes, plus a few extras like me, started clicking into their skis and shuffling to the start house. I was following Thomas but somehow ended up a dozen or so athletes behind him. It was every man for himself now. Making it inside the start tent, I looked around and found myself standing beside one of my favourite athletes, Kjetil André Aamodt, along with Manfred Pranger and a select few others who could fit inside the tent.

Trying not to step on their skis, I just stood there until I was tapped from behind to move ahead. The starter was at the front calling out, "Go... Go... Go...." every ten seconds, sending skiers out one by one onto the hill.

Pranger left the gate in front of me. I wasn't ready for this. Staring through the start tent's exit, I saw the hill for the first time and watched Pranger ski, knifing one turn after the other. He looked so good.

It's so narrow. It's too icy. Where do I even ski? My self-talk was not helping, and on the next "Go," I pushed out with maybe the least confidence I'd ever left a start gate with. My first turn was so bad. I had no grip and ended up completely in the back seat. My turns quickly turned windshield wiper-esque, sideslipping ones, as I just tried to manage my speed and not crash into the fences.

I made it down to the end of the free ski zone and came to a stop at Marc's feet. He had a big smile. "Mike, What the 'ell was this?" I could see he was holding back some laughs. I hadn't made a real turn down the whole hill.

I stood watching a few of the other guys arcing down with ease and thought *How am I ever going to do that? How am I ever going to compete with them?* I was recognizing how high the World Cup level really was.

Ryan may have been feeling some similar nerves because in the race, he only made two gates, straddling the second of the course, ending his first World Cup debut far too early. We watched the second run together from the finish area, enjoying the energy and seeing first-hand the best in the world do their thing. After the race, Tom told a story of his first time racing in Madonna when Alberto Tomba was at the height of his fame, winning the race in front of 50,000-plus fans. Our race that night had around 20,000 in attendance, which felt full to me. I tried to imagine what it would look like with 30,000 more. It was more than I could picture.

A month later, in mid-January, I was given *my* inaugural World Cup shot at one of the biggest events in ski racing, the Kitzbühel slalom. We'd been in Austria for the month, racing with the whole development group, and had just finished the famous Westendorf night race. Westendorf is a town fifteen kilometres down the road from Kitzbühel, which hosts a regular FIS slalom race the Wednesday before the main weekend events go down. It draws a handful of the World Cup racers, serving as an unofficial prep event, which in turn draws a few thousand spectators out for the show. My result was nothing special, but a spot had opened up and since we were right next door, the following day I was told I'd be racing in Sunday's slalom.

The Kitzbühel race week starts with the super G race on Friday, the main event of downhill on Saturday, and after the speed skiers are done, Sundays are for slalom. Kitzbühel is one of the few circuit stops where the tech and speed groups cross over, bringing together this great dynamic of the two groups. Marc drove me to the Canadian team's hotel Saturday afternoon, where I was soon enjoying the five-star food and the more spacious rooms.

I could get used to this, I thought while walking through the lobby after lunch.

With no other teammates from my peer group with me, no Ryan or Cousi to confide in, I was feeling a little insecure around the true veterans of the team like Ed Podivinski and Darren McBeath who were walking the halls. I wasn't sure if I should actually be in this place. Sharing a room with Thomas, I basically watched and did the same things as him to get ready for the next day's race. I was getting to learn first-hand from one of my ski-racing heroes. He rode the stationary bike, so I hopped on while he stretched on the floor beside me. While riding in the hallway outside of our room, I had to pinch myself thinking about how far I'd come. From a rambunctious kid with too much energy to Team Canada's hotel, preparing to race Kitzbühel. I felt like the coolest person in the world in this moment. I had arrived.

At the far end of this second-floor hallway, Edi came up the staircase with some friends he was showing around. This was his last season of racing and because of it, he was on a little retirement tour. Actually, I had only gotten to race because he didn't want to use the spot to compete in the combined event. He noticed us at the end of the hall and brought his group over for introductions.

"Hey guys," he said to his friends while pointing to Tom stretching on the ground. "This is Thomas Grandi, our top tech skier in Canada. And this..." he continued, gesturing towards me, "... this is... ah, what's your name again?"

What?! He doesn't know who I am. How does he not know who his teammates are? These thoughts jumped around but stayed in my head. I instantly felt naked in front of the whole class. *I shouldn't be here. I shouldn't be racing, I don't belong up here yet.* The doubts in my head continued.

While all of this was going on internally, I did manage to answer, "Mike. I'm Mike," to which Edi added, "Oh yes. This is Mike, one of our up and comers for the tech side."

I felt defeated before I even started.

It had been an honest mistake on one side, but it led to a total collapse of confidence on the other. My deepest insecurities came out... that I would be exposed as a fraud, that I didn't belong and this dream would all be taken away from me. I covered this vulnerability the only way I knew how. *They don't know who I am?! I'll show them! They're nothing but wash-ups, has-beens. Good riddance. Out with the old, in with the new.* I turned the fear into anger and anger into motivation to prove them wrong and defend my place.

I internally loathed anyone who dared question my place, and the chip on my shoulder grew.

At dinner that night, as I was feeling small pretty sitting at the end of the table, Edi's ski technician, a small-framed and tough-looking French Canadian, came over to me. "Eh Mike, I'm Paul Lavoie." He greeted me with a big smile.

His warmth instantly put me at ease.

"I hear tomorrow is your first World Cup."

"Yes," I responded.

"Who's carrying your skis for you?" he asked, seeing if I had anyone to carry up my race skis for me, as two pairs are a standard for racing: one for warmup and a fresh pair for the race.

"No one. I was going to do it myself," I shared, a little embarrassed.

"Ah, nonsense. I'll come up with you, carry your race skis, and be in the start to click you in. Everyone needs a service man in the start for a World Cup." he said. "Come on, let's go downstairs, you can show me your skis and I'll bring them up for you." He tapped me on the shoulder and we got up to head down to the ski room.

I went from feeling totally alone and out of place to feeling welcomed and looked after again. The shame of my previous resentful thoughts washed over me.

The next morning, I had a little more composure than my previous experience of Madonna, but there was still room for improvement. When inspection opened, I could barely see the gates between all the athletes, media, staff, and course workers. This was absolutely a whole new level. As I came up to the first breakover, I stood to the side and looked around. Straight below me was the slalom finish area surrounded by grandstands, creating a larger amphitheatre, which would soon be filled with 40,000 fans. To my right, a few hundred metres away, I looked at the finish of the downhill track, the "Strief" where less than twenty-four hours before, 80,000 fans had been cheering on their favourite racers and gasping at spectacular saves from near crashes.

In between the two snow-filled arenas, my eyes were drawn to a person walking up the hill. I blinked a few times and looked closer to make sure I was seeing this correctly. It was 8:44 a.m. and coming over to the slalom hill was a twenty-something year old guy, still drunk from the night before, no shirt, holding two tall cans of Gösser beer, slipping and falling as he cheered and called out at the racers passing by.

Thierry's words rang over and over in my head. This is definitely not the NorAm circuit anymore.

For the race, I started bib-84, finished sixty-first of sixty-eight finishers, and 4.75 seconds back from the leader. In World Cup, only the top thirty get to race a second run, so my day was over.

From these two World Cup experiences, I learned about two new and different distractions to manage. In Madonna, it was the athletes who grabbed most of my attention, and in Kitzbühel, it was the crowds. Being amongst the fans and the energy of the biggest show in ski racing, I realized that this was something I would have to prepare for as well.

CHAPTER 7
LEARNING FROM INJURY

LIFE ON THE ROAD ISN'T always glamorous, especially away from the World Cup venues. Living out of a suitcase, moving from hotel to hotel every few days, and being away from home more than half the year felt like a lot at twenty years old. I found myself missing a lot of the Canadian comforts I'd grown accustomed to: the foods, North American sports, and English TV. Even the little cultural differences found in day-to-day life would bring up feelings of homesickness, like entering a building with a push of the door rather than a pull, or that most stores were closed on weekends and for long periods mid-day. In the lulls between skiing and team activities, sitting in hotel rooms, one after another, surrounded by unfamiliar walls became a bit too much. My solution to all of this was staying busy and being around teammates as much as possible, but I couldn't hide from it all the time.

Halfway through the previous season, my long-time friend and team-mate Ben had decided to "hang them up" and stop racing for the national team. We were in a small Austrian village near the town of Innerkrems, which sat deep in a narrow valley, hugging the river that flowed through it. High above the town was one of the country's main north/south highways, standing forty metres over top, which all together left little room for the January sunlight to get through.

Our hotel was a little three-storey *gasthof* built on the main road. It had probably stood there for well over a century. It was the kind of building that made me wonder what it had experienced from standing through two world wars. For thirty euros per person a night with full *pension*, the place fit right into our team's budget.

Four of us bunked in the top-floor room. It was built into the attic, with ceilings sloping down into the corners, forcing us to gradually crouch lower and lower to reach our beds.

Ben just came out with it, I guess not knowing a better way to share his decision. "I think I'm done."

"What do you mean, 'done'? Like done, done?" Trevor questioned him.

Ben opened up for the first time, which wasn't easy in this group. "I don't know, this isn't for me. Being over here going from race to race, I feel like I'm missing out on something. I've always wanted to go to university in the States, race NCAA, get a degree, and go into finance of some sort."

We all just sat there in silence, nodding and not knowing what else to say.

Later that night Ben restarted the conversation. "Mike, don't you ever think about stopping and going to school? Is this it, living on the road, racing from stop to stop?" he asked sincerely.

"Yeah, sure, I guess. I mean, it's not always fun on the road and now we're seeing all of our friends going to university. I do think about what I'm missing out on, but then I also want to be a ski racer, go to the Olympics, and make a career out of this," I answered, and in the process, filled my head with even more questions.

We turned off the lights and went to bed, and the hotel walls creaked and cracked as I searched for some reassuring answers in the silence between. Slight rumbles from cars passed by overhead.

A few days after this conversation, I had a third-place finish in a Super G, scoring a result that jumped my world ranking way up for my age. In the euphoria of the result that came from a pre-race plan playing out perfectly on course, I felt like I'd stepped away from the pack and onto a whole other level. *Of course I want this. It's the best feeling in the world!* I told myself.

This was the answer I'd been hoping for, and the doubts from my conversation with Ben soon faded into the past.

• • •

The big news of this next season was the return of Dusan. After a successful tenure with the BC ski team, he was brought up and hired as the continental team head coach. Ben, along with a couple other athletes, had left the team. Brad and Paul stayed with this growing development team, and four of us, Semple, Scott Hume, Cousi, and I formed this new Continental Cup group. Marc moved up to coach with the World Cup team, so Dusan took over his leadership. His return was like coming home after a long trip and finding things right where you left them; I knew what I was in for. Under his direction, I welcomed the restoration of more structure, high-volume training, and clear team goals.

Early into the race season, though, on Friday, December 13, I sustained my second major injury and the first since my broken leg at age thirteen. While racing a GS in Racines, Italy, halfway down my second run, I dropped deep into the back seat while accelerating out of a turn, and before I could recover out of this squatted position, I felt a click in my right knee. Transferring all my weight to my left leg, I skied off course and traversed to the side of the run, falling over in pain. I was only able to bend and extend my knee a few degrees, with a lot of pain in both directions. My leg was locked in position and sat almost straight.

I was soon strapped into a toboggan for a ride down the mountain, where Dus met me and drove to the nearest hospital. It was diagnosed as a tear of my medial meniscus and after a call to my mom to let her know, we returned to the hotel. The guys were nice enough to pack up my gear while I rested on the bed, contemplating my new reality of a season without skiing. On the four-hour drive to the airport with just Dus and me, in between his calls to doctors, physios, and travel agents, he shared his perspectives on injuries: how to go through them and what's on the other side. I felt so lost at the time that I'm not sure how much I took in. The vision of my whole year had just disappeared in front of my eyes. I had no sight of the future and just wanted to cry.

Consulting with the orthopedic surgeon back in Vancouver, the bucket handle tear of the medial meniscus was confirmed and surgery was the chosen course to repair it. This officially brought my season to a close. Picking me up from surgery, Mom was ready for the recovery process. Her experience had grown over the years, with multiple injuries between Britt and me. In tears in the back of the car, I blankly stared out the window at the passing mountains on our way home to Whistler.

I was looking for sympathy. "Everything I worked so hard for in the pre-season has all been for nothing, gone down the drain."

"At least you had a good doctor this time around," Mom said, putting a smile on my face for a brief moment as we thought back to the cast-removal day of my first broken leg.

At home, lying back in bed, a little sense of relief started to seep through the sadness. The stresses of a season needing to make criteria, get results, perform at my best... all of these I could put aside for a bit and just relax. I would be put on injury status, which would freeze my points and keep my position on the team. This helped me relax a little more, and it wasn't long before this feeling continued to grow into some kind of excitement.

I can do my rehab between Whistler and Vancouver, hang with my friends at university, live a little ski-bum lifestyle for a winter, and experience every-thing I've been missing out on, I told myself. *This whole thing could be an opportunity in the making!* Slowly, the future opened up again.

Supported and funded by the ski team, I split my rehab between two physiotherapists, Rick Celebrini and Bianca Matheson. Mid-week I'd spend two days with Rick in Vancouver and time with friends going to UBC, while on the weekends, I'd be with Bianca in Whistler and work at a local ski shop. It was the best of both worlds. Bianca and Rick were estab-lished sport physios, working with a range of high-level athletes across most sports while also having experience in the skiing world, Bianca with the Australian Olympic ski team and Rick with our World Cup group from time to time. Each brought a little different approach to their therapy.

With me on crutches for the start, our rehab steps were to regain range of motion in the knee, gradually load weight back into the leg, and then build the strength up enough to walk, run, and work out normally. If all went well, I'd be back on snow in four months and training with the team in six.

A few weeks into the process, we were starting to put weight onto the leg, practicing a few steps under Bianca's supervision. Later, I kept this going under no one's direction but my own, practicing steps without my crutches around the house. A couple of days later I thought I was ready to walk and was excited to show Rick the progress we were making. In our next session together, I slowly walked up the stairs into the clinic, one by one, taking in what it felt like to have weight under my right foot again. When I got to the top of the stairs and past the front desk, I could see Rick at the other end of the clinic, about thirty metres away. I put both my crutches in one hand, carrying them off the ground, and started my long walk to the stationary bike for warmup. Like a toddler taking his first steps, I was smiling ear to ear, feeling so pleased with my accomplishments and waiting for the parental praise that was soon to come. Rick was working with another patient when he looked up and saw me wobbling optimistically across the floor.

"What are you doing?!" he called out from across the room, instantly leaving his other patient to make his way to me.

My smile vanished.

"Mike! Every step you make like this only creates and reinforces a poor movement pattern. What you're doing right now throws off your hips and back while everything else has to compensate. The only time I want to see you walking without crutches is when you can do it without a limp. Take your crutches back and use them until you're ready." There was no sound of praise in his voice.

I'd been reprimanded, and I sheepishly crutched the rest of the way to the bike having learned a valuable lesson, all before 8:00 a.m.

Gaining full range of motion back in the knee was a painful and slow process. We'd use manual manipulation, digging in to break up the scar tissue, as well as using the stationary bike to help. If I could get the pedal around a full revolution with the seat in its highest position, I'd then lower it a notch and continue to try at this level until the seat was at its lowest setting. In Bianca's clinic one weekend, I was moving the pedal back and forth, tracing an upside-down rainbow with the pedals, bringing my knee up as far as it would feel ok, and then returning the pedal downward and back up to the other side's flexion limit.

Playing with this range while Bianca was with another patient, I was coming close to getting my first full revolution, enjoying the back-and-forth feeling with no pain.

"Hey Bianca, come check it out. I'm killing it with these half pedal strokes! I think I can start to do them with one leg," I called over to her.

As I started showing off to no one in particular, I gained a little too much momentum with one of my down-pedal strokes, carrying my foot over the top with a pop! My knee made the full revolution.

"Aghhh!" I squawked out for everyone to hear. In the process, I lost my balance, fell off the bike, and buckled to the ground. I had just successfully crashed off a stationary bike.

It was only then that Bianca came out from behind the curtain where she'd been working with the other patient. Without missing a beat, she said, "Ah, I see you broke through some of the scar tissue."

I looked up from the ground in hopes of finding some more sympathy but was only met with her laugh. She had a sixth sense for the sort of pain I was feeling at any time. If it was the good kind, it was safe to push through; if it was not good, she'd stop me for the day.

Over in the clinic with Rick, he would show up at the every morning by 6:00 a.m. at the latest, always in a dress shirt, pants, and nice shoes. He was built more like an athlete than I was. In our daily two-hour routine, after the stationary bike warmup, I'd get on the physio table, free for him to dig into the back of my knee, quad, surgery scars, calf, and anywhere else that was blocked. Any mobility we could gain manually before I had to go to work on my exercises was important. We'd run through a series of movements together, working the muscles through balance, strength, and agility until he saw I was losing form and fatigue was setting in. We would then ice up and shut it down for the day.

The methods he worked with were based on the understanding that all dynamic athletic movements run through the core, on a cross-pattern x from the tip of the right hand to the end of the left foot and vice versa, proximal to distal. In this way, he and his contemporaries built their rehab and performance training on strengthening these patterns. If the right knee gave way, it was because of shearing somewhere else along this chain that caused an overloading and an inevitable "break." As I got stronger and could move with more confidence, the "exercise" portion of the sessions turned into full-on workouts, becoming more dynamic. This was where Rick's strengths as a rehab specialist really came through. He'd run me through all sorts of exercises on core boards and physio balls, with med balls, bands, and anything else to create the resistance needed to form the right movement patterns. I would be in a full sweat, and he'd be right there with me, nice dress shirt and all, still looking ready for a downtown business meeting.

The clinic was an invigorating environment, with intensity, competition, creativity, and athletes from all sports coming through it. At one time Rick was working with a horse jockey who had back pain, asking him to ride a physio ball like his horse, seeing if they could recreate the movements and find a stronger position. Another time I was paired up with a baseball player who'd recently been drafted by the Mets and was rehabbing a shoulder injury. Rick put us together to challenge our movements, pitting my quick feet against the ball player's hand/eye coordination. There was always a smile and a look of *This is good stuff, isn't it?* on Rick's face after a session was over. I loved that clinic; it felt like the next best thing to being on the ski hill.

Eventually my mind started to turn back to the ski team and my goals as a ski racer. In February, the World Championships in St. Moritz, Switzerland, kicked off and two of my three teammates, Ryan and Cousi, were racing in them, getting their first World Champs experience. On the speed side, our two other contemporaries, Erik Guay and Jan Hudec, opened the event with a bang, placing sixth and seventh respectively in the super G, and Erik followed this up with another sixth in the downhill. Both were a year older than me at twenty-two years old and making a mark on the world stage in a big way already. The fire to get back out and prove myself was growing again; I didn't want to be left behind.

On top of this, in the first World Cup following the World Champs, Britt reached her career best result to that date. It was a Thursday morning in early March, and I was warming up on the bike at the clinic in the city when my phone buzzed and started to ring with a call. In 2003, it wasn't very common to have a message or call come through, especially at 8:00 a.m.

"Michael, Michael. Britt's in first, Britt's in first!" It was Mom on the other end of the line giving me a live timing update that she was following from her computer.

The race was a night event in Åre, Sweden, and at 6:00 p.m. local time, Britt was sitting in first place after run number one. It was the first time she'd been in this position in a World Cup.

"No way! This is unreal!" I said out loud, trying to get the others in the clinic to understand just how huge this was.

Not really knowing what to do with myself for the two-hour wait until the second run, with no TV or any way to watch replays, I went about my session. But my mind was still in Åre with my sister.

I wonder what it's like to be leading a World Cup? She's the best in the world right now! This can change everything! I was having a conversation with myself, imagining it was me, living vicariously through her success.

In the second run, I was back on the phone with Mom, this time getting the live updates.

"She's on course... she's at the first split, lost some time but in second place for now... second split... she's dropped back to fifth, still on course..."

I waited the final thirty seconds of her run in silence while my mom watched with vigilance for her final time to pop up on her screen.

"Fifth. Fifth, she came fifth!" Mom was screaming on the other end of the line.

I was speechless. A little bummed she hadn't held on for the win, but what did I know? She was out there racing to fifth in the world, her best finish of her career, and I was back at home doing physio, just trying to find a friend to celebrate with.

As winter thawed into spring, I felt grateful for the opportunity to explore a life outside of ski racing. A few of my old teammates from the club and BC team were skiing for the UBC ski team, and I got to spend a lot of time with them. One day in particular, Paul, who'd been our BC team veteran and a mentor for me over the years, brought it home in a conversation. "How are you feeling about going back, Mike?"

"Ahh, I think I'm ready, my knee is strong, and I feel like I can come back better than I was before," I answered.

"Mike, you have a drive and want it more than any of us did, I can see it. University, home, being a ski bum, all these things will be there for you at any time in life if you want them. Don't worry about missing out on this stuff, you have other things to do."

We sat enjoying the silent moment that followed together.

Paul's support was echoed by a few other close friends, which helped me connect back to the inner voice. My ten-year-old self's dream was still there, waiting to be accomplished. Going back out was my choice, and I still had a lot to prove.

CHAPTER 8
RISING BACK UP AND LEARNING THE MENTAL GAME

SKI RACING IS A COMMUNITY affair. A typical ski club race requires around seventy volunteers: club members, families, and alumni coming out to run the timing, the start, finish areas, and course maintenance, and gate judges to ensure safety and fairness. When we were growing up in Whistler, the parents devoted large amounts of time and energy into our events, training, and club operations. A great representation of this spirit is the famous Whistler Weasel workers, a not-for-profit organization created in the '70s, committed to supporting, working on, and running ski races. From local events to NorAms, National Championships, World Cups, and even the Olympic Winter Games, the "Weasels" have given life to this sport, fueled by their passion for ski racing and maybe a little "Weasel water." What comes from all of these early mornings and long days in the cold is a collection of devoted volunteers with a strong sense of community and willingness to support those of us with the opportunity and drive to climb up the ranks of the sport.

As costs go for the sport, the provincial, national development, and senior teams can come with team fees. Depending on the financial health of the team, the fees for these groups can range from $5,000 to $20,000, $35,000, or even $50,000 per athlete for a single season. If you're on "B" or "A" team status, you've finally made it free and clear from team fees and are usually exempt from such things. In 2003/04, Scott Hume, his brother Jeff, and I were collectively facing around $40,000 in fees and were urged by our parents to get creative to raise the funds. With this push and help from key individuals, we put on a golf-putting tournament, using the typical golf tournament format of collecting registration from teams of four. They would play their rounds, and finish with a dinner and auction. While we were out getting players to come, our two moms ran around town collecting prizes, organizing the registrations, and calling in support from businesses. We were the faces and they were the backbone to this fundraiser.

The event was held on our local eighteen-hole putting course, which made it feel special, as all the participants were condensed into a small space and got to mingle together for the whole day. These events raised a large portion of our team fees and also had a secondary charitable portion to them, putting some of the funds towards a bursary for a younger, local BC team member. For two years, the community filled the tee sheets and prize tables, coming out to support us financially and energetically.

Over the summer, Scott, Jeff, and I formed a little home dryland-training group during the weeks we didn't have to be in Calgary. For a bit of guidance and street cred, we asked one of the veterans of the team, Ryan Oughtred, if we could train with him during our weight-room sessions. Ryan, who also lived in Whistler, had been on the team for close to ten years, and through his experiences and time with injuries, he'd learned some more progressive approaches to training. He was a stickler for technique and the unwritten etiquettes of a gym that the three of us didn't know existed.

The weight room is a sacred place for an athlete, where gains are made, abilities developed, and bonds between teammates forged. With the high demands of the sport, like holding the G forces in a 100km/h downhill turn or the repetitive pounding of a thousand gates for a single slalom session, the strength-building aspects of any program are heavy and require special care and attention. Knowing all of this gave Ryan some reluctance for us to join in with him, but he eventually agreed.

In one of our first sessions all together, we were doing a series of squats, six sets of ten reps with eight minutes of recovery riding on the stationary bike in between. Ryan went first, then Jeff, Scott, and I closed the series, all rotating one after the other.

A few sets in, Ryan called a timeout. "Hey guys, come here."

We all walked over to the squat rack.

Ryan pointed to the bar with frustration in his voice. "You see this? This is not ok."

Scott and I looked at each other, confused. The bar had three forty-five-pound plates on each side, the safety collars locked in the right place... it looked normal to us.

Ryan sensed our lack of understanding and explained our mistakes. "When the plates are stacked on the bar, the numbers face in. We're not here to show off how much we can lift. Secondly, when facing out, the weights move around, jingle, and clang against each other. Take these off and rack it properly, as tight as possible. If we're going to continue working together, things need to be done right! Do we agree?" He had finished with a question that had only one answer.

"Yeah, for sure," we agreed, feeling nervous and wondering what else we were doing wrong.

Over the next weeks, through some more mistakes, Ryan continued to educate us on the proper techniques and etiquette for how an athlete should move and be in a gym.

After a summer of rebuilding, I was hungry when we hit the snow and was trying to prove myself in every run. Armed with some extra size, coordinated movement, and body control, I was stronger both physically and mentally. Since my injury status from the season before had kept me as one of the few tech skiers on the "C" team, I had the fortune of joining Semple, Cousi, Thomas, and JP on the World Cup tech team. Dusan continued his coaching rise as well and after working through the ranks of the Canadian system for close to a decade, he took over as head coach of this World Cup team. Marc remained with the group as the main assistant, plus we had two ski service men and a physiotherapist to round out the staff.

In the training season before I hurt my knee, I was typically two to three seconds behind Thomas and JP per run in slalom. Shortly after my return, I was within one to half a second consistently, and hit a new level in my skiing. The first time I beat Thomas in a run, even though he was testing equipment and probably skiing at eighty percent while I was going full out, I knew something had changed, and a little smile of recognition from Thomas confirmed it.

My big goal for the race season was to finish top two in the overall NorAm slalom standings. Any American or Canadian athlete who achieves this in any discipline earns themselves their own World Cup spot for the next year in that discipline. The team only had four World Cup slalom and GS spots at the time. JP, Thomas, and Cousi had earned their places based on their World Cup point rankings, which left the one national spot open for us young guys to fight for and qualify for. If one of us was skiing fast, we'd get put in and try to break into the top thirty. That's why these NorAm sports are so coveted; they are assigned to the individual and cannot be passed amongst the team, giving a little more security to the racer.

In the Colorado opening NorAm series, I finished with a nineteenth in one and Did Not Finish (DNF) in the other. It was good to be racing again after almost a year away. Just before the Christmas break, Ryan and I paired up with our development teammates Nik Zoricic and Patty Biggs for two Europa Cups in Donnersbachwald, Austria. The hill was nothing special: flat out of the start, took a little turn to the right onto a mild steep section, finishing with some flats and a little terrain. But it was water injected to the max, and to this day stands as the iciest hill I've ever skied on. This hill preparation turned an easy blue square run by anyone's measures into a double black diamond skating rink. When "injection" is done right, there's still some grip to the ice, but if the injection bar's pressure is too low in relation to the outside temperatures, the cold air draws the water back up, pooling it on the surface and making it near impossible to find an edge. This is what's known as a water party gone wrong.

The four of us showed up totally ill-prepared for the conditions, and even during inspection we were Bambi on ice. I stood in the start area watching the top guys like Manfred Pranger, Jure Kosir, and Killian Albrecht actually carve their turns.

How are they even doing this? I thought to myself, absolutely dumbfounded.

Not everyone had the same skills, though, and as I watched many unable to find grip, I felt a little better about my own abilities. The conditions decimated the field, and I was the only one of us four to finish the first day, six seconds off the winner, Pranger, in forty-first place. Meanwhile, only forty-six racers finished from a starting field of a hundred and five.

In the tuning room that evening, the four of us stood around our equipment wondering what to do.

"I can't get my skis to bite. How do you even ski on that ice?!" I asked the group.

"It's not possible," Nik chimed in, unbelievably confident in his answer. "There's no way I can get my skis sharp enough. Feel them. Feel them!" he screamed in desperation, daring us to feel his edges. "Tell me this isn't the sharpest ski you've ever felt!" He threw his hands up in frustration.

We all turned back to our gear to figure out personal solutions. I ended up changing my edge angle from four to five degrees, Pat played around with his boot canting, and Ryan was convinced his skis were broken. I used to scoff at athletes who took their equipment setup too seriously, but now I was starting to grow an appreciation for the importance of it.

The next day we doubled our finish ratio; two of us made it down, not with any real speed, but surviving the two runs. I ended up 5.24 seconds out and Ryan 5.65, in twenty-second and twenty-fourth respectively, and there were only thirty-two finishers on this day.

"The guys winning these races have better skis than us." Nik was restarting his rant in the van as we drove away from the hill. "I went and flexed some of their skis between runs and I'm telling you, we don't stand a chance with what we got. Ours are terrible and theirs are World Cup!" Nik was never shy to use hyperbole and spoke it as fact.

Right or not, we all needed a good excuse to lick our wounds on the long travels home for the Christmas break.

• • •

The new year brought with it a change in my results, and things started to all come together. In Sunday River, Maine, at the second NorAm tech stop of the season, something clicked, and I felt more connected to the snow and free on my skis. My skiing was so relaxed, and the training courses felt easy, like anything was possible. I was so fired up in the start house for first run, I couldn't wait to get on course and see what I could do. This was an excitement I'd only felt a few times in my career before, mostly in training.

I didn't feel much pressure to perform, as my thoughts were not on the results, but rather on how fast I could ski.

I finished ahead of the Americans Jimmy Cochran and Ted Ligety, winning the race for my first NorAm win.

This freedom continued into the next day, and I found a similar gear. I took the lead after first run but Ted got the better of me in the second and he took the win overall. I ended up finishing second with teammate Cousi in third. As I was standing on the podium looking out at the small crowd of coaches, friends, teammates, and competitors, an enjoyable thought came back to me. *This is why I ski. This is why I race!* I gave a big smile as the feeling of being on course still ran through my body.

These results earned me the nation's spot for the next two World Cups, while dropping my FIS points and world ranking from 182nd to fifty-fifth. Ryan, Cousi, and I flew to Europe to meet up with Thomas, JP, and Dusan for the next events in Chamonix, France, and Wengen, Switzerland. Coming in, I felt way more in place than I had two years prior in Kitzbühel. I knew I had the skills to get inside the top thirty, but could I bring it together on race day at this level?

I skied out in Chamonix, posting a DNF and finished fiftieth in Wengen, 4.3 seconds out on the first run, leaving me way out of top-thirty qualifying. Cousi, on the other hand had an amazing tenth-place finish in Wengen. Here was someone I'd beaten the week before at the NorAms who was now seconds faster than me at the World Cup.

What am I missing? What does he know that I don't? These were the questions I didn't have the answer to yet.

I thought the nation's spot would stay in my hands for the next stop in Kitzbühel, but three days before, Dusan had another idea in mind.

Add competition in everything.

The day following the Westendorf night race, he sent Semple and me with Marc to Rogla, Slovenia, a five-hour drive away to meet up with the development team guys to have an open time trial for the spot.

I was furious and vented my anger to Marc on the drive down. "What the hell? This is BS! You know this is going to be a bogus race and will have nothing to do with who's skiing the fastest."

Mark remained silent.

When we came to the Rogla race hill and saw that it was flat with soft conditions, my complaining only got worse. "See, Marc, I told you, BS! Steeps and ice are my strengths, which are the World Cup hills. I don't have the touch for these soft conditions." I had my excuses lined up well before pushing out of the gate.

Paul Stutz opened the race with bib 1 and had great speed even in the first turns. He had the most magical touch for flats and could generate speed in these conditions with the best in the world. He finished second on the day and I was seventh. The spot was Paul's.

After the race, Paul jumped in the van with Ryan, Marc, and me, making the return to Kitzbühel for his first World Cup race. We arrived for the tail end of dinner, where Dusan let us know that Paul's successful time trial also gave him the spot for the Schladming night race, held on the Tuesday following Kitz. I felt a little more slighted, like Dusan was losing faith in me.

Even though we weren't racing, Ryan and I still went out for morning warmup and inspection to continue growing our comfort with these tracks and their atmosphere. I felt so good in the warmup courses, and the faster I felt, the angrier I got for losing the time trial. I couldn't let it go and vented to Ryan, who brought me back down a bit.

"Mike, chill, guy. What are you worried about? Paul gets to race his first World Cups, we get to hang out, enjoy the race, and most importantly, with Schladming already decided, get to party tonight guilt-free. It's win-win." He got me to smile, always keeping things in perspective.

We positioned ourselves in the finish area to watch our teammates and the first run. Much to our surprise and excitement, starting from bib-12, Thomas posted the fastest first-run time, two-tenths of a second ahead of the Finnish superstar, Kalle Palander.

"Oh my God! Tom's in first, Tom's in first!" Ryan and I screamed at each other, barely adding a decibel to the rest of the 50,000 screaming fans.

Tom took his spot in the leader's box and watched his time hold up for the remainder of the field.

Being the biggest stop on the circuit, Kitzbühel draws the most sponsors and VIPs of any race. To sufficiently host them, the organizers set up a large tent for them to mingle, eat, and enjoy the finer sides of World Cup racing. At around half a football field in size, the tent is walled by wrapping windows and a vaulted ceiling, and houses food stations, bars, and dozens of round tables set with white linens, polished silverware, and Riedel glass-ware. The chefs cook up anything from classic central European dishes to sushi and Mexican—really anything you want, classed up and ready for your order.

This is not your typical mid-run hang spot for the athletes, and most of us don't make it past security unless you are a big name or have a big result. But most of the time, if you can flash your race bib, they'll usually let you in. Having none of these, Ryan and I followed Thomas out of the finish area, making the trek through the hordes of people in the open crowds towards the tent. With hundreds of fans now mobbing around the first-run leader, Tom handed us his gear while he signed autographs and took pictures. It took fifteen minutes to cross fifty metres, and even this was a tough pace to keep up. At the entrance of the tent, we kept a firm grip on Tom's gear and made the *we're with him* gesture to the security guards as we walked by in tow. Tom eventually left us for his second-run inspection, while Ryan and I stayed to try and find the best strüdel this place had to offer.

When we finally left the comforts of the VIP tent and re-entered the outside world, I chose to head up for a free run before watching the second run. Ryan decided that his ski boots were off for the day and went straight back to the finish area.

Coincidentally, I came up behind Thomas on my way to the gondola. He was walking on his own, on his way to get ready for second run. "Hey Mike. Come up with me," he called over. "It's better if I'm not alone right now, and you can keep me company."

He had extended an invitation where there was only one answer. "Yeah, of course. I was just going to go for a free run, but I can hang," I answered casually while shaking inside at the thought of playing the role of calming agent to his second-run nerves.

The uploading gondola attendant made extra space for us to clear past the general public, and we got in our own cabin for the fifteen-minute ride up. The doors shut and instantly the gondola became a vacuum of silence as it bounced over the wheels, leaving the station. The snow-filled trees passed by on the outside, while the air inside hung in stillness between us. Time moved slowly. We both knew what the other was thinking, but neither would say it out loud.

"How was Paul's run?" he asked.

"Yeah, not bad, he was only 1.2 seconds out from thirtieth. Pretty good for his first World Cup. Did you have any of the strüdel down in the tent? Oh man, it was so good!" I asked and answered in one sentence.

We continued on like this, moving in and out of silence for the ride. I was letting him lead and making sure I kept it light.

At the top, we went into the restaurant/lodge where the operators kept an unofficial athlete's hospitality area set up in what was normally a kids play and lunchroom. Inside, a few other racers were also doing their own preparations, getting ready for their runs. I'd never been in a prep room before the second run, let alone with only a handful of the top racers left in it. I felt like my thirteen-year-old self was getting his Make a Wish request fulfilled.

I watched each one of them with intent, studying how they carried themselves, who listened to music, who was staying quiet, how much they were visualizing, who looked confident, who looked nervous, who was holding conversations. Everyone had their little routines, everyone dealing with the nerves in their own way.

One by one, they started to leave, until eventually it was just Thomas and me left alone again. Here I was, sitting with a pitcher who was throwing a perfect game.

Leave him alone, let him be, don't do anything to jinx it, I reminded myself internally, over and over again.

The room was so much bigger than the gondola, yet the vacuum remained, and the air still held suspended around us.

I watched Tom put out his gear and get himself ready, commenting to myself as he went.

Put on your downhill suit, training shorts over top.

Right boot on, buckle it up. Left boot, buckles up.

Shin guards in place, everything feels good.

Jacket, helmet, and chin strap clicked.

"Let's go," he said out loud while clapping his gloves together.

We stood up.

"Let's go, Tom," I replied, clapping my gloves together just like him to confirm his confidence, and I walked out behind him.

I skied down behind him until he turned to the start area, and I went around to the finish, rejoining Ryan, Paul, and JP to watch the race unfold. We were four fans, just like the rest of them.

When Thomas moved into the start gate, he stood thirty feet tall from where we watched on the jumbotron. The start house was empty behind him, and everything fell silent again. He looked so composed. I felt so nervous.

In any race, by the third gate, you can usually tell if a racer is on their game by their body language, the line they choose, whether they're attacking, and how clean the ski is picking up. This is what we all looked for when he came out of the gate. Was he feeling it? Was he on?

Tom was all these things in his run; he put it on the line but was narrowly beaten out and crossed the line second on the day. He finished just 0.08 seconds behind Palander, who took his second Kitzbühel slalom win in as many years. But even though Thomas missed the win, this was still a huge result, as it was his second-ever World Cup podium and seven years after his first, which came in GS. It was also Canada's first-ever World Cup podium in slalom. When we gathered in the finish as a team, staff and athletes together, it was clear this was the start of a new era, lead by Tom and something to celebrate.

CHAPTER 9
CRACKING THE TOP THIRTY

WE'D USUALLY GET THREE TO four weeks off after our last race, but the start of the 2004/2005 season was a little shorter than normal. With only two weeks of down time, Dusan called us for a camp of high-volume training in Panorama, where he was going to push our limits.

After the last race of every season, inevitably a coach will say something like: "I hope everyone gets some good rest because the new season starts tomorrow," always trying to keep us focussed while foreshadowing the hard work to come.

This was generally met with an eye roll while mouthing, "Oh, come on!" implying that the coaches were merely doing a parody of themselves.

But the late-spring skiing in Canada is some of the best training for us, dollar for dollar, in the world and the coaches knew it was an important time. With no races in the near future to save energy for, we could maximize our runs for technical gains, and with our touch on snow at its peak, it was also a good opportunity to test new equipment. So, on this day one of the new season, after closing out the last with my first Nationals Championship win and an overall third place in the NorAm slalom standings, I was keen to get back to work.

In partnership with the resort, Dus organized the mountain's upper chairlift to run exclusively for us from 6:00 a.m. until noon for fifteen days of skiing. The goal was to pattern in the fundamentals of slalom by skiing 150 gates per run, ten to fourteen times a day, to hit an overall magic number of 30,000 turns. Normally, 150 gates could fill two full-length slalom courses, but the coaches kept the sets short, breaking them into six sections to minimize fatigue and maximize high quality movements. This camp hit at the core of all Dusan's development philosophies: ski a lot, in all conditions, with a variety of courses, and make it competitive. For the latter, all he needed to say was, "Let's see who will be the last one standing!" and it was enough to turn our resistance into motivation.

This was the camp of his dreams, though with us it was soon dubbed "Hell Camp."

The conditions were amazing: sunny in the day and clear and cold at night, freezing the snow and giving us a hard surface every morning. There wasn't a cloud for three weeks straight. Semple, Stutz, Cousi, Thomas, JP, Brad Spence, Trevor (Tito) White, and I made up the training group, and Dus found his ways to tap into our individual and inherent drives to stand out amongst the group.

A couple days into the camp, I was catching my breath by our bags at the bottom of the run, grabbing water, and just trying to collect my thoughts.

Dusan slid up beside me. "Mike, is this all you have?"

I turned to look up from my hunched-over position, not impressed.

He kept going. "You can do more. You have more to give!" He was smiling through his bristly goatee, and this infuriated me.

"Dus, I'm so tired and mad, don't even talk to me!" I yelled, turning my back to him and putting my water bottle back into my bag. I took a few breaths more, knowing he was still standing behind me, watching, waiting. "But I'll do everything!" This was what he was waiting for and now, as I finished my sentence, I was starting to smile.

Dus skied off, leaving me on my own, knowing his work was done. I loved this part of our relationship; he poked, prodded and let me complain until I ran out of words, giving me nothing else to do but get up and go for more. He pushed, but I wanted to be pushed and thrived off the recognition that came from working the hardest.

At other times, the coach-driven motivation dried up, and a more creative approach had to come from us. The chairlift ran on the skier's right of our training run, and from the lift you could see the bottom and the top two courses. The middle two, though, were out of sight as the run followed the shape of an upside down "C," going around a patch of trees and out of view.

On day six, after 10,000 slalom turns, Tito had an epiphany. "Hey guys, we don't have to ski every course on the way down on each run."

We were intrigued, and he continued. "If you've gone past all three coaches, you know there's no eyes on anymore and just straight line to the bottom. Last run Brian was in the start, coach number one. When I was on the second course, I could see Marc riding the chair, coach number two. Dus was at the bottom of the third, which meant courses five and six were optional."

We started laughing.

Trev added more. "I don't know about you guys, but I'm absolutely gassed. How else are we going to get through fifteen runs today?!"

He wasn't wrong, and from Tito's young wisdom, coach counting was born. You had to be sharp, though, and not mistake a physio or ski tech for a coach or you'd have to face the blowback.

I can't count the number of times we collectively said no more in this camp, doubled over at the bottom of the run, until one of us stood back up and pushed away to the lift, saying, "Come, guys, one more," smiling while the rest of us groaned, knowing that this is when ski racing becomes a team sport.

This camp set the tone for the season, and we were ready to be the hardest-working group out there, putting in the effort to win.

• • •

Where last season's goals were on the NorAm circuit, this year they were dead set on cracking the World Cup top thirty. To do this starting from the back of the field, one has to go all out. It is a balancing act, though: on one side there's the desire for a great result and to go for it, but the other side holds the fear of pushing too hard and skiing out. When starting back in the forties, fifties, and sixties, with every extra racer skiing down grooving, rutting up, dishing, or chunking out the track, it's a very thin line to walk. But to make it into the thirty starting past bib-70, this is otherworldly, and always gets a nod from the rest of the field, recognizing the mastery of maintaining focus while going flat out.

Shortly into the November pre-season, we lost Cousi to a knee injury while training slalom. He got a little too far in the back seat, his skis hooked up, and shot into the air, completing a kind of rodeo flip without a landing. The result of this was torn ACL ligaments, all from the forces of the turn before he even left the ground.

As a team, we still only had four World Cup spots, and with Cousi out, Ryan and I could both race the opening slalom World Cup in Beaver Creek, Colorado. Beaver Creek is nothing too demanding as slalom hills go. The track is really known as a world-class downhill and super G track, with the slalom running on the lower part of it. But when the snow's iced up, the sponsorship banners are placed, TV crew, athletes, fans, and volunteers show up, the gentlest of hills are transformed into something that calls for your attention. The biggest challenge at Beaver Creek is the altitude. At 2,500 metres, it's the legs that stump out before the hill gets you.

Starting with bib-52, I never found the right rhythm on course and came down 3.15 seconds off the leader, Austrian Rainer Schoenfelder, finishing forty-first on the run. My race day was over, but Ryan, on the other hand, from bib-55, made his run count. As one of the smoothest skiers around when he's on, he looked like he was effortlessly creating speed and clocked in 2.49 seconds off Schoenfelder, into 26th place and cracking the thirty for his first time. Ryan kept his nerves in check for run two and finished twenty-fifth overall, scoring his first World Cup points. I watched from the finish and was fired up that he'd broken the barrier we'd been going after for a couple years now.

On the twenty-minute bus ride down from the finish to the hotel area of the resort, I sat across from him with the excitement of the race slowly wearing off. Soon some jealousy crept in and took over my mind. *Why did he get to score points today? Why wasn't it me? I deserve it more than him. I work harder, I want it more.* I didn't feel good about these thoughts, but they kept coming.

As I looked around the bus at the mixture of fans, coaches, and athletes, I wanted to bring a list of all my reasons and efforts to some deity to show that I was more deserving. But there were no answers to these questions. I slumped lower into my seat. The painful feeling of loss grew so deep in my stomach that I started to bargain with myself. *Mike, promise that we won't be in this position ever again!* My mind continued with more of these thoughts as I went through the emotional stages of grieving.

When I finally reached acceptance of my result and was thinking from a calmer state, I vowed to score points my next time out.

This next shot was a week later at the second World Cup slalom of the season in the western Italian mountain town of Sestrière. With it being an afternoon/evening race with run start times of 3:00 p.m. and 6:00 p.m., I took the time in the morning to enjoy a rare race day sleep-in and moved slowly before starting my pre-race warmup routine. I went for a jog prior to going on hill to get some blood flowing and did a series of activation jumps. As much as this routine is physical, it's also a mental warmup, being alone to connect internally to the sensations and fire that would carry me into the race.

Ok, Mike, we are with you, was the feeling I'd look for.

My insecurities and fears that I wasn't doing enough were good motivators through the week, but they didn't help much on race day. I had to switch systems. Once I put on my boots, strapped on my shin guards, and put on my helmet, I had to transform into the superheroes I watched on TV as a kid. I walked slowly across the room, heel to toe, heel to toe, listening to my boots as they clanged off the tiled floor. Solid, confident, ready to dance. This was my persona.

Starting with bib-53, I knew I had to go for it to live up to the promise I'd made myself on the bus ride back in Beaver Creek.

Front of the ski, top of the turn. You can do this. Commit from the start, find the rhythm. I repeated over and over in my head until it was my turn to go.

I clicked my poles twice as I put them over the wand, my final ritual. There was time for one last breath... in... out... and I pushed out of the gate.

On course, my mind was clear, running through every section as it came up, going through my race plan as I skied it.

Find the rhythm on the first gates, through the hairpin, quick move out, strong on the left ski, tall in the transition, work on the flats, push through the finish. Crossing the line, I quickly looked over at the timing board and saw "24" beside my name.

I was elated. "Holy shit, I did it! I broke into the thirty!"

When I looked up and around the finish area, I felt like I was seeing this view for the first time. I had found the entrance to this mysterious land called the second run, and it had let me in.

With little time to digest what had just happened, I was heading back up for second-run inspection, and my excitement carried me through the next hour.

Dusan pulled me aside after I came down from looking at the new course. "Mike, you have to go all out for the second run. There's no point finishing thirtieth for one World Cup point. Use this opportunity and go for it again."

I wanted to trust him and do exactly what he said, but easier said than done.

Skiing down to the start for second run, the mountain was empty, at 5:30 p.m. local time. I thought of home. It was 9:00 a.m. their time, and my parents and friends were for sure watching live. It was mid-December, the sky was dark, the air was cold, and the lights from the town below twinkled off in the distance. The sound of the snow crackled under my skis.

My service man at the time, Marko (Mare) Skube, and I looked at each other for a few minutes before the start with little smiles on our faces. He was in his late thirties, from Slovenia and we'd been working together for the last two seasons.

This is so cool, we were thinking in unison.

With the reverse thirty for the second run, I was starting sixth and would have a clean course in my favour.

The race ran with roughly one-minute intervals between racers, giving me ten minutes or so from the first forerunner to me. This was all a blur. Mare clicked me into my skis. Our physio, Harry, stood beside us with the radio to transmit my course report, and before I knew it, the start in front of me was empty, waiting for my entrance. I pictured my mom and dad watching from their computer screens at home.

The starter closed the timing wand, signalling I was allowed to go, but did not give a verbal command and remained silent. He didn't say "Go," "*Allez,*" or anything.

Isn't he supposed to say something?

I turned to look back at Mare to see if I could go, but all I saw was a TV camera staring back at me.

Where did he go?

I turned back to the starter.

"Can I go?" I asked, not sure if I was screwing everything up, feeling like I'd suddenly forgotten the rules of ski racing.

The starter gave me a hand gesture to let me know that it was ok to leave. I wanted to say, "Wait, I'm not ready, how can I start my first World Cup second run like this?" But the moment had passed, my poles had clicked twice without me knowing, and I was out of the gate.

Everything came back to me once I felt the comfort of the course. It was solid skiing, but I wasn't able to fully let it go. In the back of my mind, I still wanted to finish more than go for the great result that Dusan had alluded to. I had never made World Cup points, and this was a benchmark I so desperately wanted to reach.

I came down into second place, safely across the line and onto the result page. I was guaranteed at least a top twenty-five. From the athlete's zone in the finish area, I watched the rest of the race unfold, getting to watch Bode Miller have one of the greatest second runs I'd ever seen, putting everything on the line, going straighter than everyone and pulling it all off, all the while looking calm and composed.

"How is he able to do that?" I mumbled to myself over and over. "How does he ski so free?"

He won the race by 1.27 seconds, and I finished sixteenth, scoring my first points ever! I felt like I had performed a miracle, not quite like Bode, but a miracle to me.

I was proving to myself that anything was possible, and I didn't want it to slip away.

CHAPTER 10
KEEP THE TRAIN GOING

IN BETWEEN SESTRIÈRE AND THE next World Cup slalom in Flachau, Austria, there was the historical World Cup GS in Alta Badia, Italy. Arguably the most prestigious GS on the circuit, set in the stunning Dolomite mountains, the *Gran Risa* the race hill is called, has physical demands as a long, unrelenting slope, while holding historical significance that draws a certain allure to it. Racing for our team, Thomas, JP, and the rising Canadian star François Bourque were the starters while Ryan and I had the day off as we were only racing slalom. Feeling a little lazy, Ryan and I decided to watch this race from the comfort of the hotel and enjoy a real day off over huddling out in the cold to watch from the grandstands. After first run, though, Tom was sitting in second place and JP was in seventh and our priorities changed.

"We gotta get to the finish area now!" Ryan and I said in uniso to each other.

With the major team milestone of a World Cup win so close at hand, we had to get over there to witness something Thomas had been building towards for years. We were staying only ten minutes from the finish line, and we grabbed the keys to one of our team vans and headed out the door. Now safely inside the athlete's zone, in the vicinity of any potential celebratory action, we watched with excitement. With the top thirty in the second run running in reverse order, our eyes were glued to the jumbotron that stood just to the right of the finish line, counting down for Thomas's turn to go.

As he pushed out of the start gate, my focus zoned in on the all-important first few turns to see if the touch was there. I didn't see anything special on the first couple gates, but his third turn made a statement. Every racer before him had struggled to run a clean ski as it made a big swinging turn to the right, but Tom picked up the edge early and left nothing but two tracks in his path.

"He's on! He wants it, look at him!" Ryan clenched onto the back of my shoulders, shaking me with excitement. Tom was on it!

Almost every subsequent turn was perfection. Tom never broke his commitment to the carve and took every risk he needed to, while looking composed and clutch. Ryan, on the other hand, continued his clutch of my shoulders, squeezing ever tighter the closer Tom got to the finish line. The nerves and excitement were almost too much. When Tom crossed the line, he was over half a second ahead of Austrian superstar Benjamin Raich, to take the lead with only one racer to go.

Kale Palander held the lead after first run. He pushed out of the start gate and started off strong, but after only twenty seconds, he fell inside, sliding out of the course on his hip.

Tom had won!

We all stood in shock. Thomas had just won the first World Cup of his career, which was also the first GS World Cup win for Canada ever. Not to be left behind, JP finished fifth for the first World Cup top five of his career. The veterans were leading the way and showing us early on that the off season was paying off.

Two days after Alta Badia, the tour moved to Flachau, Austria, and in magical form, Thomas won his second GS World Cup in as many races. They were back-to-back wins on what were the iciest World Cup hills I've ever seen, which he made look effortless and electric. The momentum of the second win carried us into the slalom the following day. After trading point scores in the first two races, Ryan and I both made it into the top thirty, finishing sixteenth and twenty-second, with Thomas finishing twelfth.

Going into the Christmas break, Ryan and I had both scored in the points, JP had a career-best top five, and Thomas had his back-to-back wins. The team was riding a major high, and to cap things off, we'd created two new slalom quota spots, giving a chance for the next in line to have their shot at the World Cup. With only a limited number of World Cup starts each season, around ten slalom and eight GS, this was the energy we needed to keep the train going.

• • •

Chamonix, France, was our next stop in the new year, and Pat Biggs got called up to race his first World Cup, deservedly so, since after back-to-back wins at the NorAms in Sunday River, Main, he was clearly skiing with speed. On race day, Patty took quick advantage of the opportunity and landed right on thirtieth place after first run. On the second run Pat made good use of his start number, posting the fastest second-run time and finishing tenth overall for the day. In his first World Cup ever, he won the second run and finished top ten! He then followed this up with another tenth place in Wengen. We were now a World Cup team, with five racers scoring points and six spots on the start list.

By the time the seventh slalom of the season in Schladming rolled around, I had let a couple races get by me, with no points scored in Wengen and Kitzbühel. The season had started off with such promise but I feared it was slipping through my fingers. I had just made it through the breakwater and now it was about to swallow me back up. I needed to finish inside the overall top thirty for the season.

The Schladming night race is the biggest slalom of the year. Held in the province of Steiermark in Austria, it brings out 50,000-plus fans to line the hill, surrounding all sides and encircling from the finish and up to the start. As race hills go, it's one of the best. The length and consistency of steepness makes it challenging, giving no reprieve until you hit the finish line. Adding to the intensity of the hill, with the energy of the crowd, every athlete wants to put their best performance on the line for this one. This was going to be my approach, and from the moment I woke up that morning, there were no doubts that I was going to lay it on the line.

Night races have magic in the air, especially here in Schladming. Riding up the four-person, old tin gondola, I climbed above the hill and looked down at the thousands of fans below. They slowly faded away, giving the signal to turn inward, heading into my zone to connect with something bigger than me. I sat in silence, listening to my breath, repeating my race mantra. Little snow crystals danced around, suspended in air.

"*Ka clunk, ka clunk, ka clunk.*" The gondola rolled over tower wheels, bouncing me along the way. I smiled and thought back to my friends and family at home. All of a sudden, the mood shifted and I felt alone. I wondered if this was worth a life of isolation, being left to ride lifts by myself while others cheered and had fun in the party below. I got off the lift and skied down into the darkness towards the start. I didn't feel alone anymore; I had my skis, I had the snow, I had my potential.

Starting with bib-50, I went lights out. From the first gate, I was taking chances with every turn. This was my first time ever racing on this hill, but I felt comfortable and loved the energy. I finished seventeenth on the run, making my return to the second run, well within the top thirty. By the end of the first leg, four of us had finished in the thirty, marking the first time Canada had qualified this many for a second run of a men's World Cup slalom.

Second run I had my plan but barely needed it. I looked around at the fans outside of the corralled fence, screaming the names of their favourite athletes: "Benni, Bode, Giorgio!" endlessly calling out and trying to get the racer's attention, anyone's attention. I faced downhill and sat into a squat with my hamstrings resting on my calves, ski boots perched on their toes, digging them into the snow. I rested on my poles with the grips in my armpits, this being the unofficial ski racer start area position.

Looking around, I smiled. *I could get used to this,* I thought, feeling a little more at home in this new land.

It took a couple gates for me to get into the rhythm on the second run, but soon I found it, and I felt like I could do anything. As I reached the second interval, making the dogleg turn to the left to enter the long pitch down to the finish line. The roar of the crowd hit me like a wave.

"*Vorsprung! Vorsprung!*" I heard the announcer shout my split time out over the loudspeakers.

Am I in the lead? I think I have the green light! Did he say vorsprung? These were the thoughts that ran through my head as I made the next few turns.

To my surprise, this run didn't require much focused thought on the skiing and my mind could wander while my body took over, knowing exactly what to do. For moments it felt like I was just along for the ride.

I finished in ninth place overall, the first top ten of my career, right behind Thomas, who finished eighth. In the end, four of us finished in the top twenty. In slalom, where the margins for error are so small and DNFs are so common, this was another huge milestone for the team. We were raising our own bar, one race at a time.

By early March 2005, we had come to the second-last stop of the season for the GS and slalom circuit, in Kranjska Gora, Slovenia. A small and vibrant mountain town in the Northwest of Slovenia, just over the Austrian boarder. World Cup finals are the official last races of the year and are reserved for only the top twenty-five overall finishers of the season in each discipline. To make the top twenty-five, I would need another top ten. To get into the space that I needed to perform, I'd sometimes turn to the outside world for a sign. It would be nice if I could say that I wasn't superstitious, but this was not the case. Buckling up my boots a certain way, wearing the same base layers or ski socks, or a morning routine all played a role in calming me down and relaxing the nerves for the right tension to perform. On the list of routines was my pre-race jog and activation, a time to check in with the body and soul.

The afternoon before the race, I took off on a run, seeing where the road out of town would lead me. As I ran, I looked for a sign: the right road, trail, or turn to take where I could find this feeling of *self*, the ten-year-old kid who first held the spark of this dream. Fifteen minutes into my run I saw a single-track trail to my right, which followed along a river and up a narrow valley.

This is the way, I sensed.

After fifty metres of the trail, the hard-packed snow turned to untouched crust, and I was breaking through with each step. My jog turned into a walk, then into a hike, and when the trail opened out of the trees, a few footsteps led me onto a snow-covered frozen part of the river. It was a wide and dried-up outflow from the mountains above. Looking upstream, I was surrounded by huge peaks on either side of me and feeling very small as I stood at the bottom of this steep, V-shaped valley. Shade started to cover me as the sun set high behind the ridge line. I stood there looking, trying to touch something untouchable, trying to know something unknowable. I wanted confirmation that my efforts were not in vain, that my dream was still alive.

My grandfather's words rang in my head. *You never conquer a mountain; it only tolerates you.*

A feeling came over me. This valley was alive.

This was the feeling I had come looking for, like I was connected to something bigger than myself, an assurance that what I wanted was in touch. I stood in this for a while, surrounded by nature, letting the shadows slowly fold over me.

"In... Out..." a few deep breaths.

"In... Out..." a few more.

It was ok to go now. Jogging back to the hotel, through my solo prints in the snow, I felt ready to race.

I was now starting with bib-26 for my first run, and being tucked just inside the top thirty, I didn't feel the same need to go all out. In these conditions, I could ski strong and not outside myself to be in the mix. With this as my plan, I finished seventeenth on the first run, Thomas just ahead of me in a tie for fifteenth.

I stuck around Thomas before second run, trying to embody the way I saw him move, prepare, and focus. I was evolving my own race persona, taking in everything I could learn. With a top ten already under my belt this season, I didn't want to just earn a few more World Cup points this time; I wanted to take Dusan's advice from Sestrière, leave my fear of not finishing behind, and go for a great result.

Free skiing down to the start I felt good, and in my activation before clicking into my skis, my legs vibrated with energy. When visualizing the course, everything was clear. Mare banged the snow off the bottom of my boots with his screwdriver, and I clicked into my bindings listening for the loud *snap* of security as the binding's heel piece locked into position. It was satisfying to hear, and I smiled. I stared straight ahead, shifting my weight slowly from side to side, waiting for Mare to check my bindings and give me the *clack* on the back of my right boot with his posidrive screwdriver to signal *You're good to go.*

Slowly moving into the start house, I crouched low, sitting on my heel pieces, being as small as possible for just a moment. I rested and looked back at Thomas, who was starting right behind me.

"Come on, Mike, let's do this!" he called out.

I stood up, jumped up and down, smacking my skis into the ground, one leg at a time. I grabbed a handful of snow and held it to the back of my neck, the jolt of cold arching my back and straightening my spine. It was time to go.

I turned to our physio, Harry, gave him a fist bump, and then turned to Mare for his.

"Always fist bump the ski tech last," I whispered to myself while looking into his eyes for solidarity.

I moved forward to the gate and took my position, now standing alone.

"Front of the ski, top of the turn. Come on, Mike, you can do this! Feel the ski pick up, be patient, then go," I mumbled under my breath, still swaying gently from side to side.

The starter closed the wand to signal it was my time. I clicked my poles twice, planting them firmly over the wand and onto the rubber pads on the back side of the start ramp.

"Go!" the starter called, and I pushed out on course.

Right away I found the front of the ski and by the second gate felt my connection to the snow. All the ruts felt in the right place, the transitions were easy, and with each passing gate my confidence grew. When I hit the last pitch, I really let it go. I ran the third fastest bottom split, and with these risks taken in the right spots, I finished sixth overall for the day. This was my career best and was good enough to qualify me for World Cup Finals.

I couldn't believe it had all worked out. I was absolutely elated, and even though this was a moment I'd been going after for all my life, it still seemed so unreal.

Leaving Kranjska Gora later that afternoon, I got in the car with Mare, our destination Lenzerheide, Switzerland, for World Cup Finals. The day before *finals*, I went on my pre-race run around a little reservoir lake near our hotel. I thought about the weight of performance, the pressures around trying to be my best, and the worries I felt around being able to perform again and again, week in and week out.

"*Is this worth it? Is all the angst and pain still worthwhile?*" I let these questions hang in the air while staring up at the rising Swiss Alps around me.

The warm, early Spring sun was on my back as I ran along on the gravel path. I thought about the freedom I'd felt on course in my second run in Kranjska Gora, the feeling when everything comes together, in complete balance with the movements and the hill.

Crunch, crunch, crunch. The sound of the gravel echoed under my feet.

"Is it worth it?" The question came again.

I smiled. For now, in this moment, it totally was.

CHAPTER 11
COACH AND ATHLETE

IN SPRING OF 2002, FOLLOWING the Salt Lake City Olympics, the Canadian team hired an Austrian coach named Burkhard Schaffer. Burkie, as he was more commonly called, came to the team with some success behind him from the Austrian system, which drew the attention of our director. As Alpine Canada was looking for someone to lead the next generation of Canadian World Cup stars, working with young talents like Erik Guay and Jan Hudec, Burkie had the right resume to fit the bill. At first, he was hired as the men's "Combine" group head coach, then the next year he moved to become the men's World Cup speed head coach. In the 2004/05 season, he was promoted to head coach of the whole men's team, which he held in conjunction with his speed-team head coaching role.

Burkie took the traditional approach to his coaching: hard work, high volume, and a drive to deliver the best quality training for the team. This was paired with a sharp eye for technique, and a creative understanding for how to develop essential skills. He put together great programs for the athletes in this traditional mold. From all these characteristics, though, it was the all-out drive to deliver perfect training that held most of his pride. He ensured every detail of the day's training was cared for so the athletes could have all that was possible in their favour.

Doing things like driving six hours just to look at a different hill to see if the conditions were better, working through the night on the snow surface, or making deals with other teams to get the Canadians optimal lane space were common in other coaches like Dusan as well, but Burkie took his efforts to heart, and if we athletes didn't reciprocate in our actions, it was personal. If your skis weren't prepared properly because of a miscommunication to your service man, you were sent down from training. If the service man messed up *their* part of the deal for some reason, they were reamed out in front of the group. If he felt your focus given to inspection wasn't up to snuff, you were "done for the day" and sent back to the hotel.

Burkhard stood an average size, five foot ten, and around a hundred and seventy pounds, and he had a round face with the strong features of an Austrian farmer. With thinning black hair that came forward into a wispy peak at the centre of his forehead and an always welcoming smile at the onset, he wasn't too intimidating on the outside. But it was his eyes that told most of his story, holding an intensity easily overlooked that said, *When you come onto my team, what I say goes.* If you missed it in the eyes, his handshake was a final warning sign. He would quickly take a grip around your fingers so the two palms couldn't meet, resulting in a crushing of your digits and spirit.

Akin to the tactics of sending people home to uphold the old-school hierarchy of coach then athlete within the team, belittlement in front of the group was another favourite. When someone was running too high, he was sure to bring them back down. After some great results in an otherwise struggling season, Cousi came to a team meeting with his aviator sunglasses on and kept them in place while it started.

It didn't take long for Burkie to call him out. "Look at Cousi, he thinks he's a rockstar." He spoke with a high-pitched Austrian/English accent that pierced right through any armour you tried to hold up. "I tell you something, Cousi, ah, you're nothing!"

And just like that, the air was let out of Cousi's sails and he came crashing back to earth.

When Jan Hudec scored his first World Cup points, Burkie congratulated him by saying,

"You scored points one time, ah, one time! You know who else scored points one time? Max Rauffer. One hundred points, then never again." Burkie was alluding to the fact that the German racer had won once in his career and then was never able to do it again.

GO TO THE START - LIFE AS A WORLD CUP SKI RACER

Over the course of a career, an athlete comes to understand the unspoken dynamic of the athlete/coach relationship, learning to read a coach's moods, what they are saying between the words, and most importantly, what can set them off in any given moment. If the coach is having a bad day, this can easily be passed onto the athletes. Being reamed out for something seemingly small demonstrates full well who holds the power. Most of the time these situations are benign, and you learn to give the coaches what they want to see to either get in their good books, or in the case of Burkie, to stay out of his bad ones.

Anytime we trained with Burkie or knew he was around, I kept my head on a swivel and coach counting doubled as the "know where Burkie is at all times" skillset. Sometimes it was done out of real fear, but other times it was lighter and could be a game that bonded the team together.

One afternoon, while we were in the middle of a summer ski camp in Zermatt, Switzerland, Tito came bursting through our hotel room door with a story to tell. "You guys, I almost just got busted by Burkie so hard." His words barely got out because he was half panting, half laughing, and gasping for air.

Trev was dressed in his spandex bike shorts, suspenders up, no shirt, shoes on, hair wet with sweat. When his breathing slowed enough, the story started to come out. "So I was down in the gym, supposed to be doing my flush ride on the bike, but wasn't feeling it so I was going super easy at like seventy-five watts, barely spinning."

We'd been skiing high volume for a week at over 3,000 metres in altitude and trimming down our prescribed 150 to 175 watts for the mandatory forty-minute flush rides happened from time to time.

Trev continued, still grinning. "Then I heard Burkie's voice from down the hallway and thought, oh no, this won't look good."

Paul buried his face in a pillow, sensing the anxiety induced from such a situation.

Trev held on to his words for an extra moment, letting the tension we all felt fill the room.

"And...? So... what'd you do?" I asked impatiently.

"I obviously faked it," he responded. His look of urgency now shifted into a smug and satisfied smile. "I grabbed my bottle of water, quickly sprayed it all over me, cranked the wattage up to 200 and acted like I'd been there for the last thirty minutes."

Our eyes rolled, knowing only Trev would make a last-second ditch effort to fool Burkie.

"Yeah, but get this," Trev continued. "He walks in the doorway, sees me looking flush, full of sweat, comes over, checks my wattage and says, 'Ah, Trev. You're going strong today, ah. Don't go too hard, though, remember we still have to ski tomorrow.' Then he walked on."

We rolled back on our beds, dying with laughter. There had to be some joys in the predictable nature of an unstable character.

When we didn't know what was coming and plans changed on a dime, it was a little less funny, though. During a mid-season training block in our Austrian homebase of the time, Turrach, Burkhard laid out three different plans for the upcoming day in our nightly meeting.

"Ok, so tomorrow, some of you are going to Kranjska Gora for the World Cup, some are going to a FIS race down the valley, and Trev, you are going home. We changed your ticket, and you are flying back to Calgary tomorrow." His words were spoken casually.

It was this easy, like telling someone it's their turn to do the dishes, except this was sending a nineteen-year-old home on his own, from Austria to Canada, because he wasn't skiing well enough.

Turrach to the Münich airport is 300 kilometres and can be done in three hours when you know where you're going. When Trevor, on the other hand, was given the keys to one of our team vans and sent on his way, only a few clues were given. He was only told to drive to Münich, check-in to the Mövenpick, our usual airport hotel, and fly out in the morning. Key items missing from these instructions were: One, the Mövenpick hotel that was referenced is in a town called Hallbergmoos, not actually in Münich and a thirty minute drive out from the city; Two, Trev wasn't given the directions to even get there; and three, he wasn't provided a team credit card to fill up the van with gas if needed.

With confusion and fear of questioning what was happening, he took the autobahn away from the team. After making it into the outskirts of Münich, he quickly realized that he was lost. He stopped at a gas station, added two euros worth of fuel, and went inside to ask for directions.

Trev walked nervously towards the attendant, knowing this person held so much promise for his safe arrival to the hotel that night.

"*Entschuldigung, wo ist der Mövenpick?*" he asked in the German he knew, all his hopes resting in this one question.

The attendant looked very confused.

Trev's heart sank. He tried again. "*Der Mövenpick? Wo ist der Mövenpick?*" On long pause ensued.

"*Ahh, der Mövenpick!*" The attendant's face lit up, finally understanding the question, and with this, Trev's spirits lifted too.

The clerk came out from behind the cash register and confidently escorted Trev to the back of the convenience store. They came to the freezer section, and he proudly pointed with a big smile on his face to the ice cream in the freezer. "*Hier der Mövenpick!*"

Apparently the Mövenpick hotel chain also made a brand of ice cream in their same name, much to Trev's desolate frustration.

Luckily, though, there was a woman who had witnessed this exchange and seemed to understand what Tito was looking for. She kindly stepped in, and in English, figured out where he needed to go. Then she proceeded to be his guide and had him follow in the van behind her car as she took an hour out of her night to show him to the Mövenpick hotel in Hallbergmoos, where he finally arrived at his destination.

• • •

We all have our stories from Burkie's tenure. Some are more intense or traumatic, some are career ending, and some are just shocking and more easily laughed off.

This is mine.

The week before the 2005 Bormio World Championships, we were doing our prep training in Turrach. Burkhard had set up perfect training for us to peak at the upcoming big event. The coaching and mountain staff water-injected the hill in the night, arrangements were made to load the lift as early as possible, and multiple hill spaces were secured so everyone could get the training in the event they needed. We had a slalom coming down on spectators' left, a GS set up to the right, and a super G on another run out to the far right. The Slovenians and some Austrians joined in as well. Everything was set up for our success.

A normal slalom course length that we'd train during the season is between forty and sixty gates. This only requires a portion of the whole run and usually leaves empty hill space before or after the course. On this day, our course was set at the bottom, leaving more than half the run above clear of gates, probably enough room for 200 slalom turns. Occasionally we'd utilize this for focussed free skiing work, but most of the time we'd just straight-line down to the course, having fun with a teammate or simply doing what we could to manage our energy levels. Burkhard was known to hide in the trees of these zones, from time to time, to see what the racers were up to and would jump out if he felt we were wasting valuable space.

On one of my runs of the day, I was skiing lazily down the open run, leaning in from side to side at high speeds, enjoying this feeling of gravity and using little of my own effort in the process. In front of me on one of the rollers, I saw Burkhard standing in the middle of the run waving his hands in the air. Before stopping, I could hear him shouting, his voice high pitched and angry. I knew I had done something wrong but didn't know what.

He walked towards me, screaming, and grabbed onto my shoulders. "You don't ski like this! You don't ski like this!"

I pulled back and he grabbed on again. "You don't ski like this!" he repeated, still shouting and moving me from side to side.

I was in shock, trying to grasp what was going on. Pulling back again, I mustered a confused response. "What?"

I could now clearly see that he was irate, and my ignorance as to what I'd done wrong seemed to enrage him more.

"You don't ski like this." He again grabbed me, pushing me from side to side.

In fear, I realized he was signifying that I was letting my upper body lean inside, back and forth, with no discipline while skiing down. He was furious that I was not taking this open hill space more seriously.

I pulled back again, feeling my own rage building.

"You don't waste this! You ski the whole hill. You don't ski like this!" he continued to yell.

In the shock of the moment, I'm not sure what happened next; either I skied off or he did, but soon I was at the top of the course with my teammates and Burkhard was nowhere in sight.

I called Dusan on the radio which was left in the start and asked where he was so we could talk. At the bottom, I met him and told him what had happened, that Burkie had just grabbed me and screamed at me for not skiing properly. I was beside myself, but able to let the emotions out, feeling safe with Dus.

He calmed me down and said to get through the day and we could talk about it after training.

I went through the motions for the rest of the session, but my mind was somewhere completely different. I thought of home, I thought of what the right thing to do in this situation was, I thought of my mom and everything she'd taught us about standing up for ourselves. I felt very far away from all these safety nets.

After training, Burkie called a team meeting at the base of the hill. We circled up, all of us still in our ski boots, still on the snow. He ranted about doing everything we can every day, not wasting this training, and went on about how much work went into setting up these training days. In his view, we were not respecting all of this.

Feeling my own rage, I was trying to manage these emotions to follow through on my decision to speak to him afterwards. I needed to stand up for myself and set boundaries.

From across the circle, when the meeting was over, I called to him. "Burkie, can I speak to you?"

"What?" he called back.

"Can you please come here so we can speak?" I repeated, feeling like my voice would disintegrate if I wasn't careful.

"What? You come to me. I don't go to you, you come to me!" He was white with rage and not moving, so I walked over to him.

"Burkhard," I started, my voice trembling, I'm sure. I tried to call up some special forces to hide how scared I was. "You can yell at me, you can scream at me, you can threaten me all you want, but don't ever touch me again."

"What, like this?" he replied, grabbing me by the shoulders again.

I pulled back. "Yes. like that. You can yell and scream at me all you want, but don't ever touch me again!" I spoke with all the authority I could muster, wondering if our next moves were going to involve fists.

"I can do what I want! This is my team, and you do what I say. If I tell you something, you do it, this is my team!" he screamed, completely lost in his fury, with no conscious mind apparently present.

"That's fine, just don't ever touch me again," I repeated one more time.

He repeated his words about this being his team again, but with a little less *umph*, and the tension slowly diffused as both our positions were made clear.

Not knowing what else to do, I went back to my gear and started packing up my skis and bag, feeling the adrenaline rushing through me.

Walking back to the van, one of the Slovenians came alongside me. "What was that?" he asked, not looking for an answer, knowing full well what he saw. "How did you not punch him? If this were me, I would have for sure punched him out." This was his clear conclusion.

I would have said the same thing as a witness, but in the moment, I'd been paralyzed, and all my energy went into the words.

I called my mom when we got back to the hotel. With tears running down my cheeks, I shared the day's events: the exchange with Burkie and that no one came to my defense, and no other coaches had said anything to him.

"I don't know what to do," I said over and over again to her, sobbing.

Springing into action, while trying to hide their own fear and anger, my parents called the team's chief athletic officer at the time. Shortly after, I received a call from him, and we spoke at length on the phone. At first I thought this was a call of support, to show that the team had the backs of the athletes, but all that was given was rationalizations for Burkhard's actions.

"Mike, you have to understand that he's European... This is just how they are... I can't fire someone over this."

I felt my words were falling on deaf ears.

There was a promise to put this incident on Burkhard's permanent record, though, and I was told that he would be spoken to about his action.

A couple days after the incident, needing a ride from one destination to another, I was put into a car with Burkie. It was just the two of us, alone together.

"Ah, Mike, about the other day. This is all in the past, huh?"

I was silent.

He continued. "Yeah, we got excited, angry, and now it's behind us. Ok?" He put out his hand to bury the hatchet.

I wanted to stand my ground and refuse the handshake, but I was stuck in this moving vehicle with him for the next couple hours. Was there another choice?

We shook and continued to drive as if nothing had happened.

Burkhard never crossed this line with me again, and the strange thing from this event is that I had somehow earned his respect through standing up to him. It was a respect I sadly wanted, but this was too much to digest in the moment. With World Champs just around the corner and results on the line, there was nothing to do but lock this away and put the anger into my skiing. Here was someone else I could prove wrong.

CHAPTER 12
BECOMING A TEAM

THERE'S A PARADOX IN SKI racing, in that we compete as individuals while being part of a larger team. We strive for our own results but so much of this requires working within the group to push, support each other, and pool the resources needed to win. In the summer of 2005, Thomas was our clear team leader. Ranked third in GS and thirteenth in slalom, he was the veteran we all looked up to. Behind him, I was ranked seventeenth in the slalom standings, Biggs twenty-fifth, and Stutz was in the sixties, while Semple and Brad had both won NorAm spots, securing their World Cup starts for the next season. On the return to snow front, Cousi and JP were both coming back from injury, eager to find their form, and altogether, we had a budding group with the potential of becoming a full-on World Cup team.

The summer on-snow season started with a training camp in Chile, where we split our time between two resorts: El Colorado and Chillan. We flew into the capital, Santiago, a city of five and half million people, encircled by mountains. It sits an hour and a half drive from the Pacific Ocean to the west, with the same drive time for the ski resorts to the east, a beautiful area bustling with life. This was my second trip to South America after our camp in Argentina four years prior and the pace of movement and contrast between affluence and poverty still kept my eyes wide open.

We drove 2,000 metres up and into the mountains to the ski station that would be our home for the next two weeks. Up this high, walking the stairs is challenging enough, let alone the volume of skiing the coaching staff had planned for us.

As we grew as athletes, Dusan grew as a coach as well. He was able to give us a more and more complex training environment, evolving his course creativity while pushing us to adapt to these courses with more and more speed.

One evening, in the team meeting, Dus came in smiling with a plan. "Guys," he started in his never-improving English-Slovenian accent. "Tomorrow the plan is to run a slalom course of only combinations, flushes, hairpins, and delays. We're going to see how much speed we can build out there. I don't care how many times you ski out, I want to see everyone going a hundred percent in every run." Dus loved creating environments where our limits were reached and the idea of impossible was front and centre.

It had snowed a little the night before, making for soft conditions and leaving us to play a guessing game on just how big the ruts were going to be. The run the coaches had chosen was relatively flat, set off to the skier's right of the chairlift, it maximized our need to build speed. We jostled in the start to find our running order, as we followed the unwritten rule that the best ranked got first crack at the course. This honour was clearly given to Thomas, but for the rest of us, it was up to some debate.

Ryan spoke up, tapping Stutz in the leg with his pole, signalling he had rights to start before him. "Yo, out of the way, Paul."

Paul didn't move from his place. "No way! I have you on FIS points by a long shot, so I go before you!"

"True, but if you check the World Cup start list, I'm way ahead of you. World Cup points trump FIS points, so actually, I have the start." Semple's retort was delivered in a calm manner, as if Paul should have known this from the beginning.

"Hey!" Cousi called from the back of the queue in his thick Quebecois accent. "I'm ahead of both of you, so shut up and get out of the way!" This put an end to their squabbling.

We were a bunch of nervous horses jockeying for position.

As we settled into the day, the energy grew more collaborative and the fun of pushing each other took over.

"How did you run the third hairpin?" I asked Pat on the chairlift. "I can't seem to carry any speed out of it, I keep getting sucked too low before the delay."

"You gotta keep a long leg so you get into the rut early on the entrance gate and then you're fine to run a straight line," he answered. This was easy for him to say, as he stood over six feet tall with maybe the longest femur bones on the circuit.

"Hey man, come on! You both can take it way faster into the flush, just don't hesitate and trust that the ski will come around," JP goaded us in his fiery French Canadian way.

We'd watch each other, run after run, seeing who skied which sections well, and we exchanged notes while riding the chair. Someone was always ready to push the limits and try something new.

Joining Dusan and Marc on the coaching staff this year was Johnny Crichton. Johnny, who had come directly up from the club level of coaching, towered in at six foot four. He's a big guy in stature, features, personality, and heart, and he brought a contagious excitement into our team for its lifestyle, travel, and high-performance athletics.

Most nights, he'd call us outside to take in the view. "Guys, guys, come check out the sunset tonight!"

"Holy cow, did you see the food they have here? It's amazing!"

"Oh man, look at the mountains here!" He was like a kid getting his first bike, ready to see how far he could ride it before his parents called him home for dinner.

Johnny carried the fire of passion in his eyes and the warmth of invitation in his smile, which softened his imposing presence. He helped us see our lives through a fresh lens, and it didn't take long for him to be embraced by the group, clearly represented through Cousi's love-language of mockery and imitation,

"Guys, check it out, it's a rock from Europe!" Cousi would repeat to no end.

A couple days before our scheduled departure from El Colorado, the weather changed on us, and a big storm came in. In the span of thirty minutes, from the time we got off the hill to lunch, huge snowflakes started falling outside, much to the concern of the coaches. In talking with the resort manager, we learned there was a good chance that the roads would close and we'd get stuck up there to wait out the storm. By the time lunch was over, Dusan made the call to pack up and get out. Within minutes of the decision, there was a flatbed truck for our gear and a van for us waiting out in front of the hotel, with both drivers wanting to get out as soon as possible.

Personal clothing and gear are one thing to shove in a bag at the last minute, but a ski room filled with fifty-plus pairs in it was a whole other challenge. Dressed in goggles, coats, and snow pants, the entire team was outside, loading the bags and boxes one by one, piling our gear high onto this truck. A tarp was thrown over to cover this precarious mound, and the driver assured us it was safe to reach the valley below. With the final bags loaded, nine of us piled into a ten-person van with goggles still on, dragging the snow in with us. Our backpacks were piled to the roof. Laughing and cheering as the doors shut, we felt like we'd escaped by the skin of our teeth. This whole experience had played out like the most elaborate team-building exercise the coaches could have come up with and lent itself to the old adage that "those who suffer together, come together."

• • •

Along with the regular World Cup schedule, this 2005/06 season was also an Olympic year, with the games to be held in mid-February, about three-quarters of the way through the regular season. For Games qualification, the specifics range from nation to nation and sport to sport, and for us on the Canadian Alpine team, it was done with either a top five at the last World Championships or two top-twelve results on the World Cup, one of which could be from the previous season. With my top-ten finish from the year before, I was halfway there.

The second stop of the slalom tour had us back in Madonna di Campiglio. As a very welcome treat at this race, my mom had come over to watch after dealing with some family affairs in Hungary. In all the years of her skiing with me, taking me to races as a kid, helping me through my broken bones and injuries, here we were over in Europe together, and she was watching me race a World Cup live for the first time ever. I felt a comfort in having her there; it let me relax a little the night before.

The warmup courses for any level of race can be intimidating places, with competitors from every country congregating on one run to get up to speed. On the morning of the race, looking out at the three wide slalom courses set up in front of me, I felt these nerves. Athletes were going one after another on all courses, and each gate that was hit felt like gunshot to my confidence,

Bang, racer on course #1.

Bang, racer on course #3.

Bang, racer on course #1 again.

When everyone I saw looked so good, I turned to find another kind of skier. "Bourgeat totally slid that turn. Oh man, Zurbriggen barely carved these top turns." I ran my own commentary, using my competitors' flaws to help boost my confidence. This wasn't always the best strategy, but it served its purpose when I was feeling extra insecure.

I made my own turns on the warmup courses, hoping they were good enough to cast some doubt into the competition.

With a little surprise, I found myself in ninth place after the first run and let out a big exhale in the finish area.

Dusan met me with encouragement during inspection. "Mike, you have to go for it second run. You know how to do this. Come on!" His booming voice carried across the hill.

It was 6:45 p.m. local time, fifteen minutes before second run, and I found myself walking around the start area, looking up at the dark sky and out at the silhouettes of the mountains across the way. Listening to the roar of the crowd and the announcer below, I thought of my mom and our road to get here. Everything inside me was falling silent. The cold air crossed my face, and I watched my breath cloud up and freeze as it left my mouth.

I turned and looked at my competitors. *This is so cool*, I thought. *I have to finish this race.*

This for sure did not line up with Dusan's race plan, but I didn't want this all to vanish in front of me and wanted to arrive at the finish for my mom.

It took me a little bit to get into the flow of the second run, but as the hill rounded to the right and broke over onto the pitch, I felt the front of my ski bite and with it, my confidence picked up. I was aggressive down the steeps, kept my speed up onto the flats, and made it safely across the line, finishing twelfth overall for the day. I was so relieved and happy.

Dusan came and greeted me in the finish. "Dammit, Mike, I told you to go all out for the whole run, not wait until halfway down. You could have been on the podium!" he said both seriously and with a grin, knowing the fine balance between finishing with a result or walking away with a DNF beside your name.

Now he turned to my mom. "Andrée, tell him to not hold back next time. Ok?"

They both had a laugh.

I knew I held on too much out of the start. Dus was right, and this went against everything I had built my career on, but I was ok with it. Watching the prize-giving ceremony that awarded the top ten, I savoured the moment with Mom beside me.

Afterwards, Dusan came back over to me and extended his hand. "I guess congratulations are still in order, though."

I looked at him, puzzled.

"You just qualified for the Olympics. This was your second top twelve!"

"No way!"

We shook hands, hugged, and smiled deeply at this achievement. I couldn't help but think about seven years prior when the three of us, Mom, Dusan, and I, had been discussing how I didn't make the BC team, and here we were, in the finish of Madonna with the history of the sport all around... qualified for the Olympic Winter Games.

• • •

This year, for the 2005 Christmas break, we decided as a team to stay over in Europe which was a little scary for me to be away from home over the holidays. For a feeling of home, though, Thomas invited us to his family's place in Trieste, Italy, where he'd been born and his grandparents still lived. Trieste is a town on the far northeast coast of Italy, all the way up the right side of the boot and then back down towards Croatia, on the Adriatic Sea. This was one of my rare occasions of being in an actual home in Europe and not just a hotel, and it was still a novelty for me. To take part in this immersion, Cousi, Biggs, JP, and I went, along with our physio, Harry, and coach Johnny.

On our first full day in the city, it was beautiful; the sun was out, with a few white cumulus clouds in the sky and temperatures in the mid-teens. A balmy day by Canadian standards. We parked the van near the town's harbour, stood looking at the sailboats lined up in their slips, and then crossed the road towards the Piazza Unita d'Italia. On our way, we passed a couple of older ladies speaking Italian to each other and looking up at Johnny, shaking their heads.

Thomas started laughing. Fluent in Italian, he translated for us. "Ha. Those two women just said, 'Are they crazy, it's winter and they have t-shirts on. What are they thinking?!' They can spot you guys from a mile away." He pointed to Johnny and Harry, who proudly kept wearing their short sleeved shirts.

Later in the afternoon we found ourselves caught in another cultural faux pas. After a great pizza lunch, we crossed the street and went to a coffee shop to sit and enjoy the afternoon sun as the Vespas and scooters zipped by. Cousi got to the counter first and ordered a cappuccino. Pat, Johnny, and I followed suit. The man behind the bar started gesturing his hand in front of him as he walked away to fulfill our orders,

"*Che cazzo fia,*" he mumbled under his breath.

"Did we do something wrong?" we asked Tom.

"Yeah, so..." he started, laughing once again at us *turistas*, "cappuccinos are more of a breakfast drink; no one really orders them after lunch. I think you might have ruined his afternoon."

"Oh, come on, how are we supposed to know this?" I exclaimed, flailing my arms in the air, now looking more like a local.

We sipped our milky coffee, feeling the eyes of the café on us.

After an evening out with Thomas's family and friends, his cousins took us to a little hole-in-the-wall pub around 2:00 a.m. to close the night. Upon entering the narrow, twelve-person-capacity bar, Cousi spiritedly went to the bartender to place his order. "We'll have six schnapps and a board of prosciutto!" His French-Canadian accented voice boomed off the walls with joy.

The gentleman behind the bar, who was in his mid-fifties with wisps of hair combed neatly on his head, responded in his broken English, "Schnapps yes, but no prosciutto."

"Nonsense, this is Italy, every great establishment has prosciutto!" Cousi, now as boisterous as ever, was adamant and stood at the bar, sure he would receive his full order.

Tom's cousin came in with some Italian to support the cause and the bartender eventually called to his friend at the other end of the room, who left and soon returned with the request. The cured meat was sliced thin and placed directly on the wood of the bar, with fresh oil drizzled over top.

"Eh, see? I told you. Did I not tell you?!" Cousi smiled, proudly pointing to his prize like he'd been the one who had finally got the cultural secrets right.

After so many years of being homesick and feeling lonely on the road, this holiday season changed me, and I started to feel some affection growing for this continent.

• • •

The month of January is the most jampacked on the racing calendar, with lots of the classics taking centre stage. Adelboden in Switzerland hosts a slalom and GS. It's a hill that boasts more terrain, sharp breakovers, and side hills than any other and culminates on a massive basketball turn that sweeps to the right before dropping down the steepest few gates on the circuit. Then it finishes in a scaffolding made amphitheatre, creating stands filled with 30,000 Swiss fans cheering the racers on.

After Adelboden, it's the Lauberhorn weekend in Wengen, which is the next valley over, then over to Austria for the Hahnenkamm in Kitzbühel, and to close out the month, we end with the slalom night race in Schladming.

By the time Schladming came around, before the pre-Olympics break, our team results hadn't taken off to the heights we'd hoped for. With only a few top tens between all of us, we were in a lull as a team and losing momentum.

Tom decided that we needed a spark and got us together for a meeting. "Guys, we have to look at who we want to be as a team if we're ever going to succeed together."

We sat around the Keilhuberhof's lunch table, our hotel for Schladming, listening to him.

"When we show up to a race, how do we want to carry ourselves? What values do we want to race with? What do we want to be known for as the Canadian team? How we are both on and off the hill?"

I looked a little puzzled when he said this last part. *Who do we want to be as a team off the hill?* I wondered to myself.

This was a strange question for my twenty-three-year-old self. At thirty-three, Tom had had some more time to contemplate these broader questions.

"How do we want to leave our hotel rooms when we check out? Do we leave them a mess or do our best to clean up?" he elaborated.

I quickly thought about Stutz and me playing a hotel room game of *what could be used as a garbage?* finding cracks and small spaces to cram wrappers and trash in.

Tom went on, "Do we want to loudly roll our bags down the stairs, clanging them for the whole hotel to hear, or do we want to carry them down and move in and out in a respectful manner?"

I started to feel a bit sheepish, like in the midst of some success, I'd forgotten everything my parents had taught me about how to behave. Thomas was waking us up.

At the end of this speech, he proposed we come up with a team battle cry, telling us about the Haka, a pre-game ritual and Māori war dance the New Zealand All Blacks rugby team perform as a challenge to their opponents. With this inspiration, we sat together for the next hour and came up with the Canucka.

Before driving to the hill for the Schladming night race, we gathered in the parking lot outside our hotel. In ski boots and full gear, we looked each other in the eyes and recited our new ritual in unison.

For as long as I can remember I have had a dream.
Deep inside I always believed I could do it.

I have given everything to get to where I am today.
Now, I am ready to prove I belong, that I am the best.
This race can only be raced once, when it's done it's gone.
I will seize it, I will own it.
I will ski with fire and no regrets.
Because I am Canadian.

We then came together in a rugby scrum, pushed forward two steps, pushed back two steps, looked in each other's eyes and said to our teammates, *"You can do this!"*

Thomas had made the point; we had to come together as a team or we'd continue as just some more individuals on a page.

At the end of the World Cup season, the tour took us to the Far East, with two GSs in Korea and two slaloms in ShigaKogen, Japan. It was early March, and I was reflecting on the season and the opportunities that had slipped away during the year's second runs. Standing at the top of our warmup courses in Shigakogen, the day before the first slalom, I looked out at this unfamiliar terrain across from me. There was a lot of snow covering the mountains, yet the hills had a greyish tone, the trees and brush creating wave-like patterns across them.

I turned my attention down the hill to the familiar sight of gates below. *Why can't I convert my speed into a great result?* I contemplated this before pushing out of the start for my third training run of the day.

At the bottom, Thomas came down behind and I stayed to watch. When he got down, we started talking technique, what I was working on, what he was feeling in his skiing, and what our focusses were for the race. After this exchange, a little silence filled the air.

"Mike, when are you going to finally put down a charger of a second run? Stop holding back and really ski like you can?" Thomas asked me directly but in a kind and honest way.

I was a little taken aback, as I hadn't seen this coming. "Uh, I don't know. I can't seem to figure it out. I get so scared that I'm going to lose my first-run result and can't fully go for it in the second."

"Mike, one great result makes up for five or more medium results. If you're willing to go for it, it pays off. Trust me, it's worth it! Don't keep wasting your runs for mediocre results."

After his coaching, the silence returned to the air, leaving me to reflect. For the rest of the afternoon and night, his words rang in my head. *One great result is worth more than all the medium ones put together.*

He'd poked a hole in my delusion.

The next day of the race, I sat in eighteenth after first run. It was another warm spring day. The sun was out and softening the snow, so there would be some ruts to manage. In the start area for second run, there were four of us Canadians who qualified. We were all trying to find some space in the shade, to cover our boots in snow and keep the plastic relatively stiff, ensuring they could still perform as needed on course. I found a little corner off to the side and stood on my own for a bit.

You have nothing to lose, Mike. Thomas is right, let's see what happens. I stood there remembering my first National Champs win in Quebec; this felt similar.

I went over my race plan, kicked my boots out of the snow, and walked to my skis. With Mare and Harry in the start with me, I got my course report and took in what the coaches said about the ruts forming and conditions deteriorating. Standing in the gate, I stared the course down, wanting to get on it to see what I could do. I fist-bumped Harry and then Mare, squatted down low, jumped back up, grabbed a handful of snow, and placed it on the back of my neck for a jolt to the nervous system. I stood tall again, swaying back and forth.

"Come on, Mike, you got this! Come on!" Harry called from behind.

"Front of the ski, top of the turn, move, stay active. Come on." I repeated my own words out loud, clicked my poles twice, planted them firmly, and pushed out.

There was never a doubt from the first gate—this was me at my best. Dancing in and out of the ruts, taking chances, I felt in sync with the course, almost smiling as I went down. There were a few holes developing on the pitch, but I felt like I could do anything with my skis, I felt balanced and centred. I went for the more aggressive line, and it paid off. I crossed the finish and into first place. I had the lead in the second run for the first time in my career and with the green light had found my place in the leaders' box. One by one, over the next ten racers, I watched each one come down behind my time. I was still in first with eight to go; the worst I could do was ninth, a season best.

In the start gate now was Thomas. I looked on, half cheering for him, half wanting my time to hold up. Tom came down with an impressive run, beating me by two hundredths of a second overall. The teacher was not ready to hand over his class. He looked over at me in the leader's box, stoked to see me, and also to find himself in the lead. As he took my place in the hot seat, he smiled as if to say, *Nice work, but I still got you.*

He and I finished the day in third and fourth place. It was only fitting that Thomas was the one who kept me off the podium by such a small margin after showing me to the first top-five result of my career. He'd given me a glimpse into the world of real performance, and I knew there was no turning back. Before this, though, we had become more of a team.

CHAPTER 13
THE TORINO GAMES

EVERY FOUR YEARS, IN THE middle of the season, shortly after Schladming, there's a three-week pause in the regular World Cup schedule for the Olympic Games. The 2006 Torino Games would be my first. When I dreamt of the Olympics as a kid, I saw myself walking in the opening ceremonies, my country's flag waving high above and my friends and family cheering me on. As I grew, this dream filled with more and more details: seeing the other athletes, picturing the start gate, crossing the finish line, and the podium ceremonies. The sense of elation this brought also came with nerves when I thought about the possibility of reaching the Games only to fail in the race.

Don't worry, Mike, by the time you get there, you'll know how to deal with the nerves. You'll have the answers. I routinely reassured myself when these fears came up.

In November leading into the Games season, the Canadian Olympic Committee (COC) sent out representatives to meet us during our preseason camp in Colorado to let us know what to expect and to prepare us for the lay of the eventual land.

"At this year's Games, there will be three separate athlete villages: the main hub is in Torino; Bardonecchia will be home for the Nordic, ski jumping, and freestyle competitors; and then the Sestrière village is home for the alpine teams." The COC team shared the details over PowerPoint, showing pictures of what the different villages looked like, both under real-time construction and in the rendering of the finished product.

"Both mountain villages are an hour and a half drive from the main village... The alpine houses for Team Canada are standard bedrooms, two per room with a bathroom. Outside there's a common area for just the Canadians to hang, with games rooms and TV, and the food hall is in the main building..." They covered everything from security to the accreditation protocols and general logistics.

It was all so new, and my mind filled with excitement.

On the logistics front, the Alpine Canada team manager, Robert Rousselle, took the lead and went through arrivals and departures details for our group. "Due to the limited space in the athletes' village and training space available on-hill, we can only have the competing athletes in the village at a given time. The speed athletes will be there for the first week and when the super-G is over, they will leave, hand over their accreditation and in will come the tech skiers."

Robert's words caught me off guard.

Flabbergasted, I interrupted. "Wait, what?! We don't actually go into the Games until just before our event? We don't get to be there for the whole thing?!"

The images of my perfect Games experience, which I had held in my mind for so many years, were slowly fading away.

"Janyk!" Dusan called from the back of the room. "We will be training off site, on a good hill outside of the village. You slalom guys have a Europa Cup race just before to prepare as well. Remember, we're going to race, not as spectators."

"Yeah, but does this mean we don't walk in the opening ceremonies?" I asked.

There was no need for Dusan or anyone else to answer this question.

"Oh man, that sucks," I said under my breath, slumping into my chair.

With the slalom scheduled on the second last day of the whole event, it made sense. I just had never thought about the actual performance preparation piece attached to the dream of competing in an Olympic Games.

• • •

Our home base for this prep period that Dusan had alluded to was in Gressoney, Italy, a little mountain town an hour and a half drive directly north of Torino. Finding a great training venue prior to these big events is a mission for national teams in and of itself. First it has to be a place with similar snow conditions and terrain as the race hill and second, a venue willing to give a team full rein over the piste to prepare and use the hill as needed.

Driving up the Aosta Valley to Gressoney, the vineyards stretch up impossible hillsides, where terraces cut into the slopes to stabilize the land to allow for grazing of cows and farming. We passed by small towns and villages with little clusters of stone homes, all built together around a single church. As I took in the simple and quaint landscape, it felt strangely eerie to be here, in contrast to the frenzy of the Olympics just a short way down the road.

Turning right off the *autostrada,* we cut through narrow streets, passing by gas stations, pizzerias, businesses, and cafés. We proceeded to climb, driving up switchback after switchback, until eventually cresting onto a plateau where the road straightened through a basin in between two large members of the Alps family on either side of us. At the front end of town, we came up to the base of the little ski station, our training hill up to the left, and our hotel in front of us just to the right. This was our home for the next two weeks.

The hill had everything we needed: a long pitch to start, a good flat section in the middle as the hill took a long "S" across, cutting back down to the right for some steeps, and finishing with rolling flats through to the bottom. The chair was an old double lift that brought us two-thirds of the way up. For the rest, the mountain provided a snow-cat grooming machine to tow us up to the GS start. Actually, they attached a toboggan to the winch cable of the groomer, and we were pulled up in this sled three, sometimes four at a time.

With the first requirement in check, the second was in play as well and the hill manager gave the coaches full control of the run. It didn't take long for them to find the fire hoses to saturate the snowpack. Johnny, Marc, and Dusan headed up for their first water party shortly after our first night's dinner. While we went off to bed, they were on the hill and for a total of thirteen hours, sprayed over a hundred thousand gallons of water onto the surface of the run, after which the winch groomer tilled it all in. They looked just like fireman trying to put out a blaze of freezing snow. Later the next morning, when we eventually got out there after a late breakfast, the track was hard, icy, and very bumpy.

"Johnny, I think we might have overdone it a little," Dus said over the radio in his deep and booming voice, as he watched us rattle down the course in the first run.

The town's mayor had the same thought because halfway through our training session, he paid the coaches a visit to see who had drained the town's reservoir. After some smoothing over, everyone agreed that it was an acceptable use of the town's resources, and as for the track, it just needed a couple days to settle and soon was transformed into the snow surface we needed.

The town not only offered up their ski hill and water, but they also welcomed us into their community. The local ski club and school came out to cheer us on, and we were invited to their classrooms and aqua aerobics classes. We took pictures, signed autographs with the kids and eventually were guests of honour at a ceremonial dinner by our new friend the mayor and other local dignitaries.

For the races, the men's tech team consisted of me, Pat Biggs, Thomas Grandi, Ryan Semple, JP Roy, and Francois Bourque. The women's side was also training in Gressoney with us: Brigitte Acton, Christina Lustenberger, and Shona Rubens. On one of the training days, while I was riding the chair with Christina, we talked about our dreams and how cool it was that we were both going into our first Olympics. As the conversation grew, one of her responses to a question surprised me.

"Yeah, I don't know how much longer I'll race," she said.

"What!?" I blurted. "But you just had your best results, three times in the top thirty with a tenth place. Why would you want to stop?"

Our feet dangled in the air, passing above an icy creek below. The chair bounced, *keklunk, keklunk, keklunk* over the lift tower wheels.

"I want to have more freedom to tour the mountains around home, the Purcells, Rockies, and Bugaboos. Maybe get into backcountry and guiding. I just want some more time to explore these mountains beyond the racecourse."

She was being honest, but I still couldn't believe what I was hearing.

Here I was about to realize my childhood dream and the person beside me, who I thought was doing the same and with more raw talent than me, had other plans.

The chair continued to climb up through the trees, past the mountain huts, still suspended off the ground. I had never seen anything beyond this one dream. I sat there bewildered.

• • •

Together as a team, we watched the opening ceremonies from our hotel lobby, and I kept wondering if something special was about to happen to me, if I was going to be taken over by some magical power or something that would alleviate my fears and propel me into the results of my dreams. We watched country after country and seeing Danielle Goyette carry in the flag for Canada, it felt like this was becoming real.

Four days later, after an early morning training session, we gathered around the TV to watch the cross-country women's team sprint event. Of interest to us was Tom's wife, Sara Renner, and Beckie Scott competing for Canada. Sara and Becky won the silver medal in an all-out performance, with the now-famous broken pole/new pole handoff by the Norwegian coach to save their medal chances. In our small, remote group, we celebrated together. The Olympic spirit was sweeping over us.

Soon after, Thomas decided that it was time for us to go into Athlete's Village to get a first-hand experience of the Games. Jumping in the team car, we drove the two hours into Torino, calling Robert along the way to organize event tickets for speed skating, followed by the Canada vs Italy hockey game. With no official Team Canada apparel given to us yet, we only had our athlete accreditation in hand. Mine hung proudly around my neck; I was showing it off as we walked past security and into the streets of the village.

The village didn't seem like anything special on the outside: some rows of four- to six-storey apartment buildings lined the streets, all going off in different directions to places like the food hall, the residences, and the main international houses. With grey and overcast skies, it was quiet as we walked between the curbs, looking up at the different flags that hung from the balconies. France, Netherlands, USA, Switzerland, South Korea,

Sweden, Germany, Australia: every country proudly showed off their colours. With each one, I thought about the athletes who were behind them, what sport they were in, if they were winning medals, how many Olympics they'd been to, and how their Games were going.

As we were walking toward Team Canada house, we spotted Henrik and Daniel Sedin, and Mattias Öhlund, three Vancouver Canucks playing for Team Sweden. Since we were going to the hockey game, I had my Canucks jersey on. Feeling halfway between fan and peer, I figured I should ask them for an autograph.

With the midday streets empty beside the three of them walking towards the four of us, Semple nudged me. "Come on, you know you want to. I even have a Sharpie," he said with a smirk, handing me a pen.

I slowed my pace to match the approaching Swedes and gingerly asked, "Um, Henrik, Daniel, Mattias, can you guys sign my jersey?" Mattias gave a laugh, took hold of the jersey and signed first, followed by one of the Sedins. Then they continued walking in the direction of the food hall.

I turned around to see Ryan and Pat laughing, getting a kick out of my stumbling. Only feeling a little sheepish, I wasn't too bothered as only thirty minutes inside the gates, I had already run into my favourite hockey players and gotten their autographs. This part was for sure in my childhood dreams of going to the Games, and I was still a fan.

After our short taste of life inside the walls, we returned to Gressoney, but I was itching to immerse myself back into the atmosphere. Pat and I were the last two to come in, just three days before the slalom, and we'd watched our teammates have some amazing performances. Erik Guay and Kelly Vanderbeek both finished fourth in the super G events, Geneviève Simard fifth in the women's GS, and Francois Bourque an impressive fourth in the men's GS after leading the first run by 0.19 of a second. He was one of the youngest in the race and leading the first run of his first Olympics. In an event where medals are the biggest and only measurement for success, this was so close to being alpine's most successful Games ever.

Driving up to the Sestrière village, we crossed through the first line of security ten minutes down the road, at which point we transferred from our team car to the shuttle bus, taking us the rest of the way. Marked by one main spiralling tower, plus two smaller ones, the alpine village was a relatively small footprint, especially in the athletes' area. Our accommodations were built into the hillside, with the entrance floor being the highest and the apartments descending like staircases four to five stories to the ground below. It would be accurate to say that these buildings had just been finished in time, with some upgrades still required. The thirty-metre courtyard between the main international and food area to the athlete quarters was a mixture of snow and dirt, with plywood laid down to keep us from the mud. It was all part of the experience. Inside the apartments, the long hallways were lined with grey square tiles, which ran throughout into the bedrooms and bathrooms. We made our new home as comfy as possible for seemingly the biggest four days of my life.

Walking into our bedroom, Pat and I saw two single beds pushed together with a desk and chair in the corner. In front of the closet, our eyes were drawn to the two bags full of Olympic gear. This was what we'd been waiting for! It had been too long watching, feeling jealous that the rest of the team got to rock the swag.

Pat and I dove in. We took turns bringing out one item at a time. In each kit, there were four Canada t-shirts in four different colours, a track and sweat suit, the opening ceremonies gear, the podium jacket, toques, socks, gloves, shoes, boots, shorts, and the closing ceremonies gear and a cell phone.

"Hey, have you seen the mukluks yet?" I called over to Pat.

"No, but check out this bomber jacket," he responded, posing in the red suede coat, which was fully unzipped, with his hands deep in the pockets.

With all the sponsorship regulations involved with the Games, we could technically only wear our country's official supplier for the whole two weeks, which was the main reason we received so much gear. Pat and I, only there for three full days, would have to get creative to ensure we wore every piece of this new wardrobe.

• • •

The morning of my race, the Olympic slalom, to manage the nerves, I kept asking myself questions to bring some greater perspective. "Why are you here, Michael? What do you want from the day?"

I set out for a jog on the same route I'd done the year prior, before scoring my first World Cup points on this same hill. It was another afternoon/night race with a 3:00 p.m. first run start and a 6:30 p.m. second run, so I knew I had some time. Coaches talk about using the first Games for experience, or as Dusan would put it, "Go out hard and see what happens."

But I had watched my teammates' successes and seen Ted Ligety win gold in the combine event. He was someone I'd stood beside on the Nor Am podium, and I thought, *If it could be him, why not me?*

While I was getting lost in my head, imagining what the day could bring, I also got lost in person. Through the maze of security gates and fences, my regular route was no longer available. With more of a scramble and faster speeds then I would have liked to run with, I made it back with a little less time to get ready for skiing than anticipated.

On snow and in warmup, I continued to search for my special feeling.

Johnny stood at the bottom of the training course doing what he did best, directing our attention towards what I do best. "Pick up the ski early and trust it. Show us what you're capable of. Come on, Mike, you know this hill. Let it fly!" The enthusiasm emanated out of him on race days.

There had been a dusting of fresh snow overnight, and in the morning, the course workers were scraping it away with shovels and rakes, revealing the hard, icy surface underneath. There were course workers everywhere, two per gate.

I slipped down for inspection, checking the hill for myself. *Ok, the snow's a little grabby, it has good bite to it. Gotta be careful not to straddle,* I said to myself, wishing that thought hadn't popped into my head.

Partway down, I looked out at the empty grandstands, taking a moment before they'd be filled with thousands of fans. I scanned the hill, seeing the Olympic rings over and over. I was really here. I took a deep breath to savour this feeling and then turned back to the course.

After inspection, I stood in the middle of the finish corral and went through my visualization routine. My course notes ran in my head: *There's a few key breakovers, nothing too tricky, find the rhythm sections and commit. Tack, tack, tack,* I said over and over as my hands mimicked the turns of the course playing in my mind.

I stood in the finish and looked back up the hill. "I welcome this course with love…" The voice of Mom came through as I remembered our time on the tennis courts as a kid. "Here we go!"

At the start of my first Olympics, my parents and sisters were at the bottom, in the grandstands, my friends back at home were watching on TV, and all my aspirations were riding on this one run. The fear crept in. *I don't want to ski out. I want to make it to the finish.* These thoughts were not in my race plan, but I knew skiing out was a possibility.

I fought back. *Get comfortable, find a rhythm, see where you land this run, and then throw down for the second.*

The nerves subsided enough for me to move towards the start with bib-21, but they still hung over me like a billboard, trying to give me a reality check. *You didn't spend your whole life getting here just to ski out on the first run!* they read. It was too hard to get past this fear of skiing out.

On course, I couldn't find the commitment and feeling on my skis to set me free. My skis chattered, I hesitated over the breakovers, and all my actions had the undertone of *don't ski out* in them. I finished twenty-sixth after the first run. So much for making it down. I wanted to crawl up in a ball and cry. Any hopes of a great result were gone just like that.

In between runs at the Olympics, there's a three-and-a-half-hour break, thirty minutes more than a typical World Cup break. After a bad run, all I want to do is go back out there as soon as possible and ski for redemption, so this added time felt like an eternity of suffering with the feeling of sucking. In the athletes' lounges, I sunk back in a chair, put some music on and took a nap. I wanted to be consoled and left alone at the same time.

Dusan eventually came over, waking me up to give a fist bump before the coaches headed back out. "Janyk, come on. I want to see some fire out there!" He spoke calmly. I knew he felt for me and was trying to bring me back up.

By the time I reached the start area, I looked over at Mare, who was taking in his own first Olympic experience. I let the sorrow go. Clicking into my skis, I took a breath and found a little place between anger and apathy to muster the spirit for my second run.

There was some more fire and commitment on course this time around, and I moved up a few spots to finish seventeenth overall. For the rest of the team, JP was out in the first run, Pat out in the second after a great first, and Tom finished ninth, moving back from a first run place of fifth, making some mistakes as he pushed for the podium. This is how racing goes; it's rarely perfect, as much as I wanted it to be.

Following the race, I turned for the long walk through the snaking finish area. After a maze of fences, which passed by the media, the athlete areas, and fans, I was first met by my teammates, JP, Ryan, Christina, and Brigitte. They were all smiles. They knew the feeling of loss I was experiencing. It's the feeling that bonds athletes more than the successes, and this understanding from them picked up my spirits. We shared a smile.

Moving farther along, I came to the edge of the maze and saw my best friends from home and old ski teammates, Tony and Ben, hooting and hollering, waving and smiling, so stoked for me no matter what my result. I'd had no idea they were even here! We embraced, and after a few minutes of talking and sharing stories, some perspective returned and I saw how far I'd come—how far we'd all come. Farther past the finish area, through the bleachers and outside the accreditation area, I finally met up with my family: Mom, Dad, Britt, and Steph. Amid the hugs, congratulations, and sincere joy my family expressed, it took my older sister Britt to really bring me back. She knew without me saying anything what I was going through. Her season had not gone as planned. Having scored no World Cup points, she hadn't qualified for the Games, and in the face of this, was here to cheer me on. She looked into my eyes, and I knew she knew, and she knew I knew for her too.

The next day, we woke up late with one goal in mind: to walk in the closing ceremonies. This was also part of my childhood dreams, and I vowed to enjoy every moment. The remaining members of Team Canada all loaded the buses to bring us down to Torino, preparing us to march and close the Games. On board everyone was in good spirits, a mixture of the alpine skiers, the bobsled, sliding athletes, and ski jumpers filling the seats. Seeing our 140-pound ski jumper sitting beside our 230-pound bobsledder, joking around about who could best each other in which athletic feats, was as good an entertainment as we could have asked for.

The athletes from every country gathered in the large foyer of the hockey arena before the closing ceremonies, all in our respective nation's colours. Team Canada stood in our beige mukluks, white corduroy pants, and deep-red, long, and insulated jackets, clustered together, with all the other vibrant and eclectic uniforms surrounding us. It was a reunion as well, running into my old coach from when I was thirteen years old, who was there with Team China. Bianca, my old physio, was also there with the Australians and other friends from Whistler, who had been competing in snowboarding, moguls, and border cross. We signed each other's flags, shared stories, and traded scarfs for toques, or sweaters for shirts with other nations. Above us were panels of mirrors angled at forty-five degrees so we could see the whole room. I looked up with a smile at everyone together, talking, sharing, exchanging, and flirting, all inter-mixed. The Olympic spirit—it was beautiful.

They soon called us to get ready to march, and we segregated back into our nations. JP, Ryan, Pat, Harry, Christina, Brigitte, and I stood together, and then we walked outside, towards the stadium, waiting, collecting other team members, anticipating. When it was our turn, we passed under the rings above and the view opened to the sea of people, lights, and flashes throughout the stadium. I smiled again, this time with a wider intensity. My race hadn't been great, I didn't feel like I'd accomplished my goals, and the nerves had taken over my performance. I knew all of this but for a moment was able to put it aside.

We continued to march, and we waved, laughed, and spotted Canadian volunteers who had donned Hockey Canada jerseys under their official jackets. Taking our seats for the show, we saw Andrea Bocelli sing and Cirque du Soleil perform and then the mayor of Vancouver accepted the Olympic flag, signalling Canada would officially host the next one. The Olympics were coming to my hometown, and I had a lot to learn over the next four years.

Will I be ready? I let this question linger.

I returned my thoughts to the ceremonies, looking at my friends, coaches, support staff, and teammates. I had no answer, but for now I was satisfied just experiencing the closing ceremonies; they were as special as I had always hoped they'd be, like the opening ones had been in my dreams.

CHAPTER 14

DRYLAND TRAINING WITH A NEW APPROACH

TO BE SUCCESSFUL AT A high-performance level requires so many people dedicating their time, creative thought, and energy towards this one goal. There are the coaches, ski techs, physios, doctors, directors, office staff, sponsors, and partners, all of whom in their ways help to elevate the athletes. The other key roles to this performance puzzle are the strength and conditioning trainers. They are ones who help ready our bodies for what the coaches want us to do on-hill and everyone else hopes we can do in the races. Working behind the scenes, they play a significant role in the success of a team, and a lot of the time connect with the athlete to prepare them mentally as well.

From the years 2005 to 2011, our strength and conditioning trainers were two Austrians, Mike Ficta and Kurt Kothbauer, and between the two of them, they fundamentally changed how we prepared for a World Cup season.

Mike came from the Austrian National Team, working with legends of the sport such as Herman Maier, Stephan Eberharter, Hans Knauss, Hannes Trinkl, and Fritz Strobl aka "The Power Team." Mike had a lean but muscular build, an average height, and a serious look to him. He kept a shaved head and was always sure to stand in perfect posture and move with precision. Contrary to his appearance, though, he was supportive and open natured, in an Austrian, military kind of way, where direct answers were given but excess smiles, praise, or criticisms were not.

At a summer ski camp in Zermatt, Switzerland one July, we sought his advice for what food was best to bring on the hill to keep our energy up. It was dinnertime, and raclette was on the menu. We were half serious and half curious to see what he'd answer. Mike scanned the table, looking down at the boiled Yukon golds and the array of pickled vegetables, bread, and butter in front of him.

"Yoh, put some potatoes in your pocket," he replied in his assertive Austrian accent. "Yoh, grab a bag, put some potatoes in it. It's simple carbs to last the day. For me this is perfect." He shrugged his shoulders like it was simple math we should have known all along.

Kurt on the other hand, balanced Mike's tangible take on life with a big-picture perspective, having the ability to pose possible solutions while leaving it for us to discover them on our own. And where their approaches contrasted, so did their stature. Kurt stood around the same height as Mike, but his body barrelled around his frame. As an ex-shot putter, he was well built, with a big chest and arms, thick hands, and solid legs. Against his big physique, his character was gentle, and he took the presence of a teddy bear over a roaring grizzly.

During this same summer camp in Zermatt, three of us were on the stationary bikes doing our daily recovery rides in the basement gym of our hotel. Kurt gently walked in, not disturbing anyone, and stood off to the side, surveying the room. We rode the bikes, either listening to music or watching a movie from a laptop, just trying to get through the forty minutes of spinning. When I hit the end of my first twenty minutes and got off the bike for a quick stretch, Kurt came over. Seeing his invitation, I took my headphones out for a brief moment.

"You know, from time to time," he said softly, "you can try and ride the bike without listening to music." His accent seemed to be his own unique Austrian-English, with a gentle and slight lisp.

"What!? You know how boring this gets, day in and day out, forty minutes on the bike? It's hard enough *with* music. Why would I do it without?" I was unable to even conceive of his alternative reality.

He paused, looked slightly to the floor, and still with a hint of smile said, "Without your earphones in, it's possible to listen to your body, to your heartbeat, your breathing. You might learn a little more than from your shows." He looked back and held my eyes with his gaze.

I could not compute.

In the following year, at our first official dryland camp of the off season, Mike and Kurt started it by asking us to perform an ordinary task in an unorthodox way. It was early May in Whistler, and both the men's and women's senior teams were in attendance.

Kurt and Mike corralled us outside of the rec centre's fitness studio.

"Welcome, everyone." Kurt began giving us the instructions. "Behind these doors, there are two chairs. On one of them there is a pen. Go into the room one by one and move the pen from one chair to the other." Our attention was drawn to him by how softly he spoke.

Down this long, white-brick-walled hall, past the entrances for the aquatic centre's changing rooms, twenty of us stood tightly together in front of the wood veneered double doors. We looked at each other, some laughing at the simplicity of the request, others confused by it.

"This is it, just move the pen, that's all we have to do?" someone asked Ficta, who offered only a small smile in return.

Allison went into the room first, followed by Geneviève, then Jeff, each one coming back out to face the same line of questioning from us on the outside.

"What was in there? Was it really just a pen and two chairs? Were there any surprises?"

"Yeah, it was just moving a pen," they each replied, looking like they weren't sure of the answer.

After the next two participants were given the same interrogation, Alli had had enough.

"Guys! Seriously, it's just two chairs and a pen. Move it from one to the other. Get over it!"

When my turn came, I swung open the door, feeling the air swoosh behind me as I stepped through the threshold into the unknown. I scanned the room, looking for anything that would be out of place, clues to the mystery or puzzle I might have to solve. A traditional dance and fitness studio, it was a square-shaped room with shiny wooden floors, floor-to-ceiling mirrors, and a stretching dowel that ran horizontally along the walls. I walked a metre farther in, through the little foyer, and up two stairs to stand on the wood flooring. Nothing moved.

In front of me rested a chair with a plastic seat and four metal legs. Six metres away from it stood its partner, with a pen placed neatly in its centre.

"I guess it's exactly what they said, move the pen from one chair to the other," I thought out loud.

I walked slowly towards the pen and cautiously picked it up as if there were traps attached to it or something. With the coast clear, I walked the pen to the other chair, looking around, thinking, *This is strange.*

I placed the pen on its new home and left the room. Coming out, I joined in with my previous teammates' statements: "It's really just moving a pen from one chair to the other."

The remaining athletes still rolled their eyes in disbelief.

Once we completed part one, Kurt moved us all inside the studio to explain phase two of the exercise.

"Now that everyone has moved the pen by themselves, we will move the pen again, one by one, but this time with everyone watching."

We broke out in some chuckles and a series of "come-ons" at the simplicity of it all.

"Ok, here we go," Kurt commanded, unfazed by our childish reactions.

We moved the pen again, one after the other, watching each other as we went, some of us calling out or joking as we moved it. Others were taking it very seriously, but all of us were conscious of the new observers in the room. Kurt and Mike remained silent the whole time.

When we were all finished, Kurt grouped us for his final speech. "I want you to take note of the two times you moved the pen. One by yourself and the others in front of your team. How did you move it when no one was around? How did you move it when people were watching? What thoughts were going through your mind? How did you carry it? How did the action feel?"

My mind stopped when he asked these questions. There was a purpose to it after all. I stared blankly with wonder.

This concluded our mystery session, and we followed Kurt upstairs to the weight room for the main training. There were no other explanations after this; he just left us in contemplation, in our own thoughts.

• • •

Before Mike and Kurt took over our training programs, a day of off-season dryland had consisted of four hours of training split into two sessions, five or six days a week. After, our training grew to six, sometimes seven hours a day, with three-to-four-hour mornings and two-to-three-hour afternoon sessions. This philosophy for developing ski racers grew out of their understanding of the demands of the sport, both at a mental and physical level. A ski racer has to perform in two different ways. The obvious one is in short, high-intensity, anaerobic bursts for one or two minutes on race day, but the second is for training, when days are filled with ten to fifteen runs in a course, requiring a capacity for long, sustained energy output. In both, a high level of aerobic capacity is needed to successfully recover from one day to the next.

For the mental side of it, on any given race day, a skier could do their warmup runs and inspection in the first two hours of the morning, then weather could come in, delaying the start for three hours, and then, in a short window of notice, they would have to be ready to perform. Or in Mike's words: "Yoh, if you can't stay focussed here in the gym for four hours, how are you going to ski a downhill after a fog delay?" He was always matter of fact, always ready with a tangible reason.

To mimic a training day, our main lifting segments were designed accordingly. It started with thirty minutes on the bike, fifteen minutes of dynamic warmup, and then six to twelve sets of either squats, Olympic lifts, split squats, or anything legs. A typical chairlift or T-bar ride is roughly ten minutes, so in between our sets, we rode the bike for this amount of time, flushing the legs out and going back for two minutes of intense work. Everything in the gym was connected to everything on the hill; one worked to support the other. This was then followed by hamstrings, upper body, and abdominal circuit, closing with forty minutes of cardio, preferably on the bike.

To coincide with the traditional demands of a strength and conditioning program, Kurt added an eastern element through his education and practice in Feldenkrais. Feldenkrais is a method of organizing one's movements back to their innate and efficient way of functioning, while strengthening the mind-body connection. Kurt would bring the whole team in the gymnasium together and we'd unfold large, blue gym mats in the centre of the room, like the ones used for teaching kids to tumble. We'd lie down with our shoes and socks off, continuing to talk, joke, and banter with each other, waiting for his instructions. Kurt walked around, slowly moving, circling, and weaving through us, patiently pacing until we eventually quieted, lay back, and closed our eyes.

"I want you to notice how your body is lying," Kurt began, speaking in a consistent cadence, easing our attention inward. "How do your feet lie today? Does one lie differently than the other? Notice if they lie the same, or is one more off to the side than the other?"

The lights of the gym were turned off overhead, with just the daylight gently filling the room through the windows set high above.

"How do your calves lie on the ground? Does one feel softer than the other? Maybe one is tight or has pain. What is the sensation in your calves?" His slight lisp was coming through, leaving undefined starts and finishes to his words.

Step... step... step. He weaved slowly through our bodies. "Turn your attention to the space behind your knees. Can you notice the gap between the floor and the back of your knees? Is it different or is it the same? What is the distance of this space?"

Step... step... step. "Come up to your shoulders. How do your shoulders lie on the ground today? There is no need to correct anything, just notice how you lie here right now." He moved in this way, guiding us through our bodies. Body scanning moved into rolling, where he gave instructions for how to move in our habitual manner.

"If babies want to see something behind them, they turn their head first and then the rest of the body follows naturally. Follow your thumb with your eyes."

From our squatted position we moved our arms on a diagonal pattern up and behind us, trying our best to follow.

"When a baby gets up, it uses its weight to lean forward over itself to counter. And push through your bones. Come on, try it."

We rolled forward, trying to gracefully come to stand the way a young toddler would.

"Yeah, here we go, Juke." These would be Kurt's sound of encouragement when one of us would get it right.

At first this was something silly and it drew comments from the gallery,

"Kurt, when can we have another Feldenkrais session?" Manny asked after the first week of this new way. "I always have the best naps in them." He followed his joke up with a big belly laugh.

Kurt didn't mind, though, he enjoyed the banter and was aware of the effect this was having on the group. Even with the jokes, we soon grew an appreciation for these sessions and what they were doing for our bodies as a whole.

The intense months of dryland were a balance of work and play. Coming into the gym, morning after morning, Monday to Friday, this was our work, and the Bob Niven Training Centre in the Calgary Olympic park was our office. I loved walking into the facilities in the morning, ready to see familiar faces, to complain to each other about our aches and pains as we readied ourselves for the competition and output of the session. I grew up putting in the most I could in dryland, and now I had the coaches, infrastructure, and teammates around to support and push me. When we hit snow, the impacts came through, and the stage was set for the most successful World Cup season in Alpine Canada's history.

CHAPTER 15
ONTO THE PODIUM

AFTER AN OLYMPICS SEASON, THERE'S generally a reset amongst the team, signifying the start of a new four-year cycle. These changes can come in the form of coaching, sponsorship, corporate interest, team funding, and for the athletes, in their personal contracts. The main source of a ski racer's income is from their ski company, followed by prize money and their headgear sponsor, the company that pays for the right to showcase their logo on the racer's helmet. Post-Torino, at the start of the 2006/07 season. I went through two significant changes. The first was in coaching. After three seasons in this second block with Dusan, he moved up from his head coaching role and into the national team's athletic-director position. The next was changing ski companies, and after a period of testing, I switched my skis, boots, and binding set-up from Salomon to Rossignol.

Taking over from Dus to run the men's World Cup tech team was a Swedish coach named Mika Gustafsson. Mika brought a welcome change of energy and a shift in coaching styles. I would often go to my coaches looking for them to tell me what to do and then would do it, wanting them to give me the answers. The first time I came to Mika in this way, though, he turned it back on me.

"Duuude, you know what to do, you are a king." He spoke in a soft Swedish accent, emphasizing and elongating the important vowels for each word.

At five-foot eight, with a regular build, he had fair Scandinavian skin and kept a short, blond beard, with hair to match. His approach to most situations was to start with a smile, look at someone in wonder, and more often than not, qualify them as being "Ammassing!" In this optimistic approach, there was always part of his smile that indicated a wild side.

Midway through the winter, I was driving with him through Italy on a winding, single-lane road. Around one of the big switchbacks, Mika decided to overtake a slow-moving vehicle on the outside of the bend and in the oncoming traffic's lane. Going about sixty kilometres per hour in our team-branded Audi A6, we were just coming to the apex of the turn when a car came into view, lining us up for a head-on collision.

"Mika, Mika, watch out!" I screamed from the passenger seat.

He put his foot on the accelerator, cranked the wheel to the right, and squeezed into the right-hand lane, narrowly missing the car coming towards us, which was flashing its headlights and honking its horn.

"Mika! What was that!? That was too close!" I said, still yelling at him.

Mika slowly turned to me, not showing an ounce of panic, and calmly said, "Duuude, you worry about your side of the car and I worry about mine."

We both stared in silence for a moment.

"What?!" I broke out. "That doesn't make any sense. We're in the same car!" I didn't know whether to laugh, cry or keep yelling.

He smiled a little, pushed on the gas, and accelerated onto the highway.

Johnny and Marc remained on staff as assistant coaches and did well in keeping the continuity. In August we travelled to South America once again for our first big ski camp of the summer, this time to Ushuaia, Argentina. The capital of Tierra Del Fuego, Ushuaia sits on the southern tip of the continent, a three-hour flight from Buenos Aires, which in itself is a day's travel from Canada. Ushuaia is a fishing, natural resource, and eco-tourist town, a vibrant city set between the ocean and the mountains, its main streets only a few metres above sea level and gradually climbing the foothills of the snow-capped peaks above. There are countless ships throughout the harbour, a mixture of tour-guiding boats, commercial fishing, and smaller personal ones, up to big cruise ships and freighters. There's good action of locals, tourists, and transient workers filling the city's core. The streets are lined with souvenir shops, seafood and steak restaurants, travel agencies, and coffee shops. It is still rough around the edges, though, having the marks of other South American towns with bumpy roads, stray dogs, aging infrastructure, and spirited drivers. With all in its entirety, this was our home for the next three weeks.

The Cerro Castor ski area is a thirty-minute drive northeast, away from the coast and into the mountains. The resort was a growing favourite training venue for World Cup teams and for good reason. Despite the two-day travel from Europe and North America, it's a big mountain, with a variety of terrain and enough space to host a handful of teams. Starting in the trees, three chairs eventually take you into the alpine and to the tree-bare, snow-covered, rocky peaks above. Given the size of the mountain, we had flexibility to train on the lower mountain during storm days and up top when the high-pressure systems came through. And if conditions weren't great, we had the mid-mountain lodge *asado*, the local steak BBQ, to keep us occupied.

Mika's spirit further came out when we got on snow, bringing creative and playful approaches to our ever and ongoing work on the skiing fundamentals. On our first GS day of the camp, he stopped us outside the lodge to give the day's instructions. "Duudes, today we ski without poles..." – a normal exercise in the ski world to work on balance and position – "... and instead, everyone gets a piece of rope to use."

Ok, this was a little different.

"Run the rope behind you, across the back of your legs, holding the ends in each hand out in front of you," he continued to explain in a singsong way. "Wrap the ends around each leg, pulling them through and grabbing them out the other side, behind you. Pull the remaining length up your back and over your shoulders, holding them here in place."

The eight of us stood there on the flats outside the lodge, running these ropes between our legs, up our backs and over our shoulders, laughing like kids learning a fun new game. When I figured it out, the ends of the ropes I held onto pulled me forward, into a relatively good skiing position.

"Duudes, you look amasssing. Let's go free skiing and then we try it in the course."

With the tutorial finished, we skied off to the lift behind him. This was Mika, always adding an element of play into our training where he could.

The opening World Cup slalom of the season was held in Levi, Finland, 170 kilometres north of the Arctic Circle, near the Swedish border. As a prep camp for these races, we went to a ski hill named Ruka four hours southwest of Levi by car, near the Russian border. The surrounding landscape looked like rolling ocean waves made out of hills and trees. It was a relatively flat and small hill, like most in the area, and from the top, the world stretched out into a seemingly endless and untouched area of snow-covered trees and frozen lakes. With it being early November at the Arctic Circle, the sun just peeked out around 10:00 a.m. and was soon gone by 3:00 p.m., never really showing its full face. As we walked to training from our condos and back again in the minus-twenty temperatures, the snow crystals sparkled in the air, refracting the ever-present artificial lights which came from the lampposts that lined the ski runs of the hill. We were in the land of the reindeer, the home of Santa Claus, and it felt like we were training in a snow globe.

On the last night before leaving for Levi, Mika brought the team together for a final camp meeting. "Duuudes, we've had perfect training this pre-season. I know you may be thinking, but what about the other teams? What kind of training are they getting? Is their training better than ours? I tell you, this is the best training in the world. And most importantly, remember you are all kings."

We sat looking around at each other, wondering whether to laugh at his consistent statement claiming us as royalty or to take it as truth. The words felt secondary, though, and it was the spirit in which he spoke that made them special.

Mika eventually broke the silence. "Ok now, we have a special team activity to finish off with." He pulled a flyer out from his back pocket. "It's karaoke night at the bar next door. We're all going together, and everyone will sign a song, us coaches included."

An eruption of laughter and cheers ensued.

One by one and in pairs, we all took the stage and sang our chosen songs in front of the team and the thirty or so other patrons of the bar. Mika called us all on stage at the end for a rendition of "My Generation" to cap off the night. It was one of the rare occasions, and the first time since

Thomas's second place in Kitzbühel, where staff and athletes got together in celebration. We loved it.

Levi opened the season with a bang. I finished seventh, Thomas right behind me in eighth, and Pat nineteenth. In the off-season, inspired by the Calgary Flames Green Hard Hat Award, where the players give it to the hardest-working teammate after each game, we wanted to create our own peer-to-peer award. Given our summer homebase location for most of us in Calgary and our affinity for the Calgary Stampede, plus some great internet shopping by Stutz, we decided on a "hard" cowboy hat as our symbol and the prize awarded to the gutsiest performer of the day. In the Levi, it went to Patty for his jump from starting bib-53 to bib-19 and throwing down a great first run to make it into the second one.

As the plane took off from Kittila airport, heading south for Helsinki after the race, I sat up in my seat and looked out the window. As the engines roared for take-off, I felt a sense of satisfaction that I had not felt in a long time. Where my previous best results had been filled with excitement and excess energy, this one felt more like a belonging.

The lights of the ski hill and town now shrinking below me, I put on some music and submerged into this feeling of achievement. The athlete that I always knew was in me, finally was coming out.

The clouds now covered the view of the land below, I turned away from the window and sunk into my seat. I was living my dream and it felt like home.

• • •

With momentum building for the second World Cup slalom of the year, we were back in Beaver Creek, Colorado. Adding to the excitement of my opening result, thirteen friends flew in to watch me race, including my younger sister, Stephanie. Mom also came for the action, as she was volunteering on the racecourse crew. This was my first time performing in front of so many of my friends at this level, and I wanted to finish with a good result for them. Going to bed the night before the race I was restless with nerves and excitement, knowing I was in the best form of my life and a great result was close at hand.

Standing up at the top of the warmup courses, on a cold morning in early December, I looked out and saw my competitors.

I got them, I told myself as I took one of the start gates.

I no longer felt like a visitor on the circuit, this was my world now, and my time to play. On the first turn of the training course, I felt my ski pick up early and right away, ready to dance. At the bottom of this run, Johnny was watching, and I came to a stop at his feet. I looked at him smiling, hoping he would confirm the feeling I was having, giving me some reassurance that those turns were better than just good.

"Duude!" he said, imitating Mika, while nodding his head with a soft grin on his face. We stood there for a moment longer while Johnny's eyes told me everything I needed to know: that run was fast and I was on today.

The conditions on the race hill were icy, just like we'd been getting used to, and it suited my new equipment setup. The harder the conditions, the better I liked it. After inspection, saying a quick hi to my friends in the stands, I lapped around on the chair and started to do my pre-race warmup. On the flats above the start area, I slowed down and saw my mom standing on the side of the run. As a volunteer course worker, she was also lapping around to slip the racetrack, though she had pulled to the side from her crew and was waiting. I slowed down and stop beside her to say a quick hello. She added, "Good luck." I gave a big smile, we hugged and I continued on my way. A short but special moment we both felt.

In the start area, the race had just gotten underway, and with bib-16 on my chest, I had about twenty minutes to get ready. The skies were clear above, the air was cold, around minus fifteen, and the sun would be coming out from behind the mountains later. At 9:00 a.m. we were in the shadows, so I kept moving to stay warm, with my mind focussed on the plan.

After some short bursts of quick feet, leg swings, jumps for my activation routine, I got a course report from the coaches, visualized myself skiing it, locked it into memory, and then clicked into my bindings, feeling one with my skis.

Front of the ski, top of the turn. You know how to do this. Stay committed. Feel the ski bite, my mantras continued over and over.

I felt the nerves start to rise.

Just go to the start. Just go to the start. These words carried me forward to the gate.

I swayed gently back and forth, the course now coming into view.

Clack, Clack. I tapped my poles twice and placed them over the starting wand.

I sensed my friends in the stands cheering me on and my mom standing on the side of the course. I turned my focus to the course.

Just make it past the first gate, I thought.

Just make it past the first.

I pushed out.

There was a freedom I found on course, and with each section, more and more speed was possible. All my training took over the way it should, and the fear of failure easily slipped away. This was fun. This was why I loved ski racing.

I finished fifth on the run, my best first-run finish of my career, and only 0.25 seconds from second place. After such a great performance, I let myself celebrate a little inside. My friends in the finish area were greeting me with cheers, but I still felt a world away from them, knowing they represented the celebration I was hoping for, and my job was only halfway done. I gave them some time and then moved on slowly, back to the world of managing the energies and emotions and holding a focus clear enough for a strong finish.

During second-run inspection, Mika seemed calm. "That last run was amasssing!" He was smiling. "You will go for it again. I know this and you know it too!" Like Johnny from earlier in the morning, his eyes reflected all I needed to know.

The start area for second run is always quieter than the first. With only thirty competitors left in the race, it's a more intimate experience. Leaving the mid-mountain lodge all alone, I thought about being back with Thomas in Kitzbühel, and surprisingly I felt less nervous now than I did then.

I usually used music to manage the nerves and keep my mind on track. Depending on my energy level, I'd either use something like Rise Against to bring me up or David Gray to calm me down. Always trying to keep a connection to myself, this time I played a mixture of both to prepare for this run, putting me into my own world, where friends, family, and results didn't exist. Only me and the course, me and my skis. I sat on the edge of the run outside the start area and on my own. When the music stopped, I took my headphones out and looked out at the mountains across the valley, the sun resting gently on the peaks now. The roar of the crowd climbed up from below, and the nerves started to zap my energy. I slowed my movements down and carefully planned my efforts from here to the start gate, conserving all I could.

When it was time to click into my skis, I was standing beside our physio, Chris, and my new service man, Yul. Yul was kneeling beside my skis, waiting for me to do what I've done thousands of times before: pick up my boot so he could clear the snow from the bottom of it, click into one ski, and then repeat the process with the other. As Chris and Yul waited for me to move, I stood there frozen.

"*Allez*, Mike." Yul encouraged me in his native French tongue from below, but I remained stuck.

"I can't," I said under my breath, a little louder than a whisper.

"What's that?" Chris asked.

"I can't move. I can't move my legs." I turned to look at him.

"Why can't you?"

"I'm too nervous, I can't move my legs," I fearfully admitted.

Chris looked back at me, and seeing the panic build in my face, he replied, "That's good."

"It's good?" I gasped in shock.

"Yeah, it's good that you feel nervous. It means that this means something to you, that you care. It means you're alive."

I looked back at him, completely stunned now. *The nerves are a good thing?* I said to myself.

This statement was so absurd in the moment that it stopped my racing mind long enough for my feet to unglue from the snow and I lifted my leg. Yul cleaned the sole of my boot, I clicked in, and then we did the next one. He checked the bindings and then tapped the back of my boot with his screwdriver, knocking me back on track.

I had returned to myself and with it my faculty of focus. *Front of the ski, top of the turn. Don't straddle the first gate. Make it to the second gate and I'll do the rest. Get in the rhythm then go to work.* Even in the moments right before, there are always some negative thoughts that can come in. This is just normal.

After Rainer Schoenfelder left the starting gate in front of me, I inched my way closer.

"*Allez,* Mike! Come on, let's go, Mike." Chris and Yul cheered me into it.

My eyes were fixed on the first gates. *Just get past the first, then you're good. Front of the ski, top of the turn. Come on, Mike.*

With a breath to signal no return, I clicked my poles and felt them settle firmly into the snow.

"Ok, go," the starter calmly said, and when I pushed, there were no doubts in me.

I was going full out. I cleared the first gate and charged into the second, a right-footed turn that quickly accelerated me onto the opening pitch. It was steep and icy, but I felt grip under my feet, and all I was thinking about was carrying speed across the first flat bench. I let my skis run and entered the next section of the course. It was a tight and quick set with some tricky combinations, my favourite. I danced down the middle section. I knew I was carrying good speed, and I was so focussed on the turn I was in and the ones coming up at the same time.

Crossing the last flats and onto the final pitch, though, my focus was slipping and I was losing some steam. *Stay on your feet, stand tall, stay on your feet, and work it to the finish.*

The finish line was in sight.

I crossed in first place, one second into the lead, throwing my hands up in celebration and eventually falling to the ground, gasping for air while trying to scream in elation. My time stood as the best until André Myhrer of Sweden came down to take the win. I finished second, reaching the World Cup podium for the first time in my career!

I stood to face the crowd, skis raised over my head in celebration, and I was soon jumped by my teammates and brought to the ground in a pile. I heard the cheers of my friends in the crowd. It was everything I'd imagined it to be, even getting to hug my mom and sister in the finish area. Absolute magic.

• • •

Later that afternoon, following the awards, I met up with my friends, some of whom were old teammates and mentors. This podium not only felt like a reward for my life's work but the work of all of us who had come up together, from the Whistler Mountain Ski Club through the BC team, coaches, supporters, teammates—this was all ours. Dusan was in Lake Louise at the Women's World Cup, and I called him a few hours later from the car on our drive back to Denver.

"Congratulations, Mike," he answered as soon as he picked up.

"Thanks, Dus! This is yours too, you know," I responded.

The feeling was beyond anything that I'd conjured when dreaming of this moment. I wanted to hold onto it and make it last forever.

CHAPTER 16
A SEASON ON TOP

EVERY WORLD CUP SEASON, A crystal globe is awarded to the overall winner for male and female in each discipline. On top of this, there's also the overall World Cup winner of the season, which combines the points across all disciplines, this being associated with names such as Stenmark, Hirscher, Miller, Vonn, Maze, Wiberg, Shiffrin, Tomba, and Kostelić. The award is also known as the "Big Globe." To identify the real time leader within each discipline, the "Red Bib" is given out as a highlighter for this racer and to target the one to chase. Like the "Yellow Jersey" in cycling, the red bib draws the spotlight and the eyes of the sport towards it.

While I was climbing onto the podium during the medal ceremony at Beaver Creek, the technical ops manager for the men's World Cup, Mike Kertesz, also a Canadian, started calling my name. "Mike. Mike. Here, catch!" I turned to see the leader's bib in his hand.

He gestured like he wanted to throw it to me from below the stage.

"What? Me? That's not for me!" I shook my head with a smirk, looking around as if he was talking to someone else.

"Yeah, this is for you. You have the Red Bib. Put it on!" He tossed it to me with a big smile on his face.

The bib was logoed up with Beaver Creek, Rauch, and Audi across it. I put down my podium skis, removed my race bib, and pulled the new one on over my race suit. After two races, it's unusual that a second and seventh place are good enough to take the lead, but here I was, with a little luck, leading the World Cup slalom standings.

The next slalom stop was in Alta Badia and getting out of the vans on the morning of the race, I felt a little more visible walking through the parking lot. The early morning fans who usually line up to assure themselves an autograph from their favourite top racers now also came up to me on purpose.

"Janyk. Janyk." They came forward with the autograph books open and cards ready to sign.

Thomas smiled as he kept walking past me. He was normally the one getting stopped on his way up the hill, and he was enjoying the change of roles. As I was getting on the gondola, the lifties gave me little callouts as well, smiling and enthusiastically giving their thumbs up.

During inspection, the TV cameramen and photographers are usually huddled around the big names of the sport, Raich, Bode, or Palander, but today, more lenses seemed to be pointed my way. I had one mind trying to focus on the course while the other was aware of this newfound attention.

The gondolas in Alta Badia are egg-shaped, with windows all around, giving the rider a panoramic, 360-degree view of the surrounding Dolomite mountains. Sharp, jutting, and rising straight up from the earth, the Dolomites give awe-inspiring views while casting long and dark shadows.

I looked out and marvelled, *how did I get here? How do I have the Red Bib?!* These exhilarating thoughts carried me up through the early-morning light.

Soon though, the reality of having to perform again crept in and the bliss was short lived.

What if I can't do this again? What if I've forgotten how to ski? I have to ski up to the bib. I have to be the best in the world.

It's amazing how quickly little thoughts can magnify the fear and then the fear magnify the thoughts. On the outside, I tried to remain calm, but on the inside, I wanted to curl up on the gondola floor. It took all my years of mental skill training to just stay on my feet.

As these skills went, I had three steps to help keep my mind focussed and facilitate performance. One: combat the negativity with the positives using self talk. *You can do this. Ski like you know how, let the skiing take over. You have the speed. It's in you!*

This created a wall around me and slowed the entry of any potential new negative thoughts.

Step two: remember past successes. *You've dealt with pressure at nationals, you handled it in Beaver Creek, you skied great in warm up.* I'd pair this with visualizing highlights of my best skiing.

I let these images burn into better feelings and slowly my confidence returned.

Step three: get moving. As soon as I got out of the gondola, my routine started. From the way I carried my skis, to how I put them on the snow, clicked in the bindings, and pushed away down the hill, if I didn't feel secure inside, I had to embody some kind of swagger to help me believe, and if the negative thoughts were still winning out, distraction was my last line of defence. Music, talking with teammates and competitors, and joking around to fill my head with anything but the task at hand – all were in use on this day.

In any start area, there's always a nervous tension hanging in the air, keeping everyone's hopes and dreams suspended until it's their turn to race. I made my way over to our physio to get a course report, trying not to cut this invisible cord. I took off my snow pants and coat and clicked into my skis, the Red Bib now revealed. I felt its weight along with my own pride in having it on; both were things to uphold. Sliding into the start gate, with the TV camera just to my right, in my mind's eye, I saw every ski-racing viewer tuning in at this moment, everyone wanting to see what the "Red Bib" would do. I double clicked my poles over the wand and planted them into the snow.

"Let's see what happens."

The best thing about racing is when I get to feel at home while on course. All the hours between events, all the unease and fears of not being good enough, all the awkward social theatrics and functions of trying to impress this image I have of myself onto the world... all of this melts away when on course and I'm finally meant to be right where I am.

I finished eighth on the first run, a strong opening leg to my season's sophomore performance. I made a few small mistakes but felt relieved to know there was still speed in me, like the skills I'd honed over the last twenty-four years didn't suddenly disappear over night.

For second run, my urgency for success was too much, though, and I let my mind rest for too long on the possibility of repeating another great result. I pushed too hard out of the gate, my skis got out in front of me and lost the connection to the snow. I tried to ski beyond myself and was out of the course fifteen seconds into the run. I didn't finish the race and lost the Red Bib along the way.

Even though I was bummed with the DNF, there was a small sense of relief to have the eyes of the ski world off me for a bit. As much as I wanted to get there, when I finally arrived, I wasn't ready to be on top.

The next race I was back in the top ten, finishing ninth place in Adelboden, Switzerland and I was growing more comfortable in my pre-race routine. I used distractions at the right times, the positive thoughts were more present, my day of focus became clear, and I was learning how to decompress better after a race weekend to build back up in time for the next. I settled into this weekly rhythm and grew to accept the intensities and nerves of race day. I still didn't like it, but I knew it came with the territory.

Due to weather and a lack of snow this season, Kitzbühel didn't run the Hahnenkamm downhill, and in lieu of speed events, they ran two back-to-back slaloms on Saturday and Sunday. A few months prior, Audi released its first R8 and as the title sponsor of the World Cup and it was heavily on display. At the athlete public bib draw on the night before the race, the top fifteen gathered in the green room before heading on stage to draw and collect our race bibs. Snacking on the food provided and drinking some pop, we ogled over pictures of the new supercar.

"Here's the deal." Ligety was making a proposition to the group. "If someone wins back-to-back this weekend, they have to buy an R8."

Most of us were silent.

"Yeah, this is a really good idea. I'm in!" Sweden's Jens Byggmark added his support to the idea.

With the prize money for two wins coming in at 140,000 euros, it would be close to a wash for the car and very good for a weekend of ski racing. Jens smiled with interest while the rest of us took turns sharing comments for or against the wager at hand.

This mini-series was probably the most confident I've ever felt in a set of World Cup races. Looking out at the sea of hundred-plus racers, coaches, and workers during inspection, I only saw the ten others who I felt were in my race; the rest were just peripheral. Day one I finished ninth again, though I was fifth after the first run and felt like I'd let a podium slip away from me. The next day, race number two, I was hungrier than ever and was sitting in sixth place after first run. I wanted to be the first Canadian to win a World Cup slalom and in Kitzbühel no less to get my name on the coveted Hahnenkammbahn gondola.

There were ten or so athletes between me and my start time, and I was looking to click into my skis. Yul was prepared; he had found our position in the starting order line and was waiting for me to join him. I wasn't feeling the spot where he'd placed the skis down and made us move until it felt right. Yul went along with it all and clicked me in. Our dance from here was known but unspoken; he had his routine that needed to get done and I had mine.

With a few racers to go, I picked up my skis one by one, tail in the snow, tip in the air, and base towards him. He wiped them down with a cloth, making his last inspections of the skis, and I retreated into my world, swaying back and forth, mumbling mantras to myself, resetting the goggles on my face, pulling down my bib, checking the straps on my shin guards for the fifth and sixth time, re-gripping my pole straps – all the necessary nervous tics and superstitious movement needed for me to feel ready.

We moved into the start house, which was an old wooden race shack lined with white, vinyl Audi banners on the inside. Now closed off from the outside world, I was to go in three.

With eight racers left in the second run, there's always a three-minute TV time out, giving us all a longer interval to get ready. The air in the start shack didn't move. Austrian legend Benni Raich was in the gate and the Swiss racer Marc Berthod between us, all waiting for our turns. Little sounds of shuffling came from the racers, skis lightly slapping on the snow, anxious energy with nowhere to go.

In the corner behind me was a plastic chair. I looked at Yul as if asking for permission, clicked out of my skis, undid the strap on my shin pads, sat down, and closed my eyes.

Inhale... exhale. I settled in my mind.

Inhale... exhale. I stayed with my eyes closed, relaxed, and enjoyed listening to the faint roar of the crowd far below.

I opened my eyes and joked a little with Yul; he knew what was going on, he knew how to hang in this space.

I looked past Berthod to Raich, who was now getting ready to start. The cheering from 60,000 fans at the finish now grew louder, and it seemed quite strange to know that I'd be with them in only a few minutes. I finally stood, gathered myself, clicked back into my skis, and gave Yul a final fist bump, looking into his eyes. Here I was, at ski racing's biggest event, in the mix, week in and week out. This was the dream and it was time to go all out.

Out on course, it was truly a freeing performance, even more so than Beaver Creek. I had a great connection to the snow, playing on my skis and making speed in each turn. This was the kind of second-run charge I needed for a chance to win, but as perfect as this moment was, it all fell away in a flash. Slalom is truly a precision game, where inches can be the difference between the tip of your ski going on the right side of the gate or the wrong side, straddling the pole.

Halfway down the run, my ski tip just hooked a gate, and I was out of the race in the blink of an eye, left on the side of the course looking back uphill in bewilderment. This is the cruel nature of slalom. I knew I was skiing at the level needed to be on top of the podium, but it was not to be and there were no regrets on this day.

Returning to our group wager, with a stroke of good timing for a break-out performance, Byggmark actually won back-to-back races that weekend for the first World Cup podiums and wins of his career. His technique was a fresh take on the sport, showing a more wild style and use of the upper body to swing and generate speed. He opened the door for the next generation of technique, and true to his word at the bib draw, he bought himself an R8 later in the spring.

• • •

By the time World Cup finals rolled around, I had a couple more cracks at the podium, finishing fourth in Garmisch-Partenkirchen, and tenth in Kranjska Gora. I was on a little roll, now starting in the top group of seven, and I drew bib-2 for the last race of the season. Even after a season filled with so many firsts, I was still awestruck as I stared at my bib. It was like my younger self jumped out every so often to say, *Can you believe it? Can you believe we're here?!*

Finals were held in Lenzerheide, Switzerland, again, and the slalom race hill had its tough sections. The hill broke into a fairly steep section after five or six flat gates to start, taking a hard left dog leg onto an eight-gates pitch. From here the hill gradually turned back to the right and gently made its way to the finish. Being close to Spring in mid March, the warming temperatures created some extra challenges for the snow conditions, allowing ruts and holes to form throughout the course.

I felt effortless on my skis in the first run, and everything just fell into place. I crossed the line with a smile on my face, finishing third on the run, the pressures of a whole season now one run away from being behind me.

I was relaxed and joked with the coaches in between runs. This was the life I'd imagined, being part of a family, racing with the best, travelling and enjoying the world on tour.

With such a desire to ski my fastest of the season in the second run, I pushed out of the start and all my tactical focusses went out the window. I hammered the first few gates and they felt so good that I forgot about what was coming next. I was running too straight for the rutted conditions of twenty-eighth and hit one squarely, forcing me way off line just as the hill dog legged to the left. I made it back into the course but dumped a lot of speed in the process.

I skied well the rest of the way down, trying to make up for lost time, but the damage was done. I finished ninth on the day, for my seventh top-ten of the season. Even though my aim at the podium fell short, I was attacking, in the mix, and playing the game.

In the end, I finished seventh overall for the season and felt absolutely liberated as an athlete. Mika had woken something up in me; he helped me recognize that I held my own power, which allowed the kid inside to come out in my skiing. Here I was, having success with freedom, a say in my program, a coaching team I loved, equipment that worked, and a great Rossignol contract to match. I was on top, and the value of the team started to feel secondary to living out this personal dream.

CHAPTER 17
CANADIAN COWBOYS

MY GENERATION OF CANADIAN SKI racers came up in the early 2000s with a series of teams and individuals paving the way before us. Nancy Greene put Canada on skiing's world stage by winning the overall Crystal Globe in the inaugural years of the circuit and then on the global stage by winning Olympic gold at the Grenoble Games in 1968. Almost a decade later it would be the "Crazy Canucks" who took the flame, not only carrying it, but burning it brighter through to the mid-80s. Made up by its core of Ken Read, Steve Podborski, Dave Irwin, Dave Murray, and Jim Hunter, their nickname was bestowed upon them by French ski writer Serge Lang for their "seemingly reckless skiing" and aggressive line choices in the World Cup.

In 2003, Ken took the helm as president of Alpine Canada and was part of building up this new wave of Canadian ski racers. He brought with him a belief that Canada belonged as a top ski nation and should be vying week in and week out for World Cup podiums.

For those of us born in the '80s, Emily Brydon was the first to break through with the first World Cup podium at twenty years old in the 2000/2001 season. Following her was Geneviève Simard in 2002, and on the men's side, Erik Guay cracked it in 2003 with a second place at our home event in Lake Louise, Alberta. Then, at twenty-one years old in 2005, came François (Frank) Bourque, reaching the podium twice in super G and GS. The doors were now open for the rest of us to charge through, setting the stage for the 2006/07 season where between Erik, Frank,

Johnny Kucera, Jan Hudec, Manny Osborne-Paradis, and I, the men's side stood on twelve World Cup and one World Championship podiums. Kelly Vanderbeek and Emily brought in podiums on the women's side, adding to Alpine Canada's highest World Cup point total in its history.

Back in Beaver Creek, after my second place, I was still in my downhill suit and boots, holding my skis, with goggles hung around my neck and chatting away while waiting for the prize-giving ceremony to begin. My friends and the rest of the remaining crowd chanted in the background. I was leaning along the fence line that divides the press and the athletes in the finish area, talking with World Cup reporter Patrick Lang, son of Serge Lang, and Mike Kertesz, the Director of Race Operations for FIS on the men's side.

Following a short interview, Patrick started our off-the-record conversation. "Did you hear? Kelly was third today up in Lake Louise, her first podium as well!"

"No way? That's amazing!" I said, knowing the similar elation Kelly must be feeling in this moment brought on more joy.

"The Canadians are on fire right now! Manny and Kucera started it with a win and second place last weekend, now you and Kelly. Is a new era taking hold?" Patrick suggested.

Mike jumped in after Patrick finished running through the stats. "I'd say this is. I guess now the question is what will we call you? We've had the Crazy Canucks. What's this generation going to be?"

With Mike's questions, Patrick lit up, his quirky exuberance and passion for this sport showed up in his face. "Yes, yes, this is a great question! Erik, Manny, Hudec, Bourque... what will you be called?"

I laughed off this notion of being compared to the eras before us. "Ha. I don't know, but I don't think it's up to us."

We continued to muse and toss around names for fun, the athlete, the reporter, and the official, talking as three fans.

When it was time for the podium, I walked up to receive my prize while wearing our team's Cowboy Hard Hat, after being honoured with our team's gutsy performer award. On the podium I was all smiles, took the hat off my head and raised it high up, giving a resounding cheer to the crowd. Something might have clicked for Patrick at this moment because after the next weekend's World Cup speed events in Val Gardena, Italy, Kucera followed up his Lake Louise win with a third-place podium finish in super G. This prompted Patrick to write an article giving us our nickname, "The Canadian Cowboys." Solidifying that this really was a team affair, Erik and Manny finished second and third in the Val d'Isère downhill, making this the first time in thirteen years, since Mullen and Podivinsky, that two Canadian men shared the steps of a World Cup podium. A new era of Canadian ski racing was born.

• • •

Leading up to the 2010 Olympics, the coaching team decided that I should start skiing the combined events, with an outside hope of being a medal contender in four-years' time. Though speed events still scared me, I wanted to branch out, and it also gave me the opportunity to hang with the speed team for a bit throughout the winter. For what they shared in talent and drive, this core group of five had personalities that ranged across the spectrum. Erik, the true professional, did everything that was required to win perfectly to a T. If you read a textbook on how to be a professional athlete, Erik would have a full chapter.

Jan, on the other hand, was the absolute opposite. He rarely did anything by the book, but his natural touch for the snow and self-trust between the start and finish was unmatched.

Then there was Manny, the wild rebel who'd purposefully do something different just to make it seem like he was carefree, though he was absolutely calculated in his approach. He broke whatever mold was put in front of him and routinely proved that alternate routes are possible.

And then there was Frank, the Quebecois woodsman, who had little desire for the spotlight but was one of the most pure and smooth skiers of our time. He skied GS like Ligety before Ligety did.

Finally, Johnny Kucera, the most unassuming champion in the group, brought a methodical and diligent approach to his training and skiing, which would surprise his competitors if they weren't careful. He also came with a healthy chip-on-the-shoulder mentality to carve out his own place in the team.

It was so fun for me coming into this group as a neutral third party, seeing their competitiveness and desire to best each other in everything they did, and yet there was a balance in it all that created magic.

Johnny and I had developed a good relationship from being dryland training partners in the summer months and he helped me during those long downhill inspections. Whenever he saw me looking like a tourist lost in the fog, he made sure to point out the way. "Mike, you don't need to run that line. Even if you run it out there, you won't make it back in time before the breakover. You might as well take it tight and adjust after the breakover, and if it doesn't work out, you'll be in the same place you would have been from taking your high and slow line anyway."

Each one of them would offer support in their own ways. Erik would stick around to see my video at times and point out where I looked like a speed skier and where I was still skiing like a slalom skier, all twitchy-like.

Manny helped with my nerves. "Dude, it's ok to be scared in downhill. Everyone's scared in the start, and if you're not you shouldn't be here," he'd say all casual-like.

Most importantly, though, Jan gave the best tips on how to live like a downhiller, that it was ok to have two desserts with every meal, especially the tiramisu in Bormio.

• • •

At the 2007 World Championships in Åre, Sweden, I raced the combined discipline and the slalom, which meant I got to spend the whole two weeks at the event, from start to finish. Åre is one of the most popular ski resorts in Sweden. Known as one of the bigger mountains in the country, it sits on the shores of Lake Åresjön and gently rolls 1,400 metres up to its peak. The town itself has a quaint village centre with a lot of character, combining rural Swedish and mountain culture vibes. It felt a bit like Sweden's little Whistler, with an *après* and nightlife to match.

I was able to settle and immerse myself in the big-event atmosphere, spend some time with the speed group, and as a bonus, spend the week with my sister. We'd never raced in a big event together and usually had to find a TV between our own race runs to watch each other compete.

After years of talking on the phone after training and races, we could now simply head to the coffee shop or take a meal together to debrief.

The day of the women's super G, I trained slalom in the morning and then made it over to the finish area for their noon start time. Britt was on a comeback season after not making the team's official criteria. She had to pay her way and prove herself through her results in Lake Louise to even keep her spot through the season. Super G had been her strongest event in the year, and with back-to-back fourth-place finishes in the last World Cups, she was poised and ready in the start. I stood in the finish area, watching her image come onto the big screen, wearing bib-18, clicking her poles over the wand. I felt so nervous, more nervous than when I'm in the gate.

This must be how Mom and Dad feel, I thought.

As soon as she got on course, though, I could tell she was feeling great on her skis. When a skier's on, there's a way the ski enters a turn that is in perfect timing with the hill, a magical doorway when the mountain says, *Ok, you can cut in here,* in perfect harmony. She was supple and strong in her legs, committed to the line, and composed in her transitions. My nerves settled a little seeing the confidence she had in her skiing.

At each interval she was gaining speed and soon found the green light, posting the fastest splits, and the time gap was building.

I clutched the fencing in front of me and jumped up and down. "Come on, Britt, come on!" Louder and louder I shouted as she approached the finish.

She crossed the line in the lead by over six tenths of a second! She was ecstatic, throwing her hands up in celebration. She was sitting in first place for the moment, but the best in the world were still to come, and with bib-24, the hometown favourite, Anja Paerson, came into the lead, 0.59 ahead of Britt. It was a valiant performance to be within six-tenths of her, as Anja was on absolute fire. She was building towards one of the greatest World Championship performances of all time, with three gold medals and a bronze by the time the two weeks were up. On home soil, no less!

Next to pass ahead of Britt by three-tenths was the one and only, American Lindsey Vonn, who claimed the silver medal position. Then, with bib-31, the legendary Austrian veteran Renata Götschle, who already had almost every accolade in the sport to her name, just squeaked into the bronze medal position by six one-hundredths of a second. I was a little bummed to see Britt slip off the podium and into fourth place, but seeing her give everything she had on course, knowing she'd skied her absolute best on the day, was inspiring. Sometimes the result on paper doesn't show the true impact of the performance.

We got to hug in the finish area after she came out, she smiled and said, "Now it's your turn."

Five days later in the men's downhill, Jan added to the team's energy, racing to a silver-medal performance while Erik finished fourth. He brought home a medal to Canada House, and it instantly gave us status as a legit ski nation on the streets around the village. To the credit of this group, Manny, Erik, and Jan had made a bet that if any of them had won a medal, they would shave a mohawk strip into their heads. Sure enough, showing the respect they had for each other, the three of them posed with Jan's medal, smiles, and their new haircuts at the party that evening.

On the day of slalom, I continued to balance my fear of not finishing with the desire to push for speed and leave it all on the hill like Britt had done. I got ready in the start corral, clicked into my skis, slowly entered the start tent and into the gate. I looked out at the vista in front me. The hill ran down from under my feet and into the lake, which took up most of the valley bottom before the mountains began to rise up on the other side. The lake was iced over, and snowdrifts wafted across it in the wind. It was frozen for the winter and seemingly in time.

On the hills up the other side, the trees rolled on and out of sight. Nothing out there seem to have any concern for my internal battle about how hard to push. I brought my eyes back to the course again and smiled.

I raced two solid runs, had great sections, and held back on some others; it wasn't perfect, but I finished with a strong sixth place. This was my best result in a World Championships, and making some of the most enjoyable turns of my career in the process. It was a playful performance.

Britt was waiting in the finish area after second run. "I was so nervous when you were in the gate," she said with a warm laugh.

"I know the feeling." I smiled back.

There was a camaraderie developed amongst our group, speed and tech, men's and women's teams. We had all come up together over the years and were now getting to enjoy our successes on the world stage. Adding to this experience was sharing it with my older sister, the one I had constantly chased and never beaten in our hot chocolate races as kids. This turned my dream into something more meaningful than I could have imagined and done all by myself.

CHAPTER 18
A FALL FROM GRACE

AT THE END OF THE 2006/07 season, it felt like I had arrived, and with a slalom world ranking of seventh, I figured it would continue going up from there. But a few changes came quickly. First, Thomas announced his retirement before the last World Cup, and after a thirteen-year World Cup career with over 215 World Cup starts, nine podiums, and two wins, Tom had broken the barriers for Canadian technical skiers and set the bar for our generation. He'd been a mentor and had shouldered the responsibilities of leading this team so well.

The second change was on the coaching front. After only a season, Mika stepped down as head coach and returned to Sweden to be with his family. Mika's energy and presence had given me confidence to think and make decisions for myself towards my program. To soften this blow, I told myself that I'd grown up in the last year, that I still had Johnny and Marc, and whatever would come, my career would be fine. Deeper, though, I was devastated and felt like part of the magic was going away with him.

To kick off the summer training season, an idea was hatched between our trainers and media team. A road bike trip was planned from Calgary to Whistler to symbolize the Olympic torch moving from the 1988 site to the new 2010 venue. Ski teams often start this training period with a bike camp of some sort to rebuild and establish a solid aerobic base, though I'd heard of them in places like Majorca, Spain, or the South of France, not traversing the Rocky and Coastal mountains.

Starting on May long weekend, the launching press conference at the Calgary Olympic Park sent us off with cheers from supporters and reporters enjoying the symbolic mission from one Canadian Olympic venue to the other. We drove to Lake Louise, slept the night, and started on our bikes the next morning. There were twenty of us from the men's and women's teams, some coaches and office staff joining in as well, riding up through Jasper, down to Valemount and Kamloops, over to Cache Creek through Lillooet, up and over the Duffy Lake Road to Pemberton, and into Whistler. In total it was eight days of riding over ten days, with a few stops and talks with ski clubs and kids in the communities along the way.

The first morning, May 24th, 2007, I opened my motel room door and looked at the white trees and covered peaks around Lake Louise. I stood in the doorway, the cold air bit my face as the wind gusted up my shirt. I winced and shivered. It had snowed over six inches, blanketing the landscape with a fresh white carpet on the ground.

"There's no way I'm biking today! This is insane!" I was contemplating not making the walk to breakfast let alone actually doing the ride.

After finally deciding to break trail over to the main lobby for breakfast, I expressed my resistance.

"Come on, don't be so soft. It's kind of cool anyway," Kucera scorned me.

I scoffed at his acceptance of the situation and continued my complaining to anyone who'd listen. Eventually, enough of us knew it was going to happen and rallied the motivation to set off through the slush. We turned west onto the Trans Canada, then north, up to Saskatchewan Crossing where we would stay for the night before continuing to Jasper.

As we slowly climbed up the first hill, my toes felt like ice blocks, and I considered jumping in our support vehicles until the conditions were more favourable. No one was making us ride the whole way, and the coaches wouldn't have minded; it was only our stubborn competitiveness that kept us spinning, and I didn't want to stop if my teammates were riding.

I'll just bike a little farther, just a little farther, then I can get in the van, I repeated in my head.

Soon though, our collective suffering started fueling motivation, and our complaining turned to encouragement for each other. We crested a hill early on and the road flattened alongside Bow Lake, the wind howling over the rippling water. As the middle of the lake sat off to our left, the view of an enormous glacial valley opened before us. I was awestruck, staring for a brief moment while I rolled without pedalling. It was stunning. An instant later, though, a huge gust of freezing wind cut across our pack and snapped me back into reality.

"Come on, keep moving!" A shout came from behind from someone fearing we'd just fall over if the speed didn't pick back up.

On the second day's ride to Jasper, the morning sky was a clear, deep blue with a few white clouds hanging around the mountain peaks. We were the only ones on the road. Occasionally the sound of a car would come from behind and it would slowly pass, but it was mostly just us, the silence, and our breath ricocheting off the towering granite walls. The sun soon gave us some much-needed warmth and our layers of jackets and rain gear were shed and bare skin exposed once again. Our team's powerhouse on a bike was Gareth Sine; he'd put up some of our biggest testing numbers in the lab, and it felt like he was mostly toying with us out on the road. With him out front, a few of us chased and the group stretched out along the Icefield Parkway.

Big Bend Peak was looming just ahead, and the road horseshoed around and up a steep climb towards the Canadian Ice Fields, into the highest mountains in Alberta. Gareth and Brad were up ahead setting pace, Kucera and I were relatively close trying to catch up, and some others were down on the flats, still coming into the bend below. Johnny and I pushed each other up the hill, he passed and I pursued, back and forth we went until the top. There was no external need to push into our limits other than the joy of being able to. I loved this energy, getting lost in the movement and seeing what our bodies were capable of.

After reaching the summit and starting a little descent, I sat up briefly and coasted my bike, free-wheeling. *Take it in because I'll never get to do this again,* I thought, looking at the forest of trees climbing up the mountain walls.

The aroma of dry brush filled around me. We were alone in the middle of wilderness.

I'll never get to do this again, I said as a reminder to savour it one more time.

It was freeing to feel insignificant for a while, with no pressures to perform out here. I smiled and put my head down to the road again.

On our last day, after 700 kilometres of riding under our belts, we faced 130 kilometres of hilly terrain between us, from Lillooet to Whistler. The trip wasn't without its drama up to this point; we'd had a few crashes along the way, some overuse injuries, and I had developed some acute tendonitis in my right Achilles. Apparently, this was something that we should have trained for, not used it as training itself.

My Achilles was so inflamed I couldn't do a full revolution of my pedal stroke right away in the morning and needed twenty minutes of light riding before starting the stage. If I had been wiser in this time, I'd have listened to my body and physio, seen the bigger picture, and taken a day off, but in my youth and level of athletic maturity, the fear of what quitting represented kept me isolated from good decision-making. There was no way I would be left out of an opportunity to prove myself and so I rode through the pain, even if it ultimately meant nothing.

The stage was an absolute gruel-fest, with 400 metres of climbing to start the day. Gareth went out on the attack right away, and we all broke off into small groups pretty quickly, every rider for themself. Halfway through, we rebounded together in the face of a seemingly never-ending challenge. Riding down into Pemberton, now dropping 1,000 metres in elevation, I was shown another reason why downhillers are downhillers, as Kucera and Robbie Dixon dropped past me quickly around the first two corners, descending at speeds over a hundred kilometres an hour, leaving me well behind. With the whole team regrouping in Pemberton, we rode into Whistler as one team, even with Robbie's attempts to pop his tires by bunny hopping in gravel, just to get him a ride in the car to stop the pain. At this point, unlike the beginning of our trip, giving up without a mechanical was not an option.

We had started in snow and zero degrees and were finishing in thirty-plus degrees, perfectly contrasting our trip across the provinces and giving us good reason to go out and celebrate. Which of course was led by Robbie, our team's unofficial social coordinator.

The fitness and team building were amazing on this trip but unfor-tunately, the ride left me with a severe case of Achilles tendonitis. While the rest of my team started the weightlifting and working out, I was sent for physio and sidelined, left to reflect on my decision-making process. When I finally got into the gym a few weeks later, I felt behind the eight ball and wanted to catch up to my teammates. I progressed too quickly, though, and that's when the back pain started. Between the tendonitis and back, the summer dryland season felt like it never started and I had never stopped. I wanted to do everything, but my body was telling me to slow down. I wouldn't listen.

• • •

My first time back on snow was in August, down in Ushuaia, for a three-week camp. The coaches entered us into a GS race within our first few days on snow which is typical for North American and European teams to compete in these South American Cup races while training down there. It supports the local and national level of the sport, and it's always fun to do a little low-pressure racing every once in a while. Coming off the summer I'd had, though, I was unsure if it was right for me.

I pushed out of the start on the first run, and somewhere around the tenth gate, as the flats broke over on the pitch, something sharp pierced through my back.

"Aghhh!" I screamed.

The pain was shooting down my leg, up my back, and across my midsection. I skied off course and over to the side of the run, unable to stand back up, and in tears before I hit the ground. The last time I'd felt pain like this was when I was eighteen years old, and nothing felt right.

Johnny slid down to me from his position.

"Why am I here? Why am I racing? I shouldn't have run today!" I yelled at Johnny, needing somewhere to direct my anger.

Our physio joined us and with some encouragement I eventually stood up on my skis and slid down to the bottom of the mountain, hunched over. Every little bump caused agony, every change of direction was excruciating. At the bottom, I lay on the cafeteria floor, exhausted and needing help to get my boots off. Sitting down was even too painful.

What does this mean for the season? This can't be happening.

Over the thirty-minute ride back from the ski hill, the sounds in my head were drowned out by the rumblings of the aging, diesel-powered, twenty-passenger bus we were in. The smell of its exhaust helped me briefly rest until we came to a stop. Back at the hotel, my teammates carried my gear while I used my poles to assist in walking. Finally, I reached my bed, lying on my back with a pillow under my knees. I let out a big sigh and didn't move a muscle. A sneeze, a cough, or laugh was too much to bear.

We went for an MRI the next day, and I presented with a disc herniation in my lumbar spine, between L4 and L5. The imaging looked like my disc had squished out like a jelly doughnut, the fillings hitting on the nerves and causing the pain. My camp was over, hopefully not my season, and I was booked on the next flight home for further assessments. Before I left, Dusan took me out for lunch. As the team's athletic director, he'd flown in to see the team and support our training camp. We went to one of the numerous seafood restaurants in town, right on the water, with just the road between us and the bay. We sat at a table by the window.

"Mike, we have you set up with Rick back in Vancouver. You'll go recover, see how things heal in a few weeks, and then we'll bring you out to Calgary." He outlined the rehab plan.

"We should have started the season differently, I needed to rest more. I'll probably end up missing the start of the season now or the whole season!" I vented at him.

"Mike." He looked at me and spoke in his deep, Slovenien accent. "This isn't the end." He held his gaze.

I wanted to cry. I knew he meant this and cared for me. I was glad he was here.

I flew home and went for a second set of imaging, done in Vancouver. The doctor confirmed what was shown in Argentina and added that I had degenerative disc disease. I'd never heard of this before.

"It's common to see this in people as they age; not so common for a regular twenty-six-year-old, but we do see this in hockey players and other athletes from time to time. It's something you'll have to live with and manage for the rest of your life."

I was lost and had no motivation or even hope that healing was possible.

• • •

Physios and physical therapists are another key piece to the high-performance puzzle. Most of the time, the athlete knows very little about their own body and is usually learning along through injuries. In ski racing, our physios guide us in the understanding of physical health as well as the mental front, acting as part-psychologists while we vent, share, and release emotions on the table. Each rehab process has taught me more deeply about the body, mind, and motivation, the very thing my athletic success hinges on, and this one was no different.

Rick Celebrini, my previous rehab specialist from the knee injury, was once again the physio of choice, and he started where we'd left off. We met almost every day for three weeks and I saw a second physio in the afternoons. Slowly and over time, he broke down the potential causes for my herniation. I'd shut down the ability to move properly throughout my whole spine and was really only hinging in a couple of spots in my lumbar.

We started with manual manipulations, getting as much range of motion as we could on the table, then got up and started moving. We actively worked the core muscles, building back the right movement patterns again and finishing with a healthy sweat. When I would leave his clinic, it was the best I'd feel all day, a little manufactured relief. It was usually just enough to get me home, where it would all come back, leaving me lying face down on the carpeted floor of my friend's apartment. This routine went on for three weeks: see Rick, back to the apartment, lie on the ground, back up for a second round of physio or massage, some swimming, and then back to the apartment floor. Luckily, I was staying with good friends who kept me company in the evenings, otherwise it would have only added to the dark times.

By early October it was looking likely that I would miss the start of the season. I went out to Calgary to continue my rehab with our team's head physio, Kent Kobelka, and centralize with some other injured teammates. My routine closely mirrored the days in Vancouver, though with it revolving around Kent's office as home base, it gave us injured athletes a place where we could come together and still feel a part of the team. Trev White was coming back from a concussion, Jan was always in for his knees, and a mixture of other athletes came in and out, keeping the energy up initially.

As the season started, though, it grew a little lonelier, with only Trev and me left.

While on the table one day, I looked at a poster on the wall I'd signed for Kent a few months before when I was still on my high,

"Thanks for keeping 'the Franchise' going" it said, with my signature below it.

It was written as a joke, because he had called me this to poke fun at some of my egoic traits that had developed alongside my success.

"Not much of a franchise anymore," I said to Kent in shame.

It had been a good laugh between us, but while he dug his elbow into my hamstring, as I lay chest first on his table, it didn't seem so funny anymore.

"You'll get back out there," he said, knowing full well the struggle I was going through.

After another MRI in late October, the new images showed the disc had retreated slightly to less of a bulge, showing signs that some healing had taken place. It was time to ramp my return to snow plan up. I went out to Norquay for my first days and skied cautiously, barely putting any pressure into my skis.

Shortly after, back at Bob Niven Training Centre, I walked into Kent's office. "I don't think it's ready. I'm too scared it's going to pop again," I shared with frustration, Kent allowing me to vent.

"Mike, you've done the work, we're not getting a positive slump test, it's holding under weight in the gym, you're moving dynamically in the clinic, the MRI looks better. Eventually you're going to have to work through some pain. It's not going to feel great all the time, and you will have your setbacks, but if you don't push at all, you won't be back for this season. We gotta give it a real test."

I knew Kent's words were true. He'd seen the spectrum of athletes come and go over the years and had a keen sense for when it was time.

When November rolled around, the first World Cup slalom was days away, and I was still back in Calgary. It was a strange moment watching the start of the season just go walking by with nothing I could do. I woke up in the middle of the night at 1:00 a.m. to watch the first run live. Sitting up in bed, alone in my apartment with the computer on my lap, I waited for the first times to come onto the screen.

"I'm not on the start list, how can they continue?" I whimpered to myself.

Even then, just before it started, I didn't believe the race could run without me. I prayed for this moment not to be true. But sure enough, the first racer, Byggmark, was on course and his chrono ticked away on my screen. It had all slipped away from me, right in front of my eyes and my heart sank into my stomach.

I closed the screen and tried to forget about this with sleep.

Juxtaposed against this, Britt was having the season of her life. She opened with a podium in Lake Louise, her first World Cup podium, and with my parents on the finish line watching, to boot. Mom had somehow found herself present for both of our first World Cup podiums. The next weekend, Britt followed this up with her first World Cup win, winning gold in the Aspen downhill and earning the overall downhill lead, putting the Red Bib on for herself. I thought about back in Torino when she'd watched me from the sidelines and thinking of her ups and downs let me release a lot of the guilt, anger, and shame I was feeling from this injury. For a brief moment my pains were gone, and I enjoyed sharing in her celebrations from afar.

I made it back for mid-December, rejoined the World Cup circuit, and with the help of our physio did my best to manage the pain. I needed three times the amount of work off the hill to achieve half the volume on it. As an American fellow racer with a similar injury put it when I asked him how his back was doing: "Yeah, it's pretty good. I just need to warm up before I cross the street now."

This pretty much summed up my new athletic reality.

My season was highlighted by a fifteenth in Kitzbühel, but in the last World Cup slalom of my season when I finished outside the top thirty, I had to finally accept my fate. In the course of one year, my ranking had moved from seventh to sixty-seventh in the world, and everything we'd built felt gone. Before returning to North America for our National Championships, I travelled to a few lower-level races with my service man, Yul, to try and improve my FIS points.

Yul had been around the circuit for years and was even the tech for Franck Piccard's bronze- and gold-medal performances in the '88 Calgary

Olympics. I was feeling bad that my results had led him to the Europa Cup finals rather than World Cup finals.

"Hey, Mike. Come on, it's still good out there. You still have it. This is ok," he consoled me. Having seen every outcome possible and understanding the ups and downs of sport, he didn't seem to mind. We drove in silence for most of the trip from Kranjska Gora to Montgenèvre, France. It was nice to be just the two of us for a few races, no coaches, no pressure, just racing and for a moment, it was fun again.

CHAPTER 19

THE COMEBACK TO WORLD CHAMPS

I ALWAYS FELT MORE COMFORTABLE coming from the underdog position, where I had something to prove. Whether it was actually true, by creating this position in my mind, it gave me the best fuel I knew of for going past the nerves of standing alone in the start gate. This came back with a vengeance after my plummet in the ranks. Now well outside the top thirty, my spot on the team was on the rocks if I were to repeat another season like this, and I needed to show that I could be back on top again. There were also a few more things happening alongside me in this comeback.

After a year away from racing, Thomas decided to return to competition, and after two years as athletic director, Dusan rejoined us as the men's technical head coach. Dus was also determined to return the team to the strength it once had and paired up with Johnny as our coaching rock and Kip Harrington to bring fresh energy to the staff. This was the larger push we all needed to get behind the rebuild.

There was a renewed source of funding to support these efforts as well, due in large part to the excitement and buildup to the 2010 Vancouver home games. In light of this, the national team rented a *gasthof* in the town of Kirchberg, Austria, as our European team base. In the heart of the Tyrol, a ten-minute drive from Kitzbühel and an hour west to Innsbruck, the Egidihof was a four-storey, thirty-room building run by a brother and sister combo, Katrine and Giddy. They were two eccentric characters who made sure their presence was known in any room they entered, always ready to share a story, joke, or woe of life.

This became our place for the men's and women's teams to gather, have meals, socialize, and play games. Most importantly, this was a place to leave our gear, not having to lug it all around from race to race, town to town, all across Europe for three months at a time. Our gym was set up in the basement, the ski techs had their own tuning rooms, and the training hill, the Giesberg, was a two-minute drive, just beyond the center of town. It was a perfect home away from home.

Along with the hotel, the people in the town did their part to make us feel at home. Michele and his brother ran a couple of restaurants in town, and Michele's became a spot for afternoon coffee and lunches, while his brother's was a go-to for nicer dinners. The American women's team also used Kirchberg as a base over the years, and the walls around Michele's *Stammtisch* showcased the signed postcards and pictures of athletes who'd called this place a second home. Luckily, Thomas was there to start the relationship in Italian, because after this, it was our collective broken English, German, Italian, and French that sustained conversations.

Back out on the World Cup, there were successes coming through individually and as a team. I had made my way back into the top thirty, Tito scored his first World Cup points with a top ten and in Wengen, and all five of our starting athletes qualified for the second run, the most we'd ever done as a nation. Between Johnny, Dusan, and now Kip, they knew us well, and we trusted them enough to go when they said to go. This extended to our service men, trainers, physios, and our newly adopted hometown of Kirchberg. Everyone added value to the team, all helping bring us back to a good level on the World Cup and for the big event of the season, the World Championships.

• • •

The 2009 World Championships were held in Val d'Isère, located in the Savoie region of the Alps, in eastern France near the Italian border. Starting at 1,800 metres, it's one of the highest ski resorts and has been an iconic ski-racing venue, most notably for hosting the alpine events in the 1992 Albertville Olympic Games. For this event, the organizers resurrected the course from the '92 Games, racing down the front, steeper side of the mountain on the *Face de Bellevarde*. Since the Games, World Cups normally ran down the back side, offering more traditional, flatter terrain but with both genders needing two full-length race venues, this was the best option. No matter which discipline runs on this track, downhill to slalom, it feels like a free fall from start to finish, where any micro bench could only serve as a slight reprieve.

Winding up the narrow mountain road, hugging the cliffs to our left, we rose 1,500 metres in elevation over the hour and a half drive from Albertville. Cresting the last hills nearing the resort, we drove alongside a lake created when they'd made a dam over top of the old town to generate some hydro. In the middle of the lake, the steeple of the old church can be seen when the lake waters are low enough.

We continued towards the mountain walls and the road went dark in their shadows. As the feet of two mountains from left and right came together, as if there was no way through, the road S'd between them, opening to the narrow valley ahead, the start of Val d'Isère. The anticipation and excitement grew. With one main street through town, wide enough for rows of hotels, apartments, shops, restaurants, cafés, and bars on either side, it wasn't a large town in size but it was big in atmosphere. The streets were alive with tourists shopping, locals running errands, kids playing, and athletes and coaches moving about, their different national team jackets standing out.

By the time we arrived at the team hotel, Kucera had won the gold medal in the downhill. He became the first Canadian since Melanie Turgeon in 2003, and the first male Canadian skier of all time, to be crowned a World Champion across all disciplines. The mood was joyful, and little celebrations had started.

Trev, Cousi, Thomas, and I were the four Canadians qualified for the slalom taking place at the end of the two-week event. The night before the race, our strength and condition coach, Brian, ran us through the pre-race routine, involving a series of Olympic lifts and squats, all low reps designed to activate some explosive power. There was also a jump test to measure our power output and fatigue levels. The four of us were on the top floor of our hotel, bantering, watching each other lift and jump, and dispersing the nerves before race day. I stood on our jump mat, ready for my turn.

"One. Two. Three. Four." Brian called out the jump tempo and each jump felt like my head would hit the low ceiling above.

"Yoooo, fifty-four!!" I called out to Trev and Cousi, who were waiting their turn. "A new PB!"

I followed up this claim with a strut around the room, feeling full, like I had just won something of value. My legs felt light, like every neuron was connected and the cells alive, ready to do anything my mind or environment asked of them.

"I'm ready," I told Brian, and the jump test was the confirmation.

That night I didn't get much sleep. I opened my eyes and looked around the room at the chair, the desk, my bags, and clothing. Nothing moved yet my stomach churned.

"Just get me in my boots," I said. "I can take it from there. Just get me to the snow."

I'd gotten used to lying in bed wide awake before races. I knew I just had to wait it out and sleep would eventually take over. In the morning I woke from a light sleep and sauntered to the breakfast room. It was quiet and dark outside. Teammates slowly shuffled in as we went through our own routines: which food to eat, which snacks to bring, how to prepare. The scent of fresh croissants came from the oven. I took a pass on the chocolate ones as the sound of pouring coffee went around the room. Any luxuries like these made me fear that I'd lose my urgency to win.

The hill was a ten-minute walk from the hotel, and ski rooms were set up in the underground parking garage beside the base of the chairlifts. The day was beautiful. The early morning light warmed the sky from black to blue and the encircling snow-covered mountains added to the brightness. The air was cold, close to minus ten, and I pulled my jacket up over my chin, the faint sound of the spinning chairlift starting up in the distance. I walked into the ski room eagerly. Yul was already there, getting things ready.

It was just the two of us inside this twenty-by-thirty-foot temporary wood-framed space, rows of them built for each team. I sat down on one of the metal travel cases he used for his tools and looked around at the dozens of slalom and GS skis that lined the walls. We chatted a little while I put on my boots. I paused for a minute between each one, wanting to delay the inevitability of my identity being put on the line for as long as possible. Yul had my race skis on his tuning bench, working away to add the final touches. I strapped on a shin-guard, and the sound of the carbon fiber rang hollow off my plastic boots. I hit the top of my second shin pad down as well, wanting to hear a similar satisfying sound.

It was time to leave.

I grabbed my training skis off the wall, picked up my poles, and rhetorically asked Yul, "See you at inspection?"

"Ok, I'll bring your race skis up later and meet you there." His gentle French accent soothed me.

I smiled at him with excitement. *"Allez."*

"*Oui, Allez*, Mike!" His voice rose with enthusiasm as he smiled and encouraged me out the door.

I rode the chair up alongside the race run, *La Face de Belevarde*, as sponsor banners were being put in place, course workers and coaches sliding around to get in position.

Hrrgghh, hrrgghh. The sound of the icy surface vibrated off skis of the workers below as they struggled to stop at their intended position.

These conditions were my strength, and yet the thought of combining them with this race hill took me into playing out any worst-case scenarios that the future might hold. Mental skill number-one needed for the day, *focus on what's in front of you.* I turned my eyes back uphill, away from the track.

The start corral was crowded before first run inspection. It's a steep run from the chair down to the start area, with big rocks and parts of the mountain looming closely above. The hill doesn't feel like it's meant for stopping on. I let the crowd of racers disperse as inspection opened for the allotted thirty minutes of time we had to look at it. Now with a clear view, I saw the first few gates, looking for where the rhythm of the course started and how I could find my way into it. With sharp breakovers, lots of terrain changes, and a tight course set, it was tough to find the tempo of it.

Kip stood in his first position of the course, and I slid down to him, practicing a few small turns as I went.

He stood tall, looking assured in his orange and grey Spyder parka, the faux-fur collar of his hood resting regally on his shoulders. "It won't be too fast coming into my section. Commit early over this breakover and then you'll be set to carry speed off the steeps and across this bench."

I moved into Johnny and Dusan's section next, they both had their interpretations of the course. Combining it with mine, it was a lot to take in. Mental skill number two, *visualize, visualize, visualize*. I needed to know every section, every gate, every terrain feature of the course and recall them on demand if I were to have success.

Starting with bib-19, I was able to watch a few racers on TV in the top lodge before skiing down for my run. It was more of a restaurant on the hill, with just one main room for the athletes to prepare. I sat around talking, joking with the others while we waited our turns. At some point the interactions were too much, and it was time for me to turn within. Mental skill number three, *use external tools to help inward focus*. I put my headphones on and pressed shuffle on my pre-race playlist. "Wheat Kings" by the Tragically Hip came on and I instantly was able to relax, let go of some nerves, and connect to my plan. I changed the shuffle setting to repeat; this would be my song for the day.

I soon found myself next in the start gate, and whether all my prep work was done or not, it no longer mattered. It was time to race. I saw Felix Neureuther push out on course before me, his support staff cheering him out the gate. I didn't watch. I kept my eyes forward at the horizon, high above, where the peaks met the sky. Images flashed through my mind of me skiing out, slipping out on the ice, and straddling the first gate. Not optimal.

Front of the ski top of the turn, find the rhythm, come on, Mike. You can do this. I used these thoughts to conjure images of me at my best. Mental skill number four, *let positive self-talk guide to positive imagery*. I clicked my poles twice and pushed out of the gate.

It was a strong run but nothing too special. I managed the tough sections well and held on a bit near the bottom, never letting my skis run too much but keeping it in control to stay on my feet. I finished the first run in a tie for ninth, 1.88 seconds off the leader.

The winds felt like they were gone from my sails. This was not the first run I'd been hoping for.

I met up with Dus in between runs. "All the effort this morning, everything we put in, and for what? I'm too far out to contend today, two seconds, it's too far off. I could have let it go more." Dusan looked frustrated with me.

"Dammit, Janyk. You're two second out, yes, ok, this is true. But you're also in ninth. You never know what can happen, go out and race another run, this is your kind of condition and your kind of hill. You always come back strong after a run like this!"

I looked up at him in silence, wanting to argue some more but nothing came out. Resting on my poles, close to tears, I felt like my shot at a medal had slipped away.

I went into second-run inspection with a nothing-to-lose mentality, a common approach I'd used after disappointing first runs in the past. This stuck with me until the halfway point of the course, right at Johnny's sections. I was staring at a delay gate, which bellied out a right-footed turn over to the left, moving across with the natural flow of the hill. In the middle of the delay, there was a sheen off an ice patch staring back at me, reflecting the sun and the now bright-blue sky.

I shared my interpretation as I envisioned myself slipping on the ice and falling inside. "Johnny, this is a big one!"

"Mike, it's actually no problem. Come in with direction and just stand on the outside ski with everything you have. You have the grip, trust the skis and you'll be good. Once you're through, there's a tight combination, stay sharp through it and then keep your hips tall as you transition onto the last flats into Dusan's section." He worked me through the details, and I nodded, now seeing myself ski with his directions.

The nothing-to-lose mentality started to lose its footing. Who was I kidding? I still wanted this and wanted to put down my best run. Looking at Johnny for a moment longer, I felt his belief in me. There was still something on the line. I had to accept it and recommit to my race plan.

With the reverse start order of the top thirty for second run, I was running twenty-first and waited in the restaurant at the top of the chairlift, off on my own. I kept thinking of that delay gate and the challenge in front of me. The fear was building too high and wanted to run. I put my headphones in again and pressed play, "Wheat Kings" still on repeat, over and over. I listened. It reminded me of home, the oceans around Vancouver and the still lakes of Ontario. It reminded me of quieter times, the freedom of the off season, summer training; it connected me to Canada. I thought of all the years that had brought me to this point, all the races, training days, successes, and losses. I owed it to those moments and previous versions of myself to stick with this one, to play this to the end.

From outside the top restaurant, I looked 500 metres down to the finish. The crowd of 15,000-plus was roaring, standing in the sunshine, anticipating their countrymen Lizeroux and Grange, the hometown heroes, to come down with a win. Lizeroux and Grange were sitting in fourth and third after first run and had a good shot of making this come true. The announcers called out to the crowd, encouraging them to make more noise. With the sun just starting to tuck behind the mountains and the start area was now in the shade, the warmth would have to wait until the finish line. I free-skied loosely down to the start area, headphones still in, Tragically Hip still on repeat.

I skied up to find Yul, who was keeping my race skis protected. He clicked me out of my trainers, I passed them over, and he brushed the snow off, strapped them up, and laid them by his bag. With the music still in my ears, I climbed up the hill a bit, now looking down at the start tent. I ran the course in my mind while working through my physical prep as well.

Commit out of the start, find the front over the break overs, tall through the transitions, through the delay, stand strong on the outside ski, quick in the combos, length in the legs onto the last flats. This was the plan.

I looked up and saw our physio Therese calling me over for a course report. First Kip, then Johnny, and finishing with Dusan; each one spoke with certainty about what to do. I had to be sharp and could hear it in their voices. Yul was waiting for me in the start lineup with my skis, Therese and I walked over to him. He clicked me in and I ran through the course over and over and over again. An image of me losing grip and slipping out at the delay kept coming back into my head. It forced a more narrow and intense focus on my plan.

With only one racer to go before me, I slowly moved forward. I did a few jumps, lifting one leg at a time, bouncing up and down. Taking a deep breath, I looked at Therese. Her eyes were intense and unwavering; there was no fear. I hung with her for a moment longer.

Matias Hargin went out of the gate in front of me and I turned to Yul for a fist bump. His eyes were calm as well.

"*Allez, Mike, on joue!*" He tapped me on the shoulder.

I took the start gate, this time looking downward. "Focus on the course," I said to myself.

The vulnerability of the start gate can be a lonely place, but standing there on this second run, I felt like my whole team was with me. I could see Dusan, Johnny, and Kip in my mind and I sensed Yul and Therese behind me, all of us standing together.

Click click. My poles went over the wand, and I pushed out.

On course my skis felt good, but so much of my attention stayed with the difficulty of the track. The fear of skiing out was still very present, and my mind remained on the tactics and plan for the run. The cues ran through my head for each section, and with each one successfully executed, the next one popped in automatically. On the delay coming into Johnny, I could see him from the corner of my eye.

Stand on the outside ski, commit! My body listened to my mind, and I made it through but wasn't out of the woods yet. *Quick in the combos, long in the legs, use the suspension in the transition, push the line.*

I crossed the finish, exhausted.

I turned to the clock and saw a green light: in first and two-tenths ahead of Felix. My job had been done, and this run felt like work, but the elation quickly covered any form of fatigue. I pushed out of the finish corral and into the leader's box.

With eight racers left, Thomas, Cousi, and Trev crept over to me.

"Dude, this could stand for a while, everyone's having troubles out there," Trev said, smiling.

I gave a little smile back, not wanting to put a jinx on anything.

"Don't worry, I'm really good at shooting mind bullets." He could see my apprehensions and his assurance got me to laugh.

In seventh after first run, Benni Raich came down and skied out near the bottom, DNF #1. The next two on course, Manfred Moelgg and Ligety, sitting in sixth and fifth, were both taken out by the hill and the course.

Thomas tapped my shoulder, his smile was as wide as the brim of his hat. "You could be getting a medal here Mike."

"No, no, there's no way." I shrugged it off, though inside I started to think it might be possible.

The next down, Julien Lizeroux made it cleanly and took the lead by over a second, much to the celebration and roar of the home crowd.

Ok, fifth is still awesome, it would be my career best, I thought to myself as Lizeroux came into the leaders' box and I stepped aside, now standing with my teammates.

Next in the gate was the race favourite, Jean-Baptiste Grange. The crowd erupted as he slid into the start gate and filled the image on the big screen. We all watched with halted breath. He struggled to find his rhythm the whole way down, though, and in the last section joined so many others and skied out, not finishing the race.

The crowd let out a collective groan while the three hands of my teammates grabbed onto my shoulders and didn't let go. Next in the gate was the Swede and good friend Johan Brolenius. I felt conflicted; this would be an amazing result for him, a skier on the circuit with so much speed and a handful of top-tens but no podiums to his name. As a friend, I wanted it for him, but as a competitor... what will be will be. Broli came out of the gate absolutely flying, but with too much energy in the wrong direction, and was out of the course in the first fifteen seconds.

All of a sudden the hands on my shoulders were shaking me. "You won a medal, you won a medal!"

I turned to look at Thomas, my mentor for close to a decade, our team leader and inspiration, who'd come back from retirement and now was sharing this Canadian ski racing first.

"Nooo, nooo." I shook my head in disbelief. "I couldn't have done this without you." I smiled right back to him.

Before it could sink in, Lizeroux and I were ushered into the finish area to await the last racer and this potential podium. We all turned back to the big screen to watch Austrian Manfred Pranger take on the course. He skied this treacherous hill poised, and nothing fazed him. He put on a clinic and crossed the line in first, finishing three-tenths of a second ahead of Lizeroux, with me in third, the bronze-medal position. I couldn't believe it! Trev, Cousi, and Tom piled onto me. *Ok, this has to be real.*

I got up and saw Johnny bombing down the run into the finish area to join the celebration. Before he could stop, I jumped into his arms.

He embraced me, my ski boots dangling in the air off his 6'4" frame. "Dude! You killed it!"

Later Kip, Yul, Therese, Brian, and our support staff came into the finish area and hugged everyone with absolute gratitude. When it came to Dusan, we had a big embrace.

"I told you, Janyk, you were still in it. Dammit, you should listen to me more often." He laughed in his deep, booming voice.

"Can you believe it, Dus? From the BC team to a World Champ medal."

There was nothing more that needed to be said.

For the official podium ceremony, my name was called, and I jumped on the third step with my hands high in the air. Lizeroux and Pranger soon joined, expressing their own versions of elation. As the Austrian anthem played to honour the champion, the excitement settled for a moment as the crowd stood in stillness and we watched the three flags rise. I thought about all the sacrifices my parents had made; all the hardships; the injuries; the countless coaches who'd given their energy, inspiration, and guidance; the teammates from all the years; the supporters; the back injury; the lows of lying face down on the floor unable to stand without pain; the hours and hours of physio work; all the support. This was incredible.

The legendary downhiller from Liechtenstein, Marco Büchel, once told me that his favourite moment after a great result is when he finally returns to his hotel room and sits down on the bed, back in the same place that he woke up in. He thinks about the morning, getting out of bed with all his goals and aspirations for the day, knowing now that he'd done it—that he has achieved what he set out to do. He loved to just sit with this feeling, alone in satisfaction.

After the mandatory doping control for the medal winners followed by a Rossignol party for an hour, I eventually made my way back to our team hotel. I grabbed the key from the front desk, walked into the elevator, rode it to the third floor, and went into my room. I sat on the edge of the bed and thought about the sleepless night I'd had, the nerves in the morning, and all the unknowns that the day had presented. I went to take a deep breath to emulate Büchel, but before I could even exhale, the excitement took over. I had to get moving, and I left the room in search of my team-mates—this was no time to be alone.

We went for dinner as a team, celebrated, and cheers-ed rounds of génépi. Walking back, we were heading in the direction facing the race hill and I was trailing behind the guys. The hill was lit up under the flood lights, the steepness so present, and the glare from the ice still sheening off it. The silence of the surrounding mountains held me in place, lost in a daydream. *How did I do that?* I asked myself in my less-than-sober state.

It was the most scared I'd ever been, the most nerves I'd ever experienced, and yet it was one of my best performances.

I chuckled a little and shook my head. This had taken everything I had and now the energy was gone.

I picked up my phone and dialed our Australian friend on the circuit; he needed to be part of this. "Jono!"

"Mikey boy!"

"Where are you guys? We're all going out."

"Mate, I skied out the first run, so we took off out of town."

"Ah shoot, I was hoping you were still here."

"No worries, mate, we checked the results, saw you made it in the medals, turned the car around, and we'll be back in town soon. Because tonight we spell legend M-I-K-E!"

I burst out laughing.

"See you soon," I said with a smile, and I hung up the phone.

I guess there was still some energy left to celebrate.

CHAPTER 20
BUILDING TO 2010

IN THE SPRING FOLLOWING MY World Championship bronze medal, every-one's focus shifted to the next season and one that held the opportunity of lifetime. A home Olympic Games. The Canadian Olympic Committee hosted its second Excellence Series for winter sport athletes in Vancouver as preparation for the big event. This brought athletes together from all Olympic winter sports who had qualified for the Games or were close to qualifying, for three days of team building, a speaker series and info ses-sions. I kept myself distanced from most of it, participating in activities but not truly there. It just felt like more distractions and my goals somehow stood apart from all of this.

One afternoon a few of us athletes from different snow sports went to visit a performance coach, Donn Smith, who was interested in working with some Olympic athletes. The meeting was set up in part by my mom, who had met Donn earlier in the winter while they were riding the chairlift together. I had my skepticism, like I did with most new things outside my bubble, but Donn came with a resume of working with other professional athletes and corporate CEOs, so I reluctantly went along. We walked into his downtown apartment and office to hear and experience his techniques for ourselves. This was the sales pitch to see if we wanted to work with him and his team.

As we sat in a circle, Donn talked through his philosophy and process, that performance is hindered by unconscious patterns encoded in the mind, developed from early life experiences, which prevent us from always being at our best. The aim was to uncover these unconscious patterns, release them, and grow the sense of being in our best energy, which he called our "I AM Energy."

"Ok, who wants to be a volunteer?" Donn called to the room with his slight Maritimes accent still present.

A little less than average size, he was in his later fifties, with curly silver hair, and was full of energy. I put my hand up in an adversarial kind of way, thinking to myself, *I'm the one with the World Champ medal, what can you teach me about performance?*

I stood up in the middle of the circle, looking out of the windows of the 15th story apartment. I looked past our group and beyond the balcony where Cole Harbour, Stanley Park, and the Coastal Mountains of Vancouver acted as the backdrop. It was a beautiful sunny day in May, with the remaining winter snowpack still resting on top of the mountains. The horn of an outgoing cruise ship blasted through the open windows.

Donn gave the instructions with clarity and purpose. "Ok Mike, step forward for me. I want you to close your eyes and picture your worst performance. In your mind, bring yourself back to a race where you had a result you were unhappy with."

I pulled up a race from the year before where I'd skied tight, unsure, and where nothing worked.

It didn't feel good being back there.

"Ok, I have it," I said out loud.

"Good, stay in this place for me and hold out your left arm parallel to the ground. I'm going to press down on your wrist with my two fingers, and I want you to resist as best you can, trying to keep your arm level." Donn pushed and with little effort my arm fell towards the ground.

He continued the experiment. "Ok, step back and shake it off and then step forward again and pull up a great performance. One you feel you were at your best."

I pulled up my World Champs run; it was still clear in my mind. "Ok. I got it."

"Good, now hold your arm straight out again and I'll give it another push with my two fingers. Try and resist." Donn pushed but this time my arm stayed in one place, and he was unable to move it. I felt strong.

"Open your eyes, Mike, take a step back and shake it off. What did you feel?" he asked.

"Well, I felt terrible in my bad performance, I couldn't wait to get out of it, and my arm felt super weak. In my best performance, I was comfortable and loose, I didn't really need to try and keep my arm up," I debriefed the group.

We were at the peak of his pitch. "Yes. And this is exactly what we are trying to grow here—you in your best energy, your 'I AM Energy.' If you practice being in this, two times a day for ten minutes, it will become your natural state of performance, available every time you step into the start gate."

The rest of us went through a various set of similar exercises over the next hour, and with each he shared more information and practices for improving performance. As the group left the session and returned to our regularly scheduled COC conference, I felt conflicted. I'd experienced the applied kinesiology arm tests as a kid the naturopath our mom took us to, so the idea that mindsets brought about different energies that had their effects on the body wasn't too far-fetched.

Can I really train to be in my best energy more often? Is this the secret I've been missing? Is this really possible?

As skeptical as I was, I had to give it a try.

• • •

Out on the hill, all of us on the team had grown as athletes and we pushed each other a lot in training. With Thomas now retired for the second time, the slalom group consisted of Stutz, Brad Spence, Pat Biggs, Trevor White, Cousi, Ryan Semple, and JP Roy. We all had top-fifteen results on World Cup, Nor-Am wins, and national titles, which meant whoever was skiing fast on any given day knew they had real speed. The coaching staff of Dusan, Johnny, and Kip knew this as well and used it to everyone's advantage.

Back in Coronet Peak, New Zealand, in the race arena again, Dusan gave us a carrot to turn every day into a competition. Whoever won the most runs throughout the camp would be crowned the champ and awarded a flight tour over Queenstown and surrounding areas. This set the tone of intensity for the next three weeks and was a source of chirping amongst the group. Cousi took an early command of the lead, taking fastest slalom run after fastest run. Not to be outdone and always ready to put his body on the line, Stutz saw his opportunity to pick up a win partway into the camp.

It was a sunny clear day with icy, hard-injected conditions, and we had a forty-five second, close-to-full-length slalom course set. I was riding the T-bar with Cousi and as we started up the lift, Stutz was pushing hard out of the gate, his patented "strongest" start on the team.

I took notice, looking uphill at him coming towards us, just off to our right-hand side. "Man, those are some good turns, he's carrying some real speed."

The course was set on the lane just beside the lift line, so we had front row seats to the action. After the first pitch, he went out of our sight for a moment and onto the flat bench.

"Let's see how he breaks over onto the next pitch, though," Cousi said, not wanting to lose his fastest time of the day.

Stutz came back into view.

"Eh man, this is pretty good," Cousi admitted with his sharp Quebecois accent.

We both expressed our surprise. "Wow, he's still going."

Our heads turned to follow him around as we rode up and he skied down through the last ten gates of the course.

"Oh no, he's getting late, there's no way he's going to keep this together." I kept up the commentary as his line slowly got a little lower, but he clearly didn't want to break the arc, and he didn't want to slow his speed.

Cousi piped in with his predictions. "What's he doing? He's not going to be able to make the last combo, he's way too late."

Sure enough, Cousi was right, and Paul's speed and line combination were no match for the final tight hairpin section. His skis hit square to the gates, bucking him forward and double ejecting from his skis. He crashed through the finish, hitting the 2x2-inch wooden finish posts that held our timing system beams in place.

"Ohhh!" Cousi and I both gasped.

Johnny jumped into his skis and headed for the wreckage from the lower-course position he'd been taking video from. Paul had tried to pull off the impossible and now was in a heap being picked up by the coaches.

He eventually got up, slowly, put his skis back on, and slid to the bottom in a daze.

When we made our way down to him after our runs, he sat holding his arm. The finish post had given him a puncture wound in his arm, and our team doctor figured it would need a few stitches.

Cousi was never one to shy away from expressing his opinion. "Stutz, you idiot! There was no way you were going to make that!"

By now, the rest of the team had gathered around to check in. Trev followed Cousi's comment with a simpler question that we were all wondering about. "Paul, what were you thinking?"

He looked up at us and with a dead straight face said, "Dus told us to go a hundred percent, so that's what I did!" His words implied that we were idiots for not getting the instructions right.

"Bahaha!" We burst out laughing.

Cousi added salt to the wound with a punch to his other shoulder. "Whatever you say, Stutz. All I know is that you're never getting that plane ride now!"

Sympathy was hard to come by amongst brothers.

• • •

Before the second World Cup slalom of the season in Alta Badia, the coaches entered us into the classic early season Europa Cups held in Obereggen and Madonna di Campiglio, Italy. These events were always great tests where limits could be pushed with few consequences if we were to ski out. I also had a lot of confidence in my equipment, which translated into feeling a strong connection to the snow. With low nerves and high trust in my skis, I knew I could play and have fun in these races. I started off with a fourth-place finish in Obereggen, and three days later, for the night event in Madonna, I experienced one of the best performances of my career.

That morning I woke up and something felt different. There was a clarity to the day, and I was able to take my time getting ready. I had a late breakfast and went into the I AM Energy practices, which were short, ten-minute meditations set to music to build this "best energy" state. When I came out of it, I went for a light jog through town.

Running along the narrow streets, winding through the alleys, and between the old buildings, I took note of my footsteps: the different sounds they made on the gravel, pavement, and cobblestones. Normally my pre-race activation jog was used to go find something, an assurance, a sign that everything was going to be ok. But on this day, the feeling was already here before I had put on my shoes. I looked up at the sun resting on the mountains surrounding the town, felt the cold air in my lungs and the lightness in my legs, in tune with my body and its movements. I ran to the bottom of the race hill; no one was on the slope yet.

A sensation came over me like a warm blanket and was expressed without words. *I'm going to win today.*

I smiled. "I'm going to win today."

The words now came out but not from an egoic place, more in a letting-me-know kind of way.

I turned around and ran back to the hotel.

Everything moved slowly from this moment forward: getting my skis ready, putting on my boots. I was in no rush because I knew I had already won. Standing at the top of the warmup courses, I looked out at my competitors. I didn't feel threatened by any of them like I usually did. There was no sense that I needed to beat anyone. I was enjoying watching them ski, each one showing something unique, something special.

This is so nice, I thought, and I skied a few warmup runs myself, again in no rush. It felt effortless, playful, and fun to interact with the mountain and course.

"Mike, those turns were amazing. You were carrying the most heat out of anyone out there," Johnny came over to tell me,

"Yeah. It feels good today," I responded, not needing the reassurance on this day, yet it came nonetheless.

Before first run, I watched the first couple of racers and thought, *this doesn't look so hard.* I went through my warmup routine, still with no doubts.

My mind was relatively silent besides this recurring thought: *I'm going to win today.*

It was a simple statement rather than a positive affirmation. Yul and I looked at each other, and we smiled. Here was someone who had worked so diligently for my success, through all the ups and downs over the last four years, always patient, always supportive. I felt a special bond with Yul, an appreciation that words could not express. I smiled a little extra, holding a secret that he didn't know yet; we were going to win tonight. I pulled into the start gate.

It was a beautiful December night, and the surrounding mountains were now shadows in the sky. They were my spectators.

"Attention," the starter called out as he closed the timing wand. I looked down at the course and saw myself skiing each gate perfectly. I clicked my poles twice and planted them firmly on the other side of the gate.

"Go."

I pushed out and onto the same hill that had started my World Cup experience years before.

In my best runs before this, I would have to wait to the first, second, or third gate before I got the confirmation that my skis felt good under my feet. But on this run, there were no doubts, and I knew what I had before I left the gate. I could see every contour of the hill, where to make speed, over the first roller, through the hairpin, maintaining and gaining speed before the flush and onto the last pitch. Even in the compression as I came off the steeps to the final flats, my hips stayed overtop of my toes, the edge set early in the turn. This was the dance I always dreamed of.

I won the first run by half a second, and Dusan came down to congratulate me on my skiing. He highlighted what was going well, something I normally craved, but on this night, it wasn't needed, simply appreciated. There wasn't anyone to take ownership of the skiing. Between runs, I sat comfortably with the rest of my team and racers from other nations. We played cards and joked around. There were just a few nerves that didn't require much attention and no negative thoughts that I needed distracting from.

What is this I'm feeling? I asked myself. *This is so magical, this is so much fun.*

My routine before my start was similar to first run. I spent the time getting activated, visualizing, and watching some racers run under the floodlights down to the first breakover and disappear out of sight. I saw myself on course. The image of my skiing was so clear, like it already existed before I pushed out.

I took the starting gate. The feeling remained.

I'm going to win today.

Skiing this run was as amazing as the first; all my energy could be put into the skis, landing in the perfect place at the exact time it was needed. My equipment was doing everything I asked it to do and there was little thought required. I was simply free to enjoy the play of the race, and I crossed the line in first place. This was the first Europa Cup win of my career.

After the awards and prize-giving, we walked back to the hotel as a team, laughing and joking with each other. I hung back from the group and enjoyed the banter from a quieter distance.

The next morning the omnipotent feeling was gone.

"What was that? How do I get back there? Is this what Donn was talking about? How do I compete from here forever?" I asked myself.

I hung onto the memory of this day, knowing some other level was possible, but without any answers, all I could do was return to the process.

● ● ●

The rest of the slalom season evolved, and our team kept growing its success. I finished fifth in Alta Badia, sixth in Zagreb, tenth in Wengen, and all the while we consistently had two or three others finishing in the top thirty together. Around the halfway mark of the season, Trev and I had qualified for the Olympics slalom with the required two top-twelve results in World Cup. Coming into Kitzbühel weekend, Brad and Cousi wanted to punch their tickets too.

For the second time in Canadian ski racing history, we finished with four in the top thirty of a slalom race, and for the first time ever, all four inside the top fifteen. With over 50,000 fans cheering, screaming, and singing for their favourite racers, we all stood in the finish area, enjoying the satisfaction of a day well raced. As the prize-giving ceremony got underway, we high fived and hugged.

The announcer called out the top three names: "Giuliano Razzoli, Julien Lizeroux, Felix Neureuther." His voice called out over the speakers, trying to cut through the sounds of air horns and sizzling flares.

Trev all of sudden was hit with the true meaning of these results. "B! Cousi! You know this qualifies you both for Vancouver. You did it!"

Brad and Cousi were silent—their faces said it all.

We knew the special sense of satisfaction that they were feeling. We were three weeks away from the opening ceremonies of the Games, and for the first time, Canada had qualified four slalom skiers through the "A" line criteria. We were sending a team not just to participate but to compete for the podium on home soil.

CHAPTER 21
A HOME GAMES

IT'S STRANGE TO HOLD A day in your mind for six years, then wake up one morning and be standing in it. Stepping off the plane, walking through customs and out the terminal doors in Vancouver, I wondered if this was real. In July of 2003, I had stood in Whistler's Village square, surrounded by a thousand other locals, looking up at the big screen on stage, awaiting the announcement of who would host the 2010 Olympic Games. We stood shoulder to shoulder in anticipation, watching the events unfold in Prague to hear what city was inside the envelope.

"The International Olympic Committee has the honour of announcing," IOC president Jacques Rogge read, "that the twenty-first Olympic Winter Games in 2010 are awarded to the city of... Vancouver."

The square instantly erupted, Canadian flags waved with vigour, and the singing of the national anthem soon followed. In all the excitement, I turned my mind towards my own preparations. I would be twenty-seven years old in February of 2010, in the prime of my career, and I put my sights and intentions towards this day. I visualized the run, walking to the chairlift in the morning, waking up, seeing my family and friends, how I would ski, seeing myself cross the finish line with success, how I would celebrate, who I would hug first. With each year that passed I added any new details that came in. What the run would look like, the possible conditions, where we would stay, and who would be around me as teammates and coaches.

Driving across the Granville Street Bridge and into the city, I got my first look at the local mountains of Grouse, Cypress, and Seymour. The temperatures were unseasonably warm, which kept their runs green with only small patches of snow. I rolled down my window to smell the ocean air, my arm comfortably resting in the breeze. I was home.

Throughout the city the Olympic spirit was already on the rise; official and unofficial banners hung from city street posts and businesses. An arrangement of different national flags proudly draped from condo balconies, the residents expressing support for their home nations. Heading up the Sea to Sky Highway towards Whistler, a route I'd driven a thousand times before, I anticipated every turn and called out the landmarks in my mind, greeting them like old friends. These were calm moments, knowing the need to perform was still a couple of weeks out and I enjoyed the drive.

The alpine, sliding, Nordic, and ski-jumping events were all held in Whistler, and with this, there was a secondary athletes' village for these teams. Our alpine team opted to stay outside of the village and instead rented some mountainside condos for a more convenient, ski-in/ski-out location. National teams do this from time to time as a way to control the environment as much as possible in hopes of tipping the scales for success in their favour. The Canadian Nordic team did this in Torino, and we followed suit for these Games. The American alpine team had the same idea and rented a condo right across the street from us, making it our own mini village.

Only the speed and combined athletes were here to start: Erik Guay, Manny Osborne-Paradis, Robbie Dixon, and Jan Hudec were the four racing in the downhill and super G, with John Kucera out with a broken leg early in the season in Lake Louise. Those of us racing combined were me, Ryan Semple, Louis-Pierre Hélie, and Tyler Nella.

Ryan and I walked into our shared room, eyeing up the clothing bags sitting on our beds just waiting to be opened. It was swag time!

The official clothing kit was still a huge part of the experience, especially at our home Games and I wanted to represent to make this real as soon as possible. In the next room, Nella and Louis-Pierre were playing a similar game, each one of us coming out into the hallway to show off a new piece of the collection. We opened and dug into ours.

"Ryan, what's this one for?" I asked, wearing a quilted red bomber jacket with "Canada" across the chest and the HBC blanket print on the inside.

Ryan read a printout sheet that came in the bag, letting us know which outfits were to be worn for which events. "That's the podium jacket. You have to wear it with this toque and these pants."

Within the mainstays of t-shirts, sweaters, pants, and workout gear, there's always one standout piece, some unique item that's timeless. For Vancouver, this was the closing-ceremonies knitted sweater, inspired by the traditional sweaters of the Cowichan First Nations, located on Vancouver Island. Every item was combed through, all were tried on, and we were still kids opening presents on Christmas morning.

Participating in the opening ceremonies was still a dream of mine, to walk with Team Canada, especially in my home city. We were only an hour and a half drive up the highway from BC Place Stadium, so I figured that this had to be my moment. With the downhill race shortly after, though, and considering the estimated six hours total time for the two-way drive, plus the event, the ski team made the decision to stay back and watch it from TV to make use of the rest.

Feeling crushed, I walked outside of our condo to get some fresh air and stood on the road watching the melting snow pool into a little stream in front of me. A few houses upstream, the men's American alpine team were piling into a couple of minivans, all smiles and kitted out in their Ralph Lauren team gear.

Marco Sullivan rolled down the window as they drove by. "See you down there!" he called out with some hollering coming from the back seats, expecting we would be following suit.

Back inside, we settled in and watched the CTV panel prep the audience for what festivities they could expect from the ceremonies. Within the hour, our team manager, Robert, came in with news. "Hey guys, we've been informed that there will be a mini opening ceremony in Whistler tonight for the remaining Canadian athletes who didn't go to Vancouver." His gentle French-Canadian accent was a welcome sound. "We'll meet at Canada Olympic house at 6:00 p.m. and when Team Canada starts walking into the stadium in Vancouver, the athletes will start their walk through the Whistler village and onto the main stage in the square."

In a sudden turn of emotions, I felt lucky we'd skipped out of the main event, since we were now getting to walk through my hometown.

Only the four of us racing the combined chose to go, all dressed in our prescribed outfits: black cords; boots; a crisp, white sweater; a long, red expedition jacket with faux fur; scarves; and the quintessential *Strange Brew*-style Canadian toques with the pom poms on top. At Canada House, which was the local public library, we were greeted by our parents, families, and supporters who'd make the trip out. The rest of the mountain venue's Canadian athletes and coaches started filing in, around fifty of us in total, grouping together with smiles to participate in these secondary ceremonies.

To my pleasant surprise, Britt walked through the doors. The women's alpine team had decided to stay back from Vancouver as well, freeing her up to join this more intimate group. The voice of Brian Williams filled the room as the broadcast played through the sound system and the first countries started walking into the stadium. We looked up and watched the screens.

My mom had also made it to the event, and she, Britt and I posed for a picture. I put myself in my mom's shoes, thinking of her father, my grandfather, who had been part of a team trying to get the 1968 Olympics to come here. Now she stood with two of her three kids, who were days away from competing in the 2010 iteration. There was a joint smile and warmth from the three of us in this shared moment.

As Team Canada was about to be called into BC Place, an organizer called our group to the front doors and gave out the plan. It was pouring rain outside, but fans and supporters lined the routes, unfazed by the conditions.

Semple grabbed onto my shoulders from behind and started shaking me. "Guy! Are you ready for this?"

I laughed under my breath, bowing my head to the steps in front of me. "I have no idea," I called back to him.

With Britt standing beside me and a flag in our hands, the doors opened and we walked into the crowd. The rain pelted and popped off our jackets, like the sounds of sleeping inside a tent on a similar rainy night. The cheers from the fans soon took over, each one encouraging us as we passed by. Britt and I walked side by side, past the bars and restaurants, across the overpass, and turning right towards the village square. We saw friends, family friends, high-school teachers, ski-club coaches, community members—the elation was mirrored to each other in our faces. It was clear from the moment this community opened its doors to the world, that we would all be a part of these Games.

We walked around the back of the temporary stage in the main square, up a few stairs and under a covered area. We were soaked, an insignificant detail at the time. On stage and looking out over the village square, we saw a beautiful sea of people. Canadian, Australian, New Zealander, Austrian, American, French, Swedish, Japanese, Spanish; a mixture of flags and homemade cardboard signs showed the individuals' support. Canadian Mounties stood on either end of the stage, holding the country's flags.

The emcee for the event welcomed the supporters, introduced the athletes, and then turned to us. "Does anyone here want to say something?"

I was off to the side, filming from my own camera as the question was posed. Luge athlete Sam Edney pointed straight at me. "This is all you, Mike." He pushed me forward towards the mic.

I stood in front of the crowd that was waiting for me to say something special. "Hello, Whistler!"

A softball opener.

"I remember standing where you are now, six years ago when we were awarded these Games, and this moment was just a dream. Now here we are."

I paused and the crowd erupted.

"This is a special community, and it's because of your spirit that we're going to have an amazing Olympics! Thank you, Whistler!" I handed the microphone off to my sister and listened to the energy and roar of the crowd when she finished as well.

Shortly after, everyone in earshot of the vicinity started to sing the national anthem. The rain hadn't dampened anyone's spirit. The Olympic flame was officially lit and burned bright on this wet and rainy February night.

We were underway.

• • •

During the period between my own events, I went back and forth between competitor and fan. After and during training days, we gathered to watch the big events and cheer on our Canadian teammates. Who would break through and win Canada's first gold? The tension was cut early with Alex Bilodeau and Maëlle Ricker's gold-medal performances in moguls and snowboard cross. On the alpine side, the speed team was positioned for great results. Britt had been fourth and fifth in the two downhill training runs, and Robbie and Erik had both been in the top three in theirs. The men's downhill came first, and I put myself in Manny and Robbie's shoes. Both had grown up in Whistler and were raised on these mountains. I felt their nerves associated with the potential to win in front of friends and family. These nerves would soon be mine.

The intensity was high as they each took the start gate. Manny skied amazingly in the first half, but soon lost the race line and finished seventeenth. Robbie exploded from the start and this energy took him on too tight of a line, putting his head through a panel off the top, though he kept going, only to crash out halfway down. My heart sank watching him eventually sit up and throw his goggles to the ground. Their Olympic dreams of a medal were over. Erik, on the other hand, put in two amazing races, finishing fifth, a couple of tenths off the podium and in an even closer call, fifth in the super G, only a few hundredths off the podium.

On the women's side, Britt and Emily Brydon were our two medal hopefuls and faced an extremely challenging speed track, arguably harder than the men's. It was a clear and cold day with an iced up and bumpy track—gnarly conditions. Britt pushed out of the start with full commitment. She was on from her first turns, letting the skis run while keeping them connected to the snow, allowing her to start the turns early and carry speed out of them. She had the green light at the first interval and was in the lead. We stood screaming at the TV to keep it going. She attacked, took chances when she could, and was having one of the best runs of her life. Across the last traverse near the bottom third of the run, though, she lost the race line, and with it the speed needed to maintain her position across the flats. It was such a small slipup from perfection that cost her a spot on the podium.

She crossed the line and into the finish area, welcomed by the roaring crowd, in sixth place. In her hometown Games and first Olympics, it was an inspiring run. With medals the only measurement of success here, no matter how good Erik and Britt's performances were, Alpine Canada had none to show after the speed events, which meant the team's hopes came down to the GS and slalom.

In the super combined, I was well out after the downhill portion, and based off this time, I started number 42 for the slalom portion. I didn't feel much pressure standing in the starting gate; I had nothing much to lose but an opportunity to see how I raced this hill. Both my equipment setup and technique were better suited for ice and on a surface that could withstand a lot of forces. The soft conditions weren't my forte, where a gentler and even pressure is required through the turn. So, I was happy to see the snow conditions had firmed up overnight to my liking and I could attack with good support under the ski.

I had fun with this run and finished twenty-sixth overall, but more importantly, fourth on the slalom leg. To have this run from bib-42 with a handful of my other slalom compatriots in the field was the confidence boost I was looking for to take into the slalom. This run gave me a glimpse of what I could do on this hill in a week's time, reassuring me that I *had* come to the Games with speed and that the dream I had held for so long was still alive and well.

CHAPTER 22
SIX YEARS FOR ONE DAY

THE OLYMPIC SLALOM RACE HILL wasn't that challenging compared to the usual World Cup tracks as it was mostly flat with a few terrain changes in it. The main feature, and what made it of any real interest was the opening pitch just out of the start gate. A steep face that had been cut into the hill for the event, it was only about five or six gates long but could potentially make or break your run. Too much risk could have you crash out, while not enough would leave you playing catch-up for the rest of the run. For the two years prior, we had been training on this hill every April to try and get as much of an advantage as we could by finding the limit and being as comfortable as we could on it. Adding to this, Dusan had won the nation's draw a year before, which awarded our team the first-run course set, a small but welcome advantage in most races and one we were trying to capitalize on. We practiced all sorts of tricky combinations in the spring before the Games, trying to find the right course set that would throw our competitors off and tip the scales a bit more in our favour.

On one such occasion, Dus tried a unique combination of gates that was set really straight down the pitch for five gates and then tightened into a hairpin right in the hill's transition onto the flats. Six of us stood in the start, deciding who would be our guinea pig.

"I'm not going first." I piped in with a laugh. "There's way too much speed out the gate to make it through that hairpin. Dus has clearly lost his edge."

Brad, Pat, Cousi, and Trev agreed, but sure enough, we heard the famous words: "I'll do it!" Stutz called out full of confidence, pushing forward towards the start gate and getting us out of the way.

"Please, be our guest," we said as the five of us went to the edge to watch the show.

To Paul's credit he fully committed and went with a roar out of the start, but as in New Zealand, he didn't know when to pull the chute. He wasn't able to move fast enough in the hairpin and clipped his tips on the gate, sending him flying into the air. After completing a forward somersault, he once again finished in a groaning heap of limbs twenty metres farther down the hill from where he left his skis.

There were two physios in the start with us at the time, Dave and Chris, both of whom looked at each other to see who would take the call and be first responder. They were frozen for a moment until Dave broke the stillness. "I got this," he said with the same vigour that Stutz had used to get himself in this position.

Dave threw on the forty-pound medical backpack, clicked in his skis, and skated to the edge of the pitch and down towards Paul. In all his efforts, though, he forgot to properly assess the hill he was about to ski, and after one turn, slipped out on the ice, lost his balance, and crashed, sliding down right beside Paul.

We all turned to Chris to see if he would go next to rescue them both, but he was still speechless, staring down from the top. With his sense of duty taking over and a little fear in his eyes, he more wisely chose to go the long way around and safely made it to the wreckage pile below.

Once it was confirmed that everyone was ok, we yelled down to the coaches, "Dus! Johnny! I think we need a reset up here." We were all dying of laughter, and no one was willing to try again without the necessary adjustments.

We trained on this hill over a hundred times, with at least twenty-five different course sets. Every time I stood on top of this run, I pictured myself in the Olympic start gate, trying to stimulate the future, but even the best laid plans still have their foes. On the morning of the Olympic slalom, warmer weather had moved in, not allowing the hill to freeze overnight, and with this, everything we'd prepared for changed.

This new snowpack was significantly softer and unable to hold on the pitch anymore in a consistent manner. The officials felt it was too inconsistent to run a fair race on, which we found out about during the gondola ride up for the first run's inspection. Trev and I were sitting with our physio when the call from Dusan came crackling over the radio. "Attention, coaches, tell the guys that the jury decided to move the start down to the reserve position. I repeat, we will be racing from the lower start position." Dusan's voice lingered for a moment longer in the cabin. It felt like the air had been sucked out of it as the words fluttered to the ground.

"Well, there goes the race. Might as well just hand the gold over to Razzoli." Trev broke the tension with a little joke, though he was expressing what I was feeling as well, knowing the Italian was the best in the world on soft snow and flat hills.

My heart sank with this news that there would be no more steeps and with it, the loss of our extra home field advantage. The images I had built in my mind for so long were gone in an instant. I tried not to panic and to convince myself of all the positives that were still in place, but this was not easy.

Stepping out of the gondola before first run, I took a few steps forward and then stood still. Holding my skis in hand, I looked up to my right and towards Goat's Gully, a run I'd skied every day growing up with my friends. I looked over at the empty space where Orange Chair used to be, the lift we'd ridden thousands of times over the years, and then to my left, I looked across the valley at Sproatt Mountain. The familiar smell of pine boughs hung in the air. Britt had told me that on her race day, these familiarities were comforting. I, on the other hand, was finding them conflicting. How could the biggest event of my life be held in such a cozy place? This was like my living room, not an arena for performance. It felt strange.

The longer I stood there, the more I thought of how significant this whole moment was, and the pressure became too much to comprehend. I had to keep moving. I put in headphones, playing my race-day song, and went through the routine to get into my best energy. Any hopes of being in the supernatural *I'm going to win* state were not here on this day. I'd have to be proactive to find this state of performance.

I skied down feeling the front of my ski bite, carving, standing strong on the ski, from foot to foot, edge to edge. I had all the normal nerves, all the usual voices that fearfully asked, *What if?* There was also a calm feeling saying, *this is ok. This is alright.* Both were equally present and feeling consumed by the intensity of these pulling emotions, I could only do what was right in front of me.

My time in the start area moved fast—it didn't even seem like there was much of it at all. I drew bib-14, and after an activation, course report, and some alone time, I was in the start gate before I knew it.

Front of the ski, top of the turn, you can do this. Feel the skis pick up, push. The time is now!

The way the rut was developing, it was leaving a shelf around the gate, which was risky for my skis and setup. If I was too aggressive, they would pick up too quickly and I could straddle, but if I held on too much, the skis would be fighting against the shelf, killing all my speed. I had to push while also keeping it precise.

"I Am," I repeated to myself, trying to silence the mind. "I AM."

Inhale... exhale...

I looked Yul in the eyes, hoping for some last-minute assurance, and we gave our final fist bump.

I moved into the start gate, standing tall, listening to the crowd in the distance, the random calls of my name from course workers on the side, racers behind me smacking their skis one at a time on the snow. I looked out and glanced to my left—there was Mom. She was chief of the slip crew, working her position and trying not to smile. Just like in a race when I was thirteen years old, she was out volunteering, doing her part to help.

"Allez, Mike, comme tu peux," Yul encouraged me from behind.

I turned back to the course and repeated my mantra, "Find the front. Top of the turn. Attack!" There was nothing left to do but go.

"Racer ready..." the starter called, and out of trained habit, my poles clicked twice and seemingly planted themselves on the other side of the wand.

My hands were together out in front of me with my head cradled in them. My final resting position before I had to leave. I wanted to stay.

Inhale... exhale...

It's time to go, a voice said from inside my head, and in perfect sequence, the starter called his final command.

"Go."

I had to go. I pushed out and charged on course.

It was a sprint. I put everything into my turns but there was something missing. Over the years you build a feeling of when the skis are in perfect timing with the turn and the hill, and it wasn't here. There was no snap or energy coming back to me from the skis. I had to adapt and ski differently, putting more effort into them and keep moving. I fought for every turn, pushing when I felt connected and making it work as best I could for the sections when I didn't.

With only a few gates left, I knew this wasn't the envisioned run and there was no saving it now. I finished eleventh after first run, 1.39 seconds off the lead, and my medal chances had dropped significantly.

Second run was more of the same. I went over the pre-run plan, ran through the warmup routine, listened to my music, and did my self-talk. Out on course again, the belief and charge were there but the magic was still missing. I wanted this result so badly, I'd held out hope that the spark would be found in the next turn, and then the next, but it wasn't meant to be. I came through the finish, dropping a couple of places, and finished thirteenth overall.

I looked around at the cheering crowd. I could see my friends in the stands and wanted to savour the moment, but it was hard to enjoy it while feeling so much disappointment inside.

Cousi was in the leader's box when I came down, which gave me something to smile at as I pointed and called over to him. He finished with an eighth place, a great performance to lead our team on the results page. I pushed my way to the exit of the finish corral, knowing this was the end. There were no second chances—six years of putting everything into this, and it was not to be. Before I got too far, my dad was standing beside me as I clicked out of my skis. His volunteer position was with the equipment control team. Mom stood with me in the start and Dad in the finish. I smiled with him... another moment almost too special to comprehend.

We hung out in the athlete area and watched the end of the race, and I prepared myself for the media line on the way out, taking a moment alone to gather myself as best I could. I thought of Robbie's emotional interview after his disappointing DNF. I wanted to be honest, I wanted to be fair.

I got to the CTV cameras where Perry Sakowski asked his first question, "Mike, how do you feel with your performance today?"

It's hard to express anything significant only thirty minutes after the biggest event of your life. I'm not sure what I even said, but I knew Perry was being kind. He knew that I was gutted and guided the questions towards a chance to say thank you to all the supporters rather than harp on the performance. I slowly made my way through the different media outlets, eventually getting to the exit, where our coaches were waiting. The emotions I'd held in through the interviews now came out in tears as Dusan and I hugged. There weren't many words, as I was too overwhelmed. He understood. He was part of this journey as well.

I had to keep moving and I left Dus, stopping for a short moment with Johnny and Yul, and eventually making my way through the crowds to the bottom of the mountain. On my way, though, some people stopped me.

"Congrats on your race. Way to go, Mike!"

I looked up and thanked them, doing my best to smile with tears still on my cheeks and redness around my eyes.

They sensed what I was feeling. "Hey Mike," one of them continued, "we want to tell you that our son went to the Mike and Manny camp a few years ago..." They were referring to the camp Manny and I put on for a select group of young ski racers each spring. "...It was one of the best times of his life. He came back so inspired and still talks about it to this day."

I looked at them more closely, cheers and hollers still going on all around us, to see if I recognized them.

"It doesn't matter so much what you did today. What you brought to those kids, what you bring to the sport, you won before you left the start gate," the person finished.

Before I could properly respond, the crowd moved us apart, and in a flash, they were gone. I was left with a greater perspective, and with it a bit more space to grieve.

Soon I was in the comfort of my friends, and their celebrations and warmth helped ease the pain. We walked through the Weasel Worker's tent with all the course workers and volunteers who had put a month or more of preparation into these events. Their cheers and joy added to the perspective those parents had given me from before. I eventually found myself back at our condo, sitting on the edge of my bed, the same place I'd started the day.

I came all this way for thirteenth place. I loathed myself.

It was hard to see all the good around me; all I could focus on was the disappointment and loss that I felt inside.

After a night out, the sting had subsided. Personal losses could be put aside for now, and it was time to join in the celebrations for all of Team Canada. Ashleigh McIvor's gold medal, John Montgomery's win and walk through town, Joannie Rochette's courageous performance, the women's hockey team victory—there were so many incredible moments, and two more were still to come. We drove to Vancouver, and with a group, watched the Canada- USA gold-medal match from Canada House downtown. As Crosby scored the game-winning goal in overtime, you could hear the whole city erupt in elation—probably the whole country. Two weeks of people showing up for each other, supporters, volunteers, coaches, athletes... It seemed like Crosby had been born to score this goal for everyone who gave so much to these Games.

For the final act of this spectacular event, we gathered outside Team Canada House in Athlete's Village, waiting for our bus ride to BC Place Stadium for the closing ceremonies. It was a warm, overcast, late-February day in Vancouver and hundreds of athletes and staff mingled outside in our Cowichan-inspired sweaters and Canada hats. We took pictures, shared stories, and decompressed from the last two weeks of intensity. Before walking into BC Place, Clara Hughes got up and gave a speech. She spoke about the courage to compete, the spirit and drive to be our best, and said that every one of our performances was inspiring. I looked around at this group, collectively and simultaneously inspiring and being inspired by each other and a nation. For the first time as a competitor, I sensed the feeling that had started this dream seventeen years ago at ten years old. I was part of this bigger team, part of this movement, and we were bonded through our shared dreams, efforts, successes, and failures.

During the closing ceremonies, John Furlong recapped the events. There was a moment of silence for the Georgian luge athlete, Nodar

Kumaritashvili, who'd died in the opening days on the track. Furlong spoke of Bilodeau's first gold medal, all the amazing performances that followed, and the builders who dared to believe that these Games were possible. The loudest cheer that came from the athletes, though, was after he thanked all the blue jackets, the volunteers of the Olympics. The volunteerism is what made these Games stand out, and everywhere you went the volunteers greeted you with warmth and a willingness to help. They were the ones who embodied the motto "with glowing hearts" and were the lifeblood of the whole event. Every athlete from every country knew this, and we all cheered, this spirit imprinted on our lives forever.

CHAPTER 23
LOST IN MY WAY

IN MY VISIONS OF THE future, there wasn't much on the other side of the 2010 Olympics. Sure, I had some ideas in my head. I saw myself ski racing, but there was no clarity or tangible goal to any of this. Everything had been directed to this one day in February of 2010, and afterwards, with a medal, life would be easy, my questions answered, problems solved, and worries dissolved. A couple of days after the closing ceremonies, the world as I knew it still existed. The sun rose, traffic filled the downtown streets, people rushed to work, birds flew overhead, coffee shops lined up with patrons. Life seemed unfazed by my apparent devastation of this unrealized dream. There was an Olympic-medal-sized void inside me, and I had to get away from it. Something was missing, something was lost.

After the season, I went on a vacation to the beach, spending time with friends, relaxing, partying, and on the outside, having the time of my life. Everywhere skiing didn't live, though, there was that hole. One morning while on the trip, I woke up with back spasms and couldn't sit up. To get out of bed, I had to gingerly roll to my side, fall to the floor and crawl to breakfast on hands and knees. I'd managed the pain over the last couple of seasons, spending hours with our physio every day, before and after skiing, yet here I was, far away from the physical stresses of high performance and the pain still returned.

Later that afternoon, I lay on my back, looking up at the clear blue sky, feeling the warm sun while listening to the waves rattle against the shore, my frustrations slipped into apathy. Everything that I thought would bring me happiness was only bringing me more pain, and I couldn't take it anymore.

The trip and back spasms passed and we were soon back training in the gym, running through an intense week of dryland in Calgary as preparation for our first ski camp in New Zealand. After the long week, while out with some friends, I bent down too low on the dance floor and *pop*, the meniscus in my right knee tore again. A legit dance-floor injury. Eight years after the cartilage had been sewn up and repaired, the sutures had exceeded their lifespan and tore again, but this time there was no repair. The good news to this was that the recovery from having it scoped and cut out was much shorter and I was back on skis within a month. Mom again came to the rescue, flying out, taking me for surgery in Banff, and driving me back the whole ten hours to Whistler to heal up. After my short burst of feeling like I was on the upswing, I'd gotten knocked down again, back to rehabbing and sitting on the sidelines. Not the ideal way to start a season.

I joined the slalom group in Queenstown two weeks late, feeling rushed and behind the eight ball. I did my best to stay positive, reminding myself that I could still perform with less training, that I could still find success even with less volume. Slowly I gained confidence back on my skis. The knee was feeling strong again, even with only fifty percent of a meniscus left, my back was holding up, and I felt like everything had returned to normal.

Life has a way of coming up with alternate plans, though, and halfway through the camp, it all exploded.

A few runs after getting back into gates, I tore an intercostal muscle in my ribs. I tried to ski the next day but then my back went out. I tried to ski again the day after that, feeling like I could ski through the pain, but this was not the case. I could barely walk from the parking lot to the ski hill, let alone do one run, and I was forced to head back to the apartments for rest. My body was in so much pain and my mind filled with so much rage and so I turned to writing.

I had never kept a personal journal before, but a book I was reading, *The Divided Mind* by Dr. John Sarno, explored the mind/body connection and relationship between chronic pain and repressed emotions in the unconscious. One tool offered to tap into these repressed emotions was journalling. I had a ski journal where I talked about what I was working on and different technical cues, but never about emotions, never about me. I felt so trapped, though, pinned into a corner, so with my reservations thrown aside, I just went for it.

Journal entry - New Zealand, August 20, 2010

Today I went up for training feeling strong and confident that I could move past the injuries of my knee, my back, and my torn oblique, but mainly my back. I see all the other athletes training with ease, no pain, and here I am, unable to even do a ski camp to get myself ready for the season. I tell myself that I'm able to ski fast with less training and when I'm healthy I'll be able to win. Don't worry, don't stress, just be patient and let the pain subside, you'll be fine. Take each injury as it comes, heal up and when the race season comes, you can race better than your competition. But how much of this can I take?

Ever since I hurt my back three years ago it's been up and down. Right after my herniation I went from 7th in the world to 60th, 60th!!! I had to climb my way back into the top 15, though I was more pre-pared this time and able to do it in only one season, not the four it took me the first time. I fought on and that next season I won a World Champs bronze medal. Yeahhhh!!!! Sweet for me, right? Well, I thought so too, I had a World Champ medal, the first Canadian to win one in slalom and I had worked my way back to 14th in the world. Then a day into the first pre-season camp of the next year, boom my back goes again. What is it this time? Am I really going through this again? I skied four days in a three-week camp, all agonising, every turn is like getting stabbed in the back and every run I finish close to tears. Tears from the pain but more from the complete and utter dis-belief that this is happening again, starting another season behind the eight ball. I continue.

In the next two-week camp I'm able to ski more, around eight good days, the pain gets less and less but to what end? I'm a mess! I can't eat dinner with my team, I can't do dryland with my team, I can barely look my teammates, coaches, trainers, and ski tech in the eyes because I'm so ashamed that I can't be the athlete I used to be. An athlete who could take all the runs, all the sets, all the reps, all the pains and get up for more and more.

The season moves forward and my back becomes a thing of the past. It slowly gets less and less painful and I have a successful season, somewhat. I win a couple of runs, I have a few top-fives, I race the Olympics, my home Games. A race I focussed on for six years, to win a medal and all that comes is 13th place. In front of my family, my friends, and everyone that supported me throughout my career, all I can do is 13th! It was crushing. I tried to move past it. I thought nothing could be as hard or painful as the Olympics, moving forward will be a breeze. No more pains to concern myself with, just doing what I truly love, skiing, racing, and most importantly winning.

Well, the summer off-season training didn't go as planned. With multiple back flareups and then a knee scope, I started the on-snow training season behind again. I stayed focussed on my recovery and positive about my situation more than ever. I was getting amazing at being in my best energy, focussing on what made me perform at my best, and focussing on my healing, which was going fast. I was ready to get back into skiing and move into the season—nothing could stop me now. I was focussed, happy, loving what I was doing, where I was in my career and life more than I had been in a long time.

This only lasted a few days, though. I was having great training on snow, my knee was not holding me back at all, and that's when the back pain started. With all the work I had done with my back pain and working through the psychosomatic connection, I felt confident that I could ski through the pain. Sure enough, as I continued to do this, I went and tore my oblique. You have to be kidding me! I can only stay so positive for so long! Now I can't ski for the rest of the camp and the injury in my knee that I came down to New Zealand with is no problem, but I have a new one, and my back hurts again.

I tell myself I'll heal up, work my way through the season, and have some great results. But is this any way to live? Thinking you're doing something you love but to be in so much pain all the time that you can only enjoy very brief moments. I mean, I love this sport so much, it's all I've ever known, and I'm never as happy as I am winning, skiing fast, or just free skiing by myself on any mountain.

As much as it freaks me out to even think this, maybe this isn't for me. Maybe I can't handle the stress of trying to be my best all the time. Maybe it's fine for me up to a certain level but when I almost reach the top, when I almost get good enough to win, it gets too much, and I need to go and hurt myself. It's like my mind is forcing my body to quit because it knows I would never consciously do it on my own. What other reason could there be? So much of me wants to be the best, wants to win and loves this sport. Am I a fool to not listen to my body, to these signs? How can something I love so much be such a poison?

When these injuries happen, all I feel is so much anger towards everything around skiing, coaches, myself, my life, but then when I'm back in my bed resting, lying down, and the pain subsides for a brief moment, a total calm comes over me and there is no stress. It's like the injury has forced me to settle, to get off this tough schedule, taking performance out of my hands and releasing me from all the worries that come from trying to win. Is it wrong to think "Finally I can do what I want. I can just relax and do what I want?"

I sent this letter to our team's sport psychologist at the time, Kirsten Barnes, with a note stating I was retiring and that this was my resignation letter.

"Michael, there's a lot of good stuff in here we can work with, but I don't think you're ready for retirement," was her response.

You don't think I'm ready to retire?

I am ready!

Didn't you read the email?

I'm serious!

This wasn't exactly the answer I was expecting but I let her response sink in. After calming down and processing it, though, I felt relieved.

This wasn't a resignation letter; it was a cry for help, and thankfully she saw past the emotions that were bubbling to the surface. I had been bottling things up for a long time and this declaration was the only way I knew how to say I needed help and didn't want to retire.

I was twenty-eight years old and had visions of competing until I was thirty-six, to race in four Olympics, and then call it a career. There were more goals to accomplish. I wasn't ready to say goodbye, but I was at a crossroads. I was struggling with my body, injuries, relationships with my coaches, and the ownership I had over my program. I wanted to change the way I was training, but mostly I felt conflicted between the athlete I thought I needed to be and the person I wanted to become.

When I returned to Vancouver, I met with Kirsten. I was able to share more about what I was going through, the feelings I was having, and what I wanted as a next step if retirement was off the table. There was no clear vision of what this new way looked like, but I wanted to dig into these feelings and face them rather than run. If I'm fully honest, a lot of this motivation to get help was simply not wanting to feel so shitty, stressed, worried about performing, and fearful of losing what I had achieved.

It was clear to Kirsten that I was looking for someone beyond her field of expertise, and I was really asking for a professional counsellor or psychotherapist. Again, I was relieved that she read between the lines. I was starving for someone that I could open up to, who would listen and didn't know me as a ski racer. Kirsten connected me with a counsellor named Michelle and from our first meeting, she felt like the right person.

During our initial sessions, I was amazed at how attacked I felt when asked personal questions. My guard wanted to come up and start claiming and naming all my successes and achievements, as if they'd be stripped away if I were to admit I didn't know, or that I was scared. It took everything in me to stay open. I wanted to scream, hoping to be recognized, hoping not to disappear.

In the first few weeks after New Zealand, while working through these sessions, some new motivations started to come through for how to approach the next chapter of my career. I had previously lacked fulfilment in my best results and some of my biggest highs had left me in the deepest of lows. Winning for the sake of winning had lost its shine, and I asked myself three questions:

Why was I running from the nerves, fears, and anxieties experienced around performance?

What was I scared of?

What would be on the other side if I were to be swallowed up by these emotions?

Without any answers, I decided to continue my career with a promise to myself. I promised to use this process of competition and striving for excellence as a way to discover who I am rather than to prove it.

I was scared to step into this new world, but I needed to see what else was possible.

CHAPTER 24
THE FRACTURE

IN THIS TRANSITION FROM ONE Olympic cycle to another, there were many changes afoot. Some teammates retired, either from injury or because it was just time, and the team landscape shifted. Within the tech group, we started the season with two new assistant coaches as Johnny and Brian stepped down, which was a big blow to us. In their place, though, came Nick Cooper and Jan Wengelin, who did bring the ever-needed fresh energy and perspectives to the team. On the athlete front, Biggs, Trevor, Cousi, Brad, Stutz, Semple, JP, and I made up the World Cup Tech team, though as our successes grew, so did our personal interests.

Dusan's team-first commitment we had made to reach this place was starting to erode as individual desires for more program ownership started to come through. Whether the reasons were from long-term injuries, aging bodies, growing families, school commitment, or just wanting to evolve methods for training, we'd earned our place to have a say and started to push back.

With seven of us on the start list for the World Cup opening slalom, Cousi kicked the season where he'd left off in the top ten. Behind him, Brad, Trev and Pat all found the top thirty, for a strong opening. The next race in Val d'Isère we went one better, with five in the second run, and Cousi continued to lead the team with a fifth place. We were on a role. At the third World Cup slalom stop of the season though, things came to a head.

We were in Zagreb, Croatia, for their night event. To my Western eyes, Zagreb's a city with the markings of an old communist town, long, cement-walled state buildings for housing and government affairs. But it does also have a beautiful old town with a lively market, cobblestone streets, and interesting architecture. This is a rare city-centre stop for a World Cup race, and it held a little novelty.

Driving across the Slovenia/Croatian border, it's flat as far as you can see except for one small rise out from the ground and off to the left where the race is held, *Medvednica Sljeme*, or in English, Bear Mountain. All the teams stay in the downtown Westin Hotel, a large, twenty-storey building on the edge of the city centre and only a thirty-minute drive from the hill.

On the day of the race, the whole slalom circuit's teams and entourage reached the venue in one long convoy requiring closed city streets and a police escort. The different team vans, company cars, official vehicles, and media transports all took their places in the line that snaked from outside the lobby doors, down around and into the parking garage, all taking off together. With the parade leaving at noon, I rode with Yul and drove in silence, watching the scenery pass by. There were old churches, small cafés, squares with monuments commemorating the city's history, and statues of fallen heroes. I observed them one by one, wondering about the significance of them all.

Spectators lined the streets, and we passed streetcars and busses taking fans to the top as well. Most were wearing or waving the Croatian flag, hoping to bring luck to their national hero, Ivica Kostelić. The convoy climbed slowly, making our way up the mountain, which was still bare of any snow, revealing the neatly piled leaves and freshly bundled sticks that sat within the trees. It looked as if the forest had been manicured for our arrival.

As much as I tried that night, there was no spark in my skiing, and in the way of successful results, most of the team came out flat. Three of us finished outside the thirty and the other three skied out, not finishing the first run. This stung, but at least we were all in this together, just a little blip in the season. We were still skiing well and would come out firing for the next race in a few days.

Dus didn't see it this way, though. "Guys, I want to have a team meeting. We'll all go down now and when you get back to the hotel, get changed quickly and go to our meeting room."

This didn't sound good—he clearly felt immediate intervention was required.

On the drive down from the hill, I felt lighter than expected. Sure, the lack of results hurt, but it wasn't as bad as I feared. Leaving the mountain without any accolades, Yul and I still cracked jokes, we talked through the race, where my skiing was at, and how to change the season around. After arriving back at the Westin, I felt better getting out of the car.

We got changed and went up to the twenty-second floor for our team meeting. The large conference room had wall-to-wall carpets, with floor-to-ceiling windows facing the old city and the race hill off in the far distance. Our weights, spin bikes, and work-out gear for the pre-race activation were all set up, just where we'd left them a few hours ago. It was 5:30 p.m., and the city was dark and spattered with lights, a beautiful view that I wished I could have enjoyed more.

All fourteen of us filled the room: three coaches, six athletes, three servicemen, our physio, and our strength and conditioning trainer—everyone was there.

Dusan started to address the team's performance. "What was that tonight? Something has to change... we cannot continue like this... We need to be better at racing... to take more risks... this is not acceptable." He went through the list of all that was wrong.

Over ten years of working with Dusan, I had had my share of these meetings. Most were warranted and most sparked a call to action, but this one felt different.

"You don't think we were trying out there?! You don't think we pushed it?!" Cousi responded in his defence, expressing what I felt as well. "I went all out and didn't finish, this is how slalom goes. Don't tell me I wasn't going for it!"

Cousi wasn't having any of the criticism. I, on the other hand, knew I'd left something out there tonight but still didn't appreciate Dusan's assessment.

Dus came back with more of what was wrong, that it wasn't about one person, that we as a team needed to be better.

I wanted to speak up, but I couldn't find my voice and instead stayed silent, feeling like a child being reprimanded by a parent. After some more frustrations were vented by others, we all left the room angrier than inspired, pissed off at the lack of respect between coach and athlete.

My analysis for the inconsistency was more about my skis than my attack on the course, but getting caught up with equipment setups can be a finicky game. Boot alignment, canting, binding set up, ramp angle, ski construction, edge angles, too stiff, too soft, too much grip, not enough grip, skis that don't release or pick up early enough in the turn. All of this can play in the heads of a racer, and it's the work of the service man, the companies, coaches, and athletes to find the balance. I knew how good I felt when my setup fit perfectly to the snow. On one run I'd be dancing to the top five, and the other struggling to grind my way into the top thirty. After a long contemplation, I was convinced my skis played a role with this inconsistency.

In any event, Dusan had his desired effect on me, and I snapped out of my early season slump, finishing with a fifth and fourth place in Adelboden and Wengen, respectively. I felt back on top of my game, and a little redemption after the meeting as well, but this small success didn't solve the root problem. I was tired of being picked apart after a bad result, only to be pieced back together with hopes of a new and improved version of myself. After a disappointing seventeenth in Kitzbühel, where my coaches, the media, and I had thought a podium was the inevitable progression after the last two races, I was exhausted from this game. How could I be so good one day and so off the next, just because the conditions changed on me?

Two days later, at the night race in Schladming, Dusan and I got into it during second-run inspection. As I slid down the course under the flood lights, the hill lit up in red and blue gates in front of me. Courses were always hard to look at after a bad first run, and sitting in eighteenth place after the first, I was rushing through inspection and looking for redemption in the next.

Before I could do this, though, I stopped at Dusan, already sensing what he'd say before it happened.

He knew all the right triggers to set me off. "Dammit, Janyk, you held back down here and were just trying to survive. You have to fight the whole way!"

"You think I want to hold back? You think I'm trying to suck?! I can't feel the front of the ski. If I commit too much to the outside, I'll fall inside! I'm not getting the response I need from them and I'm just trying to hold on to the finish!" I lashed back, now finding my voice.

"You're not getting the response from the ski because you're holding on," he argued.

I tried to shout over him. "No! You have it backwards, I can't attack and let them run because I can't trust my skis on this snow. You don't get it because you've never felt it. You're not hearing me!"

We were now just yelling at each other in the middle of inspection while other racers, coaches, and media slid down and around us. I hoped my competitors would hear and sympathize with my struggles in some way, but this was between Dus and I, both of us desperately wanting stability in my skiing yet neither willing to let our guards down to actually discuss how. With over 55,000 fans surrounding us, we were only part of the show to them, but for us, we were furthering our division.

• • •

After a little time off, we were back in Kirchberg and starting preparations for the World Championships in Garmisch-Partenkirchen, Germany. During one of our last training days, Yul and I were trying to sort out which skis to race on and Dusan was still trying to correct my skiing. The simmering of frustrations over the last month were now at a boil and something needed a change. Back at the Egidihof, after lunch, I asked for a meeting with him, and we went off to the side for a talk.

"I can't keep going like this, Dus. I can't keep being told what I'm doing wrong and what I need to do better. I need space to make my own decisions."

"I give you plenty of space, you have a say in your programs, but sometimes I see what needs to be done more than you," he came back with.

Our opposing views were now on the table and clearly known, and we soon were yelling at each other.

"You don't give me any freedom in the program! I don't want to go race an FIS race before World Champs, I want to rest. I can't keep doing the same thing over and over again!" I screamed.

"I give you guys too much freedom, you don't know what you need!" he insisted, yelling back.

We went on like a father and son, pushing each other's buttons and going at each other's vulnerabilities until we both exploded.

"If this is how you see it, then I don't want to be coached by you anymore. I can't do this. I need a change," I yelled, trying to break free.

"Fine, then for the rest of the year, Jan and Nick will coach you, and after the season too," he screamed back at me.

"This works for me!" I yelled in satisfaction, storming out of the room, fuming and needing to get some fresh air after having almost blown out the walls of the place.

It's very hard to not see your head coach on a small ski team. After our fight, everything on the outside remained the same; we still travelled, lived, and worked together, he set up the training, I stopped at him in inspections, he gave course reports. After all our years together, there was still respect. We were cordial, I just didn't want any coaching from him, any say on my program; even having him suggest how many runs I should do in a training day was too much for me to handle. If he said to only do five runs in a day, I'd push for ten. If he said we needed more volume and the number was eight runs, I would do three. I needed to prove I could do it without him and that he wasn't always right.

The World Championships didn't go as planned for me. I was skiing with a lot of speed and had the dance I was hoping for, but unfortunately I straddled and skied out in the first run. Cousi, on the other hand, did what he had done all season and led the team with a fifth-place finish. It was a career best and the culmination of so much dedication and work to come back after multiple injuries. I found some redemption in the closing World Cups of the season, though, and with two fifth-place finishes, I felt I had enough clout built up to back up my decision to split from Dusan.

By the time National Championships came around in the second half of March, marking the final races of the year, I was ready to move on. The slalom team had four of us ranked inside the top thirty, and with everything that had transpired, it felt like a good time to do so.

The nationals were held in Nakiska, Alberta, and Dusan and I met in the back lobby of the Delta Kananaskis hotel in the middle of the race series. Set in the heart of the Rocky Mountains, the hotel is a few minutes from the ski hill and sits right at the foothills, with the sheer peaks above. As the location of the 2002 G8 summit, it had been witness to some intense discussions before, I'm sure, and probably more diplomatic than the one we were about to have.

I thought we were meeting to say our formal goodbyes, but I was soon proved wrong. Dus told me he wasn't planning to leave as the head coach, even if I tried to remind him of our fight from a couple months before.

"You can go coach another team, I can't go race for another country!" I told him, to which he showed no movement.

I felt trapped all over again, and quickly escalated my yelling to obscenities. I wanted others to hear me, friends, teammates, other coaches, hoping someone would come to my defence or at least step in to save us from each other. It was Dus who eventually got up and walked away, but I kept going after him down the hallway a little longer.

With nothing resolved between the two of us, I went to our men's team head coach and athletic director a few days later to plead my case, expressing my unhappiness and our inability to work together. In the end, Dusan did move on and became the coach of our development team. Taking his place was Kip, our previous assistant, who had been leading the development team at the time and was now coming up as our new head coach.

There was so much energy being used just to fight for my place. I was probably alienating myself from my teammates in the process while breaking a relationship with Dusan, someone who had helped bring me from a wiry fifteen-year-old to a World Champ medalist. For all the destruction, though, it still felt freeing to stand up and take a chance on a new way of being. What lay ahead was unknown but at least I was able to be in the driver's seat.

CHAPTER 25
A NEW WAY FORWARD

IN 2012, TSN HOST, MICHAEL Landsberg produced a forty-minute documentary called *Darkness and Hope*, exploring depression within sport. In it he interviews three sport heroes, Clara Hughes, Darryl Strawberry, and Stéphane Richer. They share, along with him, their experiences with depression, the highs of Olympic medals, Stanley Cups, and being on top of your sport in one moment and then off the cliff of emptiness in the next. I had met Michael during the 2010 Games. He interviewed me and my two sisters, and I'd been on his show *Off the Record.* He was so kind and engaging. During the Vancouver Olympics I had been inspired by Clara, and as a kid playing baseball, I had wanted to be like Darryl Strawberry. All of these icons were sharing their stories, and knowing that they too could feel such lows completely blew me away.

Halfway through the documentary, Michael describes the feeling of depression as "Wherever you are, you don't want to be. If you're at work, you want to be in the car, if you're in the car you want to be at home, and at home, well, many of us are out of options."

This was the first time I felt any real connection and understanding of the word "depression." Before, it was some far-off thing that didn't belong to me and the lifestyle I was living. This was my dream, I didn't feel depressed, I was just lonely and missing something. Michael's words brought me back to sitting on the edge of my bed after my World Champs medal or finding myself in the middle of any downtime. If I was home, I wanted to be on the road; if I was on the road, I wanted to be home, and when I was feeling this, nowhere felt right.

On the physical side, my back pain was still volatile. I had found some liberation from pain at times, but it was still a roller coaster. I had become less dependent on physios, which felt empowering. The psychosomatic work helped manage flare ups and setbacks, but the underlying fear of when it would come back next still thrived. Even though I was no longer experiencing acute pain on a day to day, I was growing limitations within my range of motion. During a spring camp in Sunshine Mountain resort in Alberta, I woke up one morning, rolled over to the left side, swung my feet to the ground, and used my left arm to push myself up on the bed.

"Ughhh," I moaned as my senses came alive to the feeling of stiffness throughout. I moaned again, much to Cousi's annoyance.

"'Ey, Pip, keep it down!" he shouted from the single bed beside me, using one of the many nicknames he had for me.

I stood up, slipped on my shirt and pants, and grabbed socks for the day.

I held one sock in both hands, rolled it down and held it open, ready to go. But when I bent over, lifting my right leg up in the air underneath me, I was stopped halfway to my target. The sock and foot didn't meet; both were inches from their respective destinations.

Angry and frustrated, I sat back down on the bed to do this in a more remedial way. With my left foot on the ground and just the right toes pointing up, I bent over with the sock in one hand and went for them like a child swinging a butterfly net. I hooked it around my big toe and then came in from behind to pull it the rest of the way on and over the heel. I was left perplexed. How could I be a professional athlete and not be able to put on my socks standing up?

"Uggghhh!" I groaned again, falling back onto my bed with a little crash, feeling totally broken again.

"'Eh, Pip, I said shut up!" His accent still keeping the H's far away from their place in the words.

I knew he wouldn't be too upset, though. This was just giving him more ammo to share with the team over breakfast.

In recognition that more change was needed, I nervously decided to add a yoga practice into my training. I had done classes over the years, but always feared that too much of it would take away from the training I was doing, sacrificing strength and power in its process. As the physical limitations built up, though, the scales tipped and gaining mobility seemed of greater value. With all the apprehensions of a kid going to his first day of school, I walked into this first yoga class like my first counselling session. I wanted to pretend like I didn't need this, but I knew that my current routine was broken.

Later that summer, I went on a three-day retreat in Park City, Utah, put on by Lululemon for their elite ambassadors. At the time, Lululemon's athlete sponsorship program was relatively small in the way of direct money like traditional sponsors but large in the way that they offered support and opportunities. When I first joined the program, I asked them what they wanted from the athletes: did they want a certain number of appearances, product feedback, or to promote them in some way?

The response I got back from the marketing director was, "Mike, if you'd like to send in feedback on the products, this would be great. If you want to stop by the office and say hi, we'd love it, but this isn't why we do this. We ask you to be part of this program because we think you're awesome! We think the other athletes in this program are awesome, and we want you to continue doing what you do best and we'll offer opportunities to bring everyone together and see what great things can happen."

I think my jaw hit the floor when I heard this.

In the competitive athlete's world, where you can feel like you're always trying to show your worth to sponsors for the next contract or to teams for a qualification spot, this was a refreshing wind to come across.

The retreat hosted twenty-five athletes, with activities centred around yoga, with some self-discovery workshops and play time mixed in. We were a mixture of Olympic and professional athletes from skiers, snowboarders, sliding sports, bikers, hockey, football, and basketball players. This diverse set of body types, ranging from the 230-pound football player to the 130-pound rock climber and the six-foot-four basketball player beside the five-foot-four freestyle skier, were all brought together through our common pursuit of sport.

It was exciting going away on a trip related to sport but without the pressures of performance hanging over my head. The next exciting part was getting to be around athletes from other sports. I loved hearing how other athletes lived, trained, and competed, and the stories that brought them here. Lastly, I was getting the opportunity to learn, practice yoga, be introspective, and explore parts of me that I was just coming to discover.

The yoga was led by renowned teacher Baron Baptiste, a practitioner and teacher who in the early 1990s had developed a style of power yoga that seemed to be attractive to athletes. Never too far away from team-mates, Brad was there as well, and after dropping our bags off in the room, we headed to the ballrooms for the opening yoga session with Baron.

Doesn't an athlete have to be tough, strong, to overcome, and conquer? The nervous thoughts swirled around in my head; these qualities were how I had learned to measure courage. Yoga felt like the opposite, learning to be warm, soft, open, willing to say "I don't know." Everything seemed to contrast what I knew about being a competitive athlete.

In so much of my training on and off the hill, I was trying to build confidence to confirm all the things I could do. *I can lift this weight, I can run this fast, jump this high, do this many reps, ski this many runs, pick up the ski this early in the turn.* Yoga, on the other hand, seemed to expose all the things I couldn't do: touch my toes, clasp my hands behind my back, hold a simple pose, sit cross-legged on the floor, do a back bridge. All the things a class of kindergarten kids could do were now beyond me.

Just staying in the room for the whole session required a new kind of courage.

In the break between sessions, Baron shared some of his history and how he found himself here, teaching yoga to a room full of professional athletes. He talked about starting out in the Boston area and working with some Bruins players, moving to LA and working with basketball players like Kareem Abdul-Jabbar, and then being hired on by the Philadelphia Eagles.

"Wait, what? All these sports icons practised yoga and used it in their training?" I was stunned.

A new world suddenly opened, and it instantly became ok to continue with this path.

In another session, our facilitator, Tracy, was going around asking why we did our sport and what we enjoyed about it. Only a couple of years before this, I would have thought this was a strange question.

"What do you mean, why do I ski race? To win, to be the best, obviously!" The question in itself would have been offensive.

After experiencing the lows of high performance, though, I was starting to wake up from the dream and dip my toes in the waters of reality. To ask "why" or "am I happy" was no longer offensive; rather, it was scary, because I might discover that the one thing I had devoted my life to couldn't bring me complete fulfilment, and admitting this would be betraying everyone who had helped me get here: parents, friends, coaches, sponsors, and community.

A few spots away from me, one of the hockey players was the first to answer Tracy's question. He started with the usual aspects of why: the lifestyle, the teammates, the rewards success brings, but he then opened up about how most of this pursuit was actually his dad's dream, not his. Here he was, in the NHL, a top player, and sharing that he was unhappy.

How can this be? I asked myself, unsure of the words I was hearing.

Darkness and Hope had shown me that this was possible, but to hear it in real life brought it home on a whole other level... to learn that even an NHL hockey player can feel unfulfilled in their career, like they didn't have full ownership of their dream, that they too could feel compromised in their pursuit. His words helped validate my own experience, and I was grateful that he shared them. I left the retreat feeling like I had permission to keep going in this new way.

• • •

On March 10, 2012, everything I'd fought for all these years: the results, the dream, the desire for World Cup success, all came to a halt. Our friend, teammate, and brother Nik Zoricic died in a ski-cross World Cup race in Grindelwald, Switzerland. Nik's parents had emigrated from Serbia when he and his sister were young, and they soon enrolled them in the Craigleith Ski Club. Nik was a bit of a phenom as a kid and soon was one of the best in the country for his age and then overall. With long, flowing, brown hair full of "product," as Semple used to say, Nik brought a swagger that only a ski racer from Southern Ontario can bring. You could often see him sitting in the corner of a room, one leg crossed over the other, reclined in a chair, his arms out, wrists turned up and cocked back. With a slight smile, a shrug to his shoulders, and a wink in his eye, as if to say, "Come on, why wouldn't you want to join this party?!"

Nik was younger than me, and yet I looked up to him like an older brother. He encouraged me to listen to myself and fight for what we wanted in our programs, sometimes pushing me to speak up on behalf of all the athletes.

It was a Saturday when we heard of Nik's death. Brad, Stutz, JP, and I were at the World Cup in Kranjska Gora, Slovenia. JP had just raced the GS, and the three of us racing slalom had just done some free-skiing on the race hill. We drove back to the hotel, I grabbed my bag and headed to my room. I walked in, put my gear down, and shortly after, Paul walked in through the open door.

"Nik died," he said. That was it, nothing more.

I looked at Paul, who was standing just inside the doorway, still in his long underwear, reading this message on his phone. I gave out some kind of awkward teenage laugh. This had to be some sort of strange joke he was playing with me, but the look on his face said otherwise.

"Whaaat?" I half said with a laugh again, having no real control over my reactions.

"Nik died today in a World Cup ski cross," Paul said.

"No, what do you mean died, what happened?" His words weren't making sense.

Surely we'd talk through what was going on, that Nik was still alive, and in understanding this situation better, we'd be able to save him. But Paul just kept saying it over again: "Nik died."

He was also trying to comprehend the situation, only having learned of it moments before telling me.

We both sat on the ends of our beds—we didn't know what to do or even how to feel.

Soon after, we met as a team and learned he'd gone off the last jump on a wrong line and hit a wall of snow that had built up and frozen in front of the finish hut.

No one wanted to be alone at this point. We hugged, cried, and tried to better understand this situation together. We soon had to discuss if we were going to race the next day.

"How can we race, why would we race?" We talked it over.

Our coaches Pete and Kip left it up to us. Kip had coached Nik from when he was fifteen and knew him and his family very well—this was all our loss.

With no real wisdom about the right thing to do, we decided to race. We told ourselves this is what Nik would have wanted, which is probably true; he wouldn't want us to waste an opportunity on his behalf, but it didn't make the day any more inspired. You hear of athletes coming out with amazing performances the day after the loss of a parent or friend, but I didn't feel any of this.

We wrote his initials, NZ, in black sharpie on our helmets, before going up for our runs. Paul took black electrical tape out of his backpack and wrapped a band around our arms. This is all that we knew to do. At least our fellow competitors would know of the pain we were in, which already felt like a lot. We weren't the first team to lose someone in a race or training; it's a known possibility of the sport but one that before this had remained a distant hypothetical. I raced and spent the day mostly in a fog; all I wanted to do was be around our teammates, current and past, to get together and console each other. After the race, Stutz and I drove back to Austria. We called teammates from the car, cried a lot, told a few stories, and wished the truth was not real.

At Nik's service back in Toronto, there were many friends from different walks of life, all of us trying to cope in our own ways, few knowing what to do. As I looked around, I kept going back to the last time we'd seen each other: did we hug, did I tell him I loved him, that I was appreciative for everything he'd brought to my life and the ways he'd pushed me? Probably not in this way.

I looked around again. Nik had struggled just like all of us. He wasn't perfect, had failures and frustrations. It was all his flaws that made him so authentic, and we loved him for this. I wanted to say this out loud but didn't have the words at the time. Instead, I hugged a few more friends and cried on a few more shoulders.

I stood beside Semple. *How can we honour Nik's life?* I thought. *How can I honour his spirit with my own actions?*

I needed these questions just to make it through the next few days, and I thought about the confidence Nik had showed, probably over-confidence at times. I also thought about seeing him at his lows, being vulnerable, hurting, talking about sadness, frustration, or the loneliness of being out on the road. These memories were enough to make me smile; we had experienced our humanity together, and there was a deeper connection.

I felt closer to him again. I felt closer to the team.

CHAPTER 26
MOVING INTO A LEADERSHIP ROLE

WHEN I FIRST CAME ON the national team as an eighteen-year-old, I thought that by the time I reached veteran status, being a leader would be second nature. I observed the older athletes, how they interacted with each other and engaged with the whole team, what they did well, and where they messed up. Later I learned from Thomas, how he led a team full of kids ten years younger than he was, actively improving the culture and raising our maturity. I felt like after years of experiences and good results under my belt, it would be easy.

Almost a decade later, the team landscape was changing. Some of my contemporaries were still racing: Trev, Cousi, JP, Brad, and Paul, while others like Biggs and Semple had retired, and I found myself in a similar position to Thomas, travelling with teammates now ten years my junior. Trevor (Junior) Philp, Erik Read, Phil Brown, and Sasha Zaitsoff were the next wave, eager for their turn, and the opportunity for me to step into a leadership role opened up. I felt a sense of responsibility to be this figure and some days I was, but on others, when my fears of losing my place took over, I was less successful, and it was the younger ones who kept me in check.

By February of the 2012/2013 season, when the World Championships rolled around in Schladming, Austria, it was only me and the young ones, Trev, Sasha, Phil, and Dustin Cook, racing in the tech events. Without the other veterans around to help shoulder the leadership role, I felt a greater sense of responsibility to fill it with a little more consistency.

Schladming was one of the first places I'd heard about as a ski-racing destination in Europe. At sixteen years old, Britt had competed here in her first World Junior Championships, with Mom and Stephanie travelling over to watch her. I was fourteen at the time, and when they came home, Steph told stories of the travels, the town, the food, and Britt talked about the race hill and how steep and icy it was. It sounded like the hardest hill I could imagine, and I wanted to go. As a souvenir, Britt had been given a plush bunny of the town's mascot, Hopsi, who wore a red toque and scarf. When I was a kid, it had embodied everything I wanted to achieve and was the coolest thing to me.

The finish area for all the events came right into town, and with this World Championships, came big upgrades to the base station and finish arena. Gone was the old rickety aluminum gondola; it was replaced by a brand-new, ten-person comfortable one with a state-of-the-art base station that came with its own escalator, gift shop, and sliding-glass doors. Outside and on hill, they installed new, giant towers with dozens of lights on each for the night races; set up scaffolding bleachers all around and up the sides of the hill; and capped it off with a metal arm that reached over top of the last part of the slope, a little artsy architectural touch for TV cameras and extra lights. All together the finish area looked like half of a football stadium shoehorning the bottom of a ski run and ready to welcome 60,000 fans. With Britt now retired from racing, she and Steph were there as spectators, taking in the different landscape that they had both experienced sixteen years earlier.

In the middle of the two-week event, between the speed and the technical races, the team event took place. Only at big events like the World Championships, Olympics, and World Cup finals, this format is a dual, panelled slalom, which pins nation against nation with teams of four on each side, two from each gender. I loved the dual format, a head-to-head style that brings an element of play and posturing not found in individual racing. The team event is full of surprises and is a race where anything is possible, which was the part I was most looking forward to.

Each racer pairs up against an athlete of the same gender from the other nation to race head-to-head, and the team that takes the most head-to-head victories wins the heat and moves onto the next round. In the event of a two/two split in the heats, the overall time difference is used to break the tie. The gates are set at a distance somewhere between GS and slalom. In action, the event lends itself to favouring slalom skiers and therefore these are the athletes who usually get the nod to compete.

Our team consisted of Phil Brown and me for the guys and Erin Mielzynski, Marie-Michèle (Mitch) Gagnon for the girls, plus Britt Phelan and Elli Terwiel as alternates. Phil and I had no backup on the men's side. On paper we were ranked tenth out of the fifteen nations, mostly due to Phil's and my current high world rankings, but I knew we stood a far better chance than this in reality and had a real shot at a medal.

This was a night event, the kind I was used to on this hill, and I felt comfortable out there. The six of us grabbed our warmup skis from the technicians and made our way through the fancy new sliding-glass doors, past the fans waiting for autographs and pictures of their favourite athletes, and onto the escalator taking us up to the gondola. We climbed into the gondola, the doors slowly closed, and as the cabin moved onto the cable, it gradually built speed, bouncing as it rose up and out of the station. It carried us above the skier's left side of the race hill, over the fans, giving us a clear view of the two parallel courses, about twenty-five gates that would add up to twenty seconds of action each run.

The lights were starting to flood the hill as the sun fell from the sky and with it, the town and its fans came alive. As we continued to climb up for the inspection run, I sat back and rested, looking out the window at the mountains across the valley. The cold air came in from the side, refreshing my lungs. Phil had his helmet off, making some minor adjustments, and my mind drifted away in the breeze.

This season was not going the way I'd hoped for; with a series of DNFs, and only one top fifteen, I was frustrated at my lack of speed and consistency. My back, on the other hand, was the best it had felt in years. I'd made a deal with myself a year prior where I said I'd be willing to trade my success for a pain-free life, and it seemed it was coming to fruition. In all of this, I was still trying to find who I was and how to authentically express this in a high-performance environment.

I bent over and adjusted my shin guards, listening to the tearing of Velcro and resetting the straps to find the right tension. The fidgeting was a good distraction. I thought back to all the times I'd ridden this gondola, or rather its predecessor, over the years: my first-ever top ten, the DNFs, the race days filled with success and the others with failures. The one common thread to them all was these quiet moments in the gondola, forever lonely and yet ever connected. I took a deep breath in, and the sound of the gondola grew louder as we passed over the tower. I looked down at my boots, finally letting my breath out, watching it freeze into a cloud in front of me. It was time.

As the six of us disembarked and walked to the snow, I felt the urge to say something to the group. This was a team event, and I wanted to share with them the feeling I had about anything being possible, that we had a shot at a medal. We each clicked into our skis and started to push away, traversing a bit before heading downhill.

I felt awkward.

Who was I to lead this group pep rally? Erin was a World Cup winner; I'd never won before. Mitch had been on the podium last season, and I hadn't reached the podium in four years. My idea of a team leader was still entangled with this notion that it had to come with results.

Eventually, the urge to at least address the group as a team before we all went into our own individual performance zones was strong enough that I had to say something.

"Hey, everyone," I called out.

They looked up at me, giving their attention.

"Before we get racing, I'd like to say something." I gestured for them all to come together for a little huddle and I went for it. "Team events can be wild, where anything can happen. If we race hard in every heat, I know everyone here has the speed to win their runs. Let's give it all we've got and see what's possible tonight. Let's go and see what we can do."

There were some smiles. I think Erin said a little piece in agreement, and Phil might have started a little cheer. It was a small speech, far from an *Any Given Sunday* moment, but at least we came together. As we skied away, I was physically shaking from the nerves, feeling self-conscious about putting myself out there in a way that felt more dangerous than anything I was used to on skis. I laughed it off and turned my attention back on the race.

In the first round, we were up against the Swiss, ranked seventh on paper, but going up against the ski-power nation of Switzerland at any time is a daunting task. In a dual, the desire is to focus on the person you're racing against, but it's your own skiing that's going to get you down the mountain the fastest.

In the start area it was a flurry of action, the different teams lining up on either side of the starting area, technicians, and coaches trying to find their athletes, course reports coming over radios, and we, the racers, arranging ourselves in coordination with our opponents. This was a steep hill for a dual slalom; normally set on flatter slopes, it provided way more risk, calling for a greater focus to stay in the course. In my own skiing, when starting the turn, I have a tendency to rush in with the upper body, meaning I fall victim to gravity and lean inside when I should stay committed over the outside, driving real power into the ski. I know when I do this, I can run the fastest line, create speed, and arc turn after turn. This was my whole focus for the race: committing to the most aggressive line on every turn and moving over top of the outside ski to pull it off. These are basic principles in theory, but on a steep, icy pitch racing head to head with the best in the world in front of thousands of fans, easy becomes hard real quick.

Mitch ran first for us, up against a rising star, Wendy Holdener. With the countdown of a series of beeps and flashing lights, like the start of a drag race, the mechanical gate dropped down and they were off. Mitch lost this round and so it became my turn, second out of the gate for our squad.

I was up against Markus Vögel, one of my contemporaries, who was having a solid season. I looked over at him, trying to see what state he was in, if there was anything I could pick up on. With nothing to read, I turned back to my own state. My energy was high—the nerves were present, but the balance was just right to find my tunnel of focus. I grabbed the handles of the start gate. In duals, the start gate is an actual gate that we rest our ski tips up against, grabbing onto handles to pull ourselves out onto the course.

"Commit to the outside, commit to the line," I said to myself as I took my position and listened to the starter's commands.

"Red course ready?"

I nodded yes.

"Blue course ready?"

He nodded yes.

"Attention." And the beeps started: *Beep, beep, beep, BEEP!*

The gates opened and we were off.

Every inch of the hill came into sight. I saw exactly where I wanted to put my skis, asked my body to perform this task, and it did. I accelerated with each turn and fought the whole way down. I was so honed in I didn't notice that Markus had crashed out beside me. I won the heat, and we were now in a tie with one win each.

Erin was next, and with a little stumble on her timing out of the start gate, she skied unbelievably to catch up and pass her opponent, taking the heat by two-tenths of a second. We were up two to one, with Phil and another young rising star, Gino Caviezel, against him.

Erin, Mitch, and I stood under the bright flood lights in the finish area, the fans cheering around us and the announcer's voice playing overhead. We all turned uphill to watch Phil. This was his first time racing this hill, and he was maybe too young and naive to even know what he was in for. He skied very solidly and took the win over Gino by 0.15 of a second. Canada had beaten Switzerland to move into the second round! We jumped on Phil in the finish area. This felt like the giant had been slayed and we could settle in.

In the next round, we found ourselves up against the Czech Republic, the last-ranked team who had just knocked out the second-ranked Italian team, giant-killers in their own right. Erin ran first and took the win in her heat, followed by Phil, who cruised to victory as his competitor crashed out. Mitch ran third and lost by 0.5 of a second, which meant it was up to me to close it out. I was up against Filip Trejbal, and for some reason I didn't feel that nervous. I saw my teammates way down in the finish, looking like ants waiting for me. I knew Filip well; he stood a good few inches over six feet, rocked a biker-style goatee, had bolts for earrings, and loved techno. Intimidating on the outside though an incredibly nice in person.

I knew how he skied and felt confident that I'd easily be able to beat him, a false sense of security. I grabbed the handles and listened to the beeps. We pulled out on course and the spots I asked my body to put my skis drifted past me, my turns a little less precise.

Out of the corner of my eye, I saw Filip pass me. *Oh my God, I'm losing this. How am I losing this?* I thought and tried everything to regain the lead.

He got the best of me by 0.07 seconds. We had tied two/two in the heats and waited together as a team, staring up at the big board to see what the timing would say to break the tie. Within a long minute, we had our answer.

"CANADA," flashed onto the jumbotron, and we advanced by two-tenths of a second into the semi-finals.

Between rounds, not feeling well in her heats, Mitch stepped out and Britt Phelan came in to fill her spot. In the semis, we came up against the Swedes, who brought with them two World Cup winners and two other podium-level athletes of the time. Britt went first, up against Frida Hansdotter, a big ask for being thrown into the race halfway through the running. Frida came away with the clear victory, and I was next. I was up against my friend Mattias Hargin, a fiery competitor I admired a lot for his tenacious spirit. As the nerves rose with the thought of racing against him, a calmness also came to meet them, and when they came together, my focus returned. I love standing in the start gate with this feeling; it's like a superpower. I'm able to harness the energy of the moment and channel it into my skiing, performing the way I always dream of.

"Racers ready... Attention," the starter called out and the beeps were on. This was going to be a great race.

We pulled out on course and everything I had went into my turns. I could see him out of the corner of my eye as we skied gate for gate, neck and neck. There was a tough gate a few from the finish line that I knew I had to nail if I had a shot. I committed to my line and my outside ski picked up early and brought me on a tighter line than expected. I closed my eyes and went through the panel of the gate, making it through cleanly and with good speed out the other side. We crossed the line and I finished

0.10 ahead of him. Mattias and I met in the finish area and hugged, congratulating each other on a great race, recognizing the level we'd found was only thanks to the effort given by the other.

After this, Erin narrowly lost to Maria Pietilä Holmner, and Phil, up against the reigning World Cup overall slalom globe winner in André Myhrer, lost in a valiant effort, a mountain too high to climb. We lost three to one but were moving on to the small finals against the Germans and competing for a bronze medal. We were still alive!

Taking the quick chairlift ride to the start, we regrouped in a little huddle again before our time.

"See, anything is possible, let's keep focussed, go out hard, and we never know what can happen," I said while Phil and Erin led us in another little cheer.

Britt was first up again for the team, against Lena Duerr, a strong slalom skier who had won this similar event a few weeks prior in Moscow. I was next up, going against another friend, Felix Neureuther, who was currently ranked third in the slalom overall title race and was also a fan favourite. He definitely had the crowd behind him. Then it was Erin against Maria Höfl-Riesch, also ranked third in the slalom standings, and Phil would bring us home against Fritz Dopfer.

I looked around the start area. The ski technicians moved more slowly now; with fewer athletes around they more easily matched the skis in their hands to the feet of their athletes. The head coaches stood around a small TV, watching the race, as the start installation blocked any chance of viewing it live. It was quiet in our little dark area behind the big Audi start wall. On the other side of it, gunpowder burned and a sea of red smoke filled the air; the fans were setting off their flares early in anticipation of an Austrian victory—a quintessential piece of a Schladming night race.

Britt and Lena left the start and I watched from behind, hoping for the best. Britt had a great performance, her best skiing of the night by far, but was outmatched by Duerr, who took the win. Felix and I then came into our respective gates, and I looked over at him, knowing what it would take to beat him, knowing he was at his peak.

I turned back to see the course. *Pick up the ski early, move over the outside, commit to the line*, I said to myself, swaying back and forth gently. The sound of the crowd was just a vague roar in the background.

My nerves called for my attention, and my attention came to meet my nerves—the balance was there again.

"Attention, racers."

There was no other time but now.

On the final beep, we pulled out on course.

I knew Felix was a fierce competitor and he wasn't going to give me an inch. *Find the front of the ski, move over it.* I was committed from the first gate.

As the hill broke over and got steeper, the demand on our bodies grew and the force to need to hold the line was intense. I couldn't see Felix at all. He must be close.

At the tough gate near the finish, I again committed to taking the aggressive line, inside the rut. This time, as my skis picked up and I felt a familiar pain in my ribs. The intercostal muscle tear from a couple of years ago had come back, but the piercing sting didn't do anything to slow me down in the moment. It would only be later that I'd have to deal with this. I kept up my intensity to the finish and crossed the line 0.07 seconds ahead of Felix.

I couldn't believe I'd beaten him. This was the closest to perfection in a run that I'd ever experienced in my career. Every turn was exactly where I needed it to be and had been performed exactly how I'd envisioned it. This was magic in movement.

Felix and I hugged in the finish. I was ecstatic and he was disappointed, but we both showed our respect. I found my way to Britt in the finish, and we turned back up to watch Erin take the gate. She shot out of the start, nailing the timing with the dropping of the gate and was neck and neck with Höfl-Riesch. The two of them went back and forth, slightly exchanging the lead as Britt and I held our breath. Near the bottom Erin pulled slightly ahead and took the win by the narrowest of margins in an outstanding performance, 0.01 seconds ahead. We were up two to one for the bronze medal.

Erin came over to us with her hands still in the air and a big smile across her face. The three of us stood together and sent our energy back to the start with Phil.

"Attention." We felt like we could hear the starter getting them ready.

They burst out of the gates, with neither one looking like they held a clear advantage. This would be a big upset for Phil as Fritz had consistently been in the top ten in both GS and slalom this season. Like Erin, Maria, Felix and myself, the two of them came down head-to-head, no one willing to give an inch. Something was calling Phil to ski the most disciplined run I'd ever seen him ski—it was beautiful to watch. Britt held on to Erin, with Erin clutching her hands together in front of her face and me shouting, "Come on, Phil!" louder and louder.

As they crossed the line together, we turned to the timing board. Fritz had beaten him by 0.01 seconds; we were tied 2/2 in the heats.

Phil came to join the three of us as we congratulated him and looked at the big screen to see how the tie-break would unfold.

"GERMANY," came across the screen.

They had edged us out for the bronze medal by 0.03 seconds. Their team celebrated and we felt wounded in defeat.

We had come within a hair of a medal but more importantly, we had competed as a team, everyone pulling their weight when needed. We hugged, smiled, and took in the atmosphere around us. Under the lights, in front of the amazing fans, on one of the biggest stages in our sport, we had given our best. This had been a performance to fill our spirits.

Back at the hotel that night, I winced at the pain in my rib as I sat for dinner. Phil and I shared stories from the heats: what he was thinking in the start gate on the last run, what I was going through in the finish. I thought some more about what it meant to be a leader on a team, how to act, what to do, how to inspire. I thought about all Thomas had done for us as I came along, and of the other athletes I admired for the qualities they brought to the team. Tonight felt like my first stab at genuine leadership, a chance to bring everyone together to believe in a common goal. For all the different ways leadership can come through, two things were for sure: it felt far from natural and was something I needed to work on.

CHAPTER 27
YOU KNOW WHEN YOU KNOW

FOR THE LONGEST TIME I imagined I'd race until I was thirty-six years old, compete in four Olympics, win a World Cup, an Olympic medal, and maybe even an overall Globe. Going into my last season, the 2013/14 Sochi Olympic season, I was thirty-two years old, had a chance to compete in my third Games, and had no idea I was going to retire. There were some extra changes within our team; I switched ski technicians, as Rossignol moved Yul to work with their young superstar, Norwegian Henrik Kristoffersen. Some more athletes also retired, like teammate Trev White, and an uncommon change happened for an Olympic season: two new lead coaches were hired, Italians Max Carca and Paulo Deflorian, to take the helm.

On a personal level, I made changes in my own approach to competition. All the techniques I'd built up over the years to facilitate performance: the distraction tools, positive self-talk, walls of mental toughness built to block out the negative thoughts and avoid the fear no longer were of interest. I'd lost all energy to use them. In their place, I decided that I would be committed to feeling the nerves, being with the emotions and the firestream of negative what ifs. It had been three years of wanting to do this and finally I stopped running, ready to see what was on the other side.

Life on the road also changed for me, and I found myself paying more attention to the places I was going and the people who were helping us along the way. On the flight down to Ushuaia, rather than bombarding myself with movies, music, books, radio shows, and entertainment, I sat longer with nothing in my ears, listening to the noise of the flight and looking around. During a short stopover in Santiago, Chile, before continuing to Buenos Aires, I got off the plane and started walking up the jetway. Through the windows I looked outside and there in the sky was a beautiful full moon. I stopped and stared, my ski boots slung over my shoulder, swaying a bit as my teammates and the other passengers brushed by. When we arrived in Ushuaia, I stood outside of the airport terminal, waiting for our team bus and looked around. The snow-covered mountains were directly to my left, the ocean and long coastline in front, blowing cool, salty air past me while the city sat just up the hill, bringing with it the smell of smoke from burning fuels.

"It's so beautiful here," I said, like this was my first, not fourth, time landing here.

During the camp, in the afternoons between skiing and dryland, I would have normally spent my time napping or watching movies or TV shows on my computer. I now found myself going for walks through town, heading down side streets, along the ocean, and paying more attention to the historical landmarks and the people making them up. I was less inclined to judge it so quickly as good or bad, a common practice when travelling with the team, but rather coming to understand it and seeing how it all ticked.

When back at home, I settled into a similar routine. My trips to and from the gym were part of the day rather than an obstacle to my destination, and I was also exploring new ways of training, trying to incorporate more creativity into my sessions. A lot of this wasn't due to some virtuous sense, though—most was from the physical limitations I had after years of pushing my body. I couldn't handle the same forces, sustain the same intensities as I once could, and my range of motion had diminished along with max strength. This was not easy to accept, and there were times that I didn't and pushed too much, but slowly I was learning to listen and give in to what my body was telling me.

In October 2013, before heading to a pre-season camp in Hintertux, Austria, I felt like I didn't want to go back on the road. Not a totally unusual feeling, it had been there at other times in my career, but back then it had soon been followed by a rush of excitement at the hopes of a potential result. In the middle of the night before leaving for this trip, though, I woke up with piercing pains in my stomach. I sat up and rested on the edge of my bed, my feet on the ground, and I winced as waves of this pain washed through me. Eventually deciding it had to be food poisoning, I went to the bathroom and sat on the toilet.

"Ugh," I groaned loudly to an empty house—there was no one to hear me. "What do I do? Do I go to the clinic, do I call my mom, what should I do?"

Another wave of pain came through my stomach, like a series of hands clenching at my insides.

"Ughh!" The more I groaned, the more it blocked out this sensation.

Be with the pain. A voice had come into my head. *Be with the pain*, it said again.

I wondered if this was the same as being with the nerves at a race. *What do I have to lose?* I thought.

In this moment, rather than avoiding and fighting the pain, I turned my focus towards it and gave it my attention. It was searing, sharp, and blinding. I shut my eyes, held back any groans, and did everything I could to keep my attention on the pain. Maybe this wasn't food poisoning but severe nerves about the travelling itself.

The next thing I remember was waking up on the bathroom floor, dazed and confused. I opened my eyes and pushed myself to my feet, using the vanity to prop me up. When I stood up, I looked to the floor; there was blood on the ground. In a panic, I looked in the mirror. I was bleeding from a cut just above the middle point between my eyes. Still very confused and unsure of how long I'd been out for, I cleaned up. I had passed out from the intensity of the pain, fallen off the toilet, and cut myself on the tiled floor.

I slowly made it back to bed, the pain in my stomach dissipated, and I fell asleep. The next morning, I got up, continued my pre-travel preparations, made my way to the airport, got on the plane, and flew to Europe... all the while trying to make sense of this strange event.

• • •

I was hot and cold in the opening races of the season. There were some fast sections, some good runs, but I was never putting it together. I struggled to find consistency in my equipment setup, but the biggest challenge was the intensity of nerves I was feeling on race days. This declaration about wanting to experience fear rather than block it out seemed to have opened some flood gates, and the sensations were almost too much.

The third World Cup slalom of the season was in Bormio, Italy and just after the New Year. On the drive to the resort, heading north from Milan, through Como and Lecco, my mind toiled over what was happening to me. I felt like I had regressed twenty years in my performance skills and searched for answers for what was wrong. It was taking up so much energy to even get to the start gate, let alone to push out and ski.

The morning of the race, I woke up and felt scared to put myself out there. I loved skiing, I loved racing, yet I was beginning to feel too vulnerable out in that space. Even before breakfast I felt paralyzed, and the techniques I'd developed over the years no longer felt relevant. Our drive to the hill wound down the valley. The snowbanks were piled ten feet high on either side, walls of white with only some blue sky above.

I looked back from shotgun as Cousi chirped Phil in the backseat for something he'd previously done in the summer. "Eh Phil, remember when you... haha." Cousi laughed at his own comment, clearly not ready to let Phil live the event down. Even though I was going through the motions, I still felt bogged down and the phrase that had come to me fifteen years prior in Sun Peaks came into my head: *Go to the start.*

I started bib-25 this race and with the top seven of Matt, Kostelić, Hirscher, Hargin, Neureuther, Myhrer, and Mölgg having already left the gate, I had about twenty minutes until my run and the nerves were starting to take over. I put in my earphones to block the internal noise and hit play on my favourite songs, but soon even this felt like wasted energy.

What am I running from? I thought.

I looked around at all the athletes doing their routines, going into their corners, and preparing themselves mentally and physically for the fight. I stood still, returning to my thoughts, feeling so scared but unwilling to do anything to combat it. Clicking into my skis and sliding into the lineup behind the Slovenian Mitja Velenčič, bib-24, the fear grew more intense. I told myself that I knew what to do, that I just had to commit to the front of the ski, that this wasn't as big a deal as my body was telling me it was.

Here I was starting my 108th World Cup, and I felt like a total beginner. Every muscle in my body tightened up. I stood tall and tried my best to play the role of a confident athlete, but there wasn't a cell in my body that believed this.

Go to the start.

"Racer ready, go!" the starter called.

I pushed out. This was the only thing I could do.

The run felt manufactured, like I was skiing from an instruction manual on this turny course set, and I laboured my way to the finish. I came down into twenty-third, in the last of the finishers so far in the run, and slowly watched as racer by racer came down with faster times, pushing me out of the top thirty and into thirty-fourth place. My race day was over.

Our Rossignol team manager, Jeff, came over to talk and strap up my race skis. "Mike, you looked a little tight out there. It didn't seem like your day." He was trying to be supportive, but I just felt embarrassed and couldn't leave the finishing area fast enough.

What is wrong with me? Why can I no longer handle the nerves? I was distraught.

For the following four World Cups, the classics of January: Adelboden, Wengen, Kitzbühel, and Schladming, I was a little more comfortable with the nerves. With no distractions like music or repetitive self-talk, all my energy was put into feeling the nerves, and to cope with them, I turned to noticing the world around me. In Wengen, I was in awe of the mountains, and in Kitzbühel, I marvelled at the crowd like it was my first race. The intensity remained, and though I continued to feel like a total newbie in the start, there was an acceptance starting to grow with this as well.

Well, I'm here. I might as well just go to the start.

By the end of the Schladming night race, I was so exhausted from the rollercoaster of the last month, I was ready for a break. With some top-thirty results, I'd qualified for the Olympic slalom through the B criteria, and even though I hadn't found my form yet, I was hoping for some magic to come for the big event. There was something developing in this new way, I just needed to keep with it.

• • •

Back home in Whistler, I had a week to rest and recover before flying back over to Italy for a pre-Olympic prep camp and then on to Sochi, Russia.

The first few days were spent reflecting a lot on the season, wondering if I was making the right decision with this approach, seeing as my results were so far from where my goals were set.

I woke up one morning with an urge to reignite the spark I'd once had. "I need to find the fire again!" I told myself and went out to the trails behind my house.

It was a mild, Coastal Mountain winter's day, and the sun was out. I started hiking behind the row of houses that sat on the edge of the trees, through the forest and up the mountain.

"Where is my hunger? Where's the Mike who brought the energy, who always had the drive to win?" I put these questions out there, feeling, wishing that something would come. After forty-five minutes of hiking up at a good pace, I reached my destination, a little lake tucked in the crater of one of the old volcanoes of the area. There was no one around, just some warming snow falling from the trees in the afternoon sun. With no real appetite to hang around for too long, I turned back the way I'd come and started to walk slowly, no longer asking and searching, just enjoying the trail.

At the midway point of the return, in a favourite part where the old-growth trees spaced the canopy out enough to let the light reach the forest floor, my pace slowed to a light walk. I savoured the smell of pine and cedar coming out from the snow, where patches of moss were uncovered and sparkling in the sun. In this unexpected moment of clarity, a voice came through once again: *It's time,* it said. A flash of insight,

It's time. These words came to me again, and with them a heaviness I didn't even know I was carrying fell from my shoulders.

It was time for me to retire.

This moment was like a match igniting in a dark room, and I could see everything so clearly. "Ahhh!" I let out a career's worth of breath with a big exhale.

Everything was silent as I smiled and looked around. I had been given permission to let go, and it was such a relief. I continued down the trail, completely empty except for this feeling of peace.

I sat in this bliss for a little over an hour on my couch, just enjoying the feeling. But after a while, this doorway started to close, and like a wave of necessity, the fear came crashing back and panic set in. *No, no, no. I can't retire. I'm not ready, I still have more to accomplish. I've never won a World Cup, I haven't won a globe, I can't do this yet.*

Even as I floundered in these waters, the memory of the hike was still there. The feeling about retirement was so strong, I knew it was the right thing to do. It didn't even feel like my decision; it had been given to me ready-made, and I just had to follow through with it. Still, at first I tried bargaining and thought about holding off my final decision until after the Olympics. *Maybe with a great result I can keep going?* But deep down I knew I had to make it official before I got on the plane. I had to honour this gift, but who could I tell?

I chose to tell my friend Nenad. Nenad was in charge of Rossignol ski racing for Western Canada and was a big reason I had made the switch to the company in the first place. Over the years we'd become friends, routinely talking through different stages of my career, a confidant and mentor on many occasions.

We met for a coffee.

"Nenad, I have to tell you something. Can I trust you not to say anything?" I spoke in a quiet voice, looking around, worried that someone else would hear my secret.

"Mike, yes, of course. Come on. For sure you can trust me," he replied, repeatedly moving his upward-facing hands towards himself and back to me again, a gesture you might see in a *Goodfellas* movie.

"Ok." I paused for a moment, knowing once I said it out loud it would be real. "I've decided that I'm going to retire at the end of the season."

With no more than a second going by and a simple wave of his hand, Nenad responded, "Yes, I know this." He picked up his cappuccino and sipped the coffee through the foam.

"You know this? How could you possibly know? You're the first person I'm telling!"

"Mike." He put down his cup. "I know you for how long now? I first met you when you were twelve years old. When I would see you working out in the ski club gym over the years, you always did more, pushing harder, you had a fire in your eyes. I knew you wanted to win."

As I listened intently through his Serbian accent, he surprised me with his insights. He continued, "Last summer, I saw you working out—it was nice, but it wasn't the same. You have new interests, other things in life, this is ok. You're ready, Mike, it's a good decision." He spoke so matter-of-factly, like a similar premonition had come to him as well, to which he most likely responded by saying, "Yes, I know this."

The second person I needed to tell before leaving was Mom. The next day, we went for a ski together up Blackcomb. I had grown up learning on Blackcomb, skiing as a family, going through all the little tree runs, chasing my sister, thinking one day I'd be as good as my mom. The two of us did some of these runs for old time's sake, while Mom reminded me of all the stories and where they'd happened. For lunch we went to Christine's, the sit-down, fine-dining restaurant built into the lodge at the top of the mountain. Mom had some vouchers given to her by clients that she was excited to use. We were seated at a table beside a window looking north-west, facing towards Sproatt and Rainbow mountains, with the valley lakes frozen below. A favourite view of ours. We'd come here as kids for special occasions, and I'd always order the black bean soup. I reminded Mom of this, and she smiled.

We poured each other some water and both turned back to look out the windows. After all the years that had passed, from racing my sister down the mountain to joining the ski club, going through the injuries, the financial challenges, the highs and lows, and now I was sitting here realizing I'd lived out my ten-year-old self's dream and was ready to call it a career. The scenery had remained the same through all of this, still neutral and providing a sense of home.

I turned back to Mom. "I've decided to retire," I told her.

She looked a little surprised but was smiling. "I figured something was up." Her smile grew bigger.

She shared a similar sentiment to Nenad—she had seen a change in me as well, that the fire was not the same and other interests had grown. I thanked her for everything she'd given us: for her and Dad's countless hours of volunteering, for driving us to all our commitments, for supporting me and being with me through all the lows.

We hugged and cried. "It was all worth it," she said as she wept. "It was all worth it."

My decision to retire wasn't a calculation, it wasn't forced or sought after, and I hadn't even had an inkling that it was coming. It was only in that moment of clarity where I could see, and not a moment before.

You know when you know. Was a phrase I'd heard from retiring athletes in the past.

I understood this now, and it was time.

CHAPTER 28
THE SOCHI GAMES

MY RELATIONSHIP WITH THE OLYMPICS had always been conflicted: on one hand, this was the event that had sparked my athletic dream, and on the other, I'd never come out on top. Before the Vancouver Games, I had heard an interview with Bode Miller saying that he wanted to be more part of Team USA, and other athletes had shared similar sentiments over the years. This was going to be my goal for Sochi. No longer seeking isolation and not scared I wouldn't achieve my desired result, I made a choice to be a part of the team, to get over myself and participate. I wanted to join in.

In the spring of 2013, the Canadian Olympic Committee (COC) hosted another Excellence Series in Vancouver. The three-day event again brought potential Team Canada winter athletes together for team-building exercises, to listen to guest speakers, and to learn logistical details about the upcoming Games in Russia. We arrived at the Sheraton Wall Centre on a May spring day, most of us coming off our down time or light training schedules. Once checked in, our gear placed away in our rooms, we headed for our welcome event in one of the banquet rooms. I loved walking the hallways and seeing the athletes I admired, some friends, others I'd never met; I was still a fan of sport, and this was still a childhood dream come true.

The first team-building exercise was to come up with team values, who we wanted to be, and how we wanted to be seen. There were about a hundred coaches and athletes in the ballroom, all sitting at round tables of ten to twelve, spread throughout to fill the space. Each person had to write ten words down that they felt best described who they wanted to be as an athlete for these games. Then the table came together to narrow everyone's words to the best ten for the group.

Once each table was done, we then gathered with a few more to bring our thirty or so words down to ten. We continued this pattern of gathering into larger groups, combining and whittling down our lists until the room was split in two and each side called out their top eight. After cancelling out the duplicates, our facilitators wrote out the final twelve words on separate pieces of paper, each held up by their own easel in front of the room. From these, we had to narrow them down to five. Everyone was given a bunch of colourful dot stickers, and in small groups, we came forward in our time, placing the stickers on the words that resonated with us the most. This was our voting system and everyone was cracking jokes, laughing and having fun.

When the votes were tallied, we had our final words: *Fierce, Proud, Unstoppable, Stoked,* and *Inspired.* Actually, there was one word that received the most votes, which was *Sexy,* and though it had received more than double than any other words, the COC figured that it wasn't suitable for the ad campaigns. So, the official five words were the former, but Sexy was kept for us athletes, which embodied them all.

With a team identity established, we moved into the guest speakers. The first was John Herdman, head coach of Canada's women's soccer team, which was fresh off its bronze-medal performance in the 2012 London Games. He spoke about his coaching story of coming to the Canadian team, the power of being vulnerable, and how he built trust with the group. After his talk, the athletes around my table were all expressing a desire to have him coach their teams. I felt the same way.

Clara Hughes and Jean-Luc Brassard were two other speakers who stood out. Clara, always open and gregarious, stood in front of her athletic peers and started with, "I'm nervous speaking in front of all of you. It's such an honour to be here."

She shared her story of what had inspired her to be an Olympian, watching Gaétan Boucher skating on TV and saying, "I want to do that." I thought of my own inspiration. She spoke with such vigour, such life. I was moved.

When Jean-Luc spoke, he opened up about his story with the media during his Olympics in '94 and how a misunderstanding can turn into a disaster. He spoke with such a deep perspective and acceptance of the situation.

I was in awe of all of them; they were superheroes yet so deeply human at the same time. Participating in the activities over the three days, I worked on putting my ego aside and slowly started to feel the power of a team. I don't know if I left feeling *Fierce, Proud, Unstoppable, and Stoked,* but I was *Inspired* and maybe just a little more *Sexy.*

• • •

Our Olympic prep camp for the slalom team started in Val di Fassa, Italy. The opening ceremonies had already happened when we touched down in Europe, and it was still a strange feeling to be so far away with only ten days to our race. But this was to be expected by now, and was the life of a slalom skier, always competing on the last day. Our new Olympic gear waited for us in Italy, and the men's slalom team was Trev Philp, Phil Brown, Brad Spence, and me. The Christmas morning excitement with the new apparel had worn off slightly, except for watching Trev and Phil go through their stuff, each one finding a new piece, coming out with it on display.

"Check out this hat! Did you see the closing ceremony coat?!" Their excitement was enough to bring a smile to my face.

For the final leg into Russia, we flew on an FIS charter from Zurich to Sochi, the plane full of slalom skiers and staff, the last load into the village for the tail end of the Games. I sat beside one of the young up-and-coming Swiss skiers, Michelle Gisin. This was her first Olympics, and with it, she had some questions about what my experiences had been like. We talked back and forth about ski racing, competition, and the life of high performance.

"I get so nervous in the start," she shared. "When I'm in the start gate for a slalom, so many things can happen, you can ski out so easily, and I think that I'm never going to do this. Sometimes I can hardly move."

At this point in her career, she had won some Europa Cups, had finished a few times in the top thirties in World Cup, and even had a top ten. She had results and yet was almost at a loss for how to manage the stress.

"Have you felt this before? Do you feel like this?" she asked.

I wanted to laugh when she asked this. "Oh, yeah! And for some reason, now more than ever." I shared my experiences with nerves and being paralyzed by fear in the start gate, though being almost twelve years her senior, I felt a little sheepish to admit that. Neither of us had any answers, it was just nice to know that we weren't alone in our experiences.

We circled the Black Sea a few times before the plane touched down in Sochi and we stepped off to a balmy fifteen degrees, with palm trees lining the road. On the drive into the main athlete village, I wondered where the snow would be; these were supposed to be the winter Olympics. I'm sure some people thought the same when they had come to Vancouver four years ago as well.

We walked the main village streets since we had a few hours before bussing up to the mountain village of Rosa Khutor. Of course, we had to use our credentials in as many places as possible in the meantime: to the athlete meal tent, Canada House for the public, and the Canadian Athlete House. I had learned enough over the years that I could enjoy these moments and that the worrying about performances would come soon enough.

On our hour and a half drive up to Rosa Khutor, the nerves did come. Soon my stomach felt upside down, and all the what ifs around performance started to arise. I knew my skiing had been nowhere special this season, but I was hoping for something magical. *Go be a part of the team. Feel inspired. Take in this experience,* I told myself, knowing this was my last Games.

Successfully going through all the security checkpoints, we finally stepped onto the grounds of the Olympic Mountain Village. The mountains were big, similar to the Coastal Mountains of BC, and given the right temperatures, this place received a lot of snow. Now in mid-February, though, it was warm, and bare patches were starting to show through. All the buildings were new, apartment complexes ranging in size from four to eight storeys high, with different nations housed in each. The flags hanging from the balconies were to let the village know who was where. Spread out over a kilometre or so, the buildings staircased up the slope, climbing until the base of the mountains, where the different events like ski cross, nordic, alpine, slopestyle, and halfpipe took place. There were communal international zones with a gym, the food hall, and Games pavilions. The grounds around the buildings were still unfinished, which was to be expected, and it was the people who filled the streets and buildings that made it feel like home soon enough.

Our Team Canada group of mountain athletes was big enough to have our own building, and inside we were escorted to our alpine floor and shown to our rooms. The hallways were cold, with tiled floors and cement walls, and they were painted with neutral colours. Luckily, the COC staff had been there for a bit and had warmed the place up with decor and reminders of home. We walked to the wood-veneered door that had our names on it: *Spence/Janyk*, it read on a print-out piece of paper.

Brad and I walked into a simple room with two single beds, a bedside table, closets, and a bathroom, just the necessities for the trip. Our room had a special surprise in it as well.

"Jan, what the hell are you doing?" Brad called out.

Lying on one of the beds, curtains drawn, sleeping in the dark, was Jan Hudec, catching a little cat nap. Two days prior, Jan had pulled off a feat no Canadian had managed in twenty years, since Ed Podivinski's bronze in 1994; he had won an Olympic medal. Known as a race-day performer, Jan had capped his career with a bronze medal in the super G, tying with Bode Miller.

"Oh, ugh, hey, guys. I hope you don't mind, I don't have a room anymore," he said, rolling over to face us.

"Of course you don't, Jan," Brad and I said in unison while laughing. This was a classic Jan moment.

After the speed events, Jan had decided to stay in Sochi to do some media and enjoy the rest of what the Games had to offer for a medal winner. The one thing they didn't offer was a consistent bed, and he'd been bouncing between the coast and mountain villages, wherever his next engagement took him. It was a wild ride for him, but even more so for his media attaché, our alpine media person, Keith Bradford, who did his best to try and keep up with the whirlwind that is Jan.

"What time is it?" Jan asked.

"It's 3:00 p.m." we replied,

"Oh frick, I'm supposed to be doing something on the coast in thirty minutes. Has anyone seen Keith? Frick, has anyone seen my medal?"

We chuckled and shook our heads, so happy for our friend and teammate. His result was a stamp on our whole generation of Canadian ski racers.

Jan got up and headed for the door. "Hey, good luck, boys. Go for it, I'll be watching!" he said as he dialled Keith on his phone, returning the multiple missed calls from him.

• • •

Over the next few days we settled into a routine of training in the morning, mixed with dryland and viewing some Alpine events while lying low. At this point in our preparation, the time on snow was really to keep our timing up, get a feeling for the conditions, and raise the intensity a little. Three to four runs in the course per day, nothing much, just a little tickle.

Britt was over here commentating for the Olympic broadcasting consortium, and I met her for coffee in one of the hotels down in Rosa Khutor, another newly constructed town. The main stroll sits along the river that runs through it, down from the mountains, with paved walking streets on either side.

Britt and I ordered a couple of cappuccinos and sat at a window seat overlooking the river. It was raining outside.

"Britt, I'm retiring after the season," I said to her matter-of-factly and went on to tell her how I'd come to this decision.

She sat there smiling and listening, the way we'd listened to each other throughout our whole careers, knowing no matter what, that when it came to ski racing, the other would understand. We took a sip of our coffees again, and I looked out the window to the river and people passing by.

"It sounds like you've made your decision," she eventually responded, and I nodded my head in agreement.

"I'm happy for you," she said. There wasn't much more to say.

We got up and hugged. This was the end of an era for us, a small moment for the family that we got to share.

Canada House had a few common rooms set up to watch TV, and sitting there with the athletes from other sports, watching all the remaining events and hearing the athletes' insights was so much fun. Even more so was celebrating as a team at moments like when Marielle Thompson and Kelsey Serwa won gold and silver in the women's ski cross. We had felt the nerves collectively and cheered and celebrated our teammates from the comfort of the couches, knowing our turn was next or that for others it had come and gone.

Another room set up was a relaxation, yoga, meditation room, a place to get away from the noise if needed. The room was filled with some mats, shelves with books, bean-bag chairs, speakers to play music, and an air diffuser.

The nerves were getting more and more intense as the days went on and finding my ability to be with this feeling was becoming harder. "Don't run from this," I told myself, "Stay with the feeling."

The night before my race, I woke up just before midnight and couldn't fall back to sleep, a normal experience before a big race. I lay there, my mind racing over all the possibilities, all the things that could go right or wrong, one keeping me up with excitement, the other with worry. After thirty minutes of this, I got up and went down to the relaxation room. I went through the books on the shelf, which had some titles like *Be Here Now* by Ram Dass or *The Little Book of Wisdom* by the Dalai Lama. Also on the shelves was a series of Canadiana books, stories of Canadian history and heroes. I picked up one, which went through the different landscapes and main landmarks of the country, a book you'd see on a cottage coffee table. Flipping through, I read about the Atlantic provinces, to the Great Lakes, the prairies, Northern Canada, across the Rockies, and to the West Coast. Every page told me a different story. I thought about my drive across the country and all the places I had yet to visit; there was so much I didn't know.

When I got to the West Coast section, there was a picture of the Capilano Suspension Bridge, set deep in the old-growth coastal rainforest of Vancouver. I was instantly teleported back to my childhood, seeing Mom driving us across the city, from sport to sport and picturing my grandfather first coming to Canada and falling in love with the mountains. I thought about all I'd been given just to be here, that all of us athletes had been given by families, coaches, friends, and community members from across the country. I started to cry, weeping in big sobs. All the emotions I'd been holding in were finally free to come out, and there was nothing but silence between my whimpers.

This is what is meant by feeling the support of a country behind you, I thought.

After three Olympics, five World Championships, and nine seasons on the World Cup, I was experiencing it, and when I settled, I closed the book and put it back on the shelf. It was 1:30 a.m. and time to go to bed.

• • •

The morning of the race I was still hoping for a miracle result but had made peace with myself and felt like I was ok with whatever would happen. It was a night race, with first run at 5:00 p.m. and second at 8:00 p.m. I had time in the day to prepare and stew in the discomfort of the unknown.

Just go to the start.

Part of me wanted to run away, to call it quits right there in the morning. It was really strange to think this on the morning of the Olympic slalom, but there was rarely logic to the thoughts and emotions that ran through my mind on race days.

Just go to the start.

Brad, Trev, Phil, and I left for the hill at different intervals, and I left thinking how in these next six hours I could return with a medal, and everything could change. Part of me knew, though, medal or no medal, nothing would change at all. We got on the bus, which drove us to the base of the chairlift and finish area for the alpine event. We then went to the ski technicians' trailers to get warmup skis, to the athlete lounge to boot up and suit up, and then headed out for warmup and inspection.

The hill was interesting, a narrow start area and opening pitch with some cool little micro terrain, side hills, rollers, and break overs onto a flat section before breaking over one last time onto a medium steep pitch and into the finish. The hill had character. With the warming temperatures, it was very spring-like. After the race organizers had already put a ton of fertilizer on it to try and keep it hard for the men's and women's combined slalom races, plus the women's slalom event the night before, we were left with a rotten snowpack, over-saturated with chemicals that crumbled underfoot. These were unique conditions, something I'd experienced before but not too often, and yet somehow the organizers had found a way to get some water mixed back in, doing a good-enough job to harden the surface back up for two more runs on it.

I rode the high-speed quad chairlift up for my first run. Inspection was done and there was little to do but find my zone to perform. I stood at the top of the hill with my nerves and the worry of what ifs still trying to take over my body.

"Just stay with this feeling, be with it," I told myself and pushed off for a free ski turn as I made my way down to the start.

I made it to the start area with seven racers before I had to go, and my service man, Juri, spotted me to check my skis and prepare us for the run. In the start I felt the nerves—all the time leading up to this, all the sleepless nights, the epiphanies, and decisions, here we were, back in the start, back in the gate.

I gave a fist bump to my physio, Stefania, and then to Juri. The technician is always last.

"Come on, Mike," Stefania called out from behind me as I clicked my poles twice and placed them over the wand.

"Come on, guy," Juri shouted in his Italian accent.

This was it, there was no turning back.

I pushed out and instantly went searching for the feeling I'd had free skiing down. It was there to some degree but not fully; the spark was missing, and I felt a little flat. I knew without the confidence in my skis and on the snow, I couldn't take too many risks.

I finished the first run in twenty second, only two seconds out. My chances for a medal were most likely gone but in this tight race, I still had a shot at a good result.

For my second run, the fire wasn't there at all. I tried to manufacture some intensity but to bring myself to a level required to be competitive with the best in the world, it can't be forced. I crossed the finish line with a sense of relief. I was both sad and happy, a rare moment where these emotions could coexist. I watched as the veteran Mario Matt won his first Olympic medal, well deserved, and behind him the next generation of ski racing, Marcel Hirscher and Henrik Kristoffersen in silver and bronze. I finished sixteenth for my last Games.

I did the media scrum walkthrough; there wasn't much to do besides one stop with CBC. In my interview, I announced this was my last Olympics, that I would retire at the end of the season. It felt good to let it out.

Following the snake of fencing to the exit, I thought back to Torino and seeing my hometown friends Tony and Ben unexpectedly greet me with an embrace. Then in Vancouver, the families who so kindly had lifted my spirits by sharing the inspiration the Mike and Manny camp had on their kids. Now here in Russia, at my exit, there was my old Whistler Ski Club teammate and life-long friend, Ashleigh McIvor who was over here commentating the ski cross events. She gave me a big hug. We walked and talked a bit. I told her that I was retiring, and her face lit up.

"I'm so happy for you, Michael." She's one of the few besides my sisters and mom who calls me Michael. "Life's good on the other side," she said, understanding this moment since she'd retired from ski cross after the Vancouver Games.

"There's so much to do, so much else to life, you'll be fine." She had supported me many times in my life, always there to reignite my love for the sport and self.

Later that night, back at Canada House, I told my teammates and coaches I was retiring.

"No, no, you're not, are you?" Trev said to me, smiling.

Our coach Max enthusiastically tried to convince me otherwise. "Ah, come on, Cico, you still have more to play with."

This felt right, though. It was time to step away.

The next day we went down to the closing ceremonies in Sochi. All the excitement behind me, I was going to enjoy the little moments along the way before we flew out. Morgan Pridy had had a career best, finishing tenth in the super G, and he and I rode bikes around the village, exploring and soaking in the warm, midday sun. All of us skiers who were still left got tickets for the gold-medal hockey game between Sweden and Canada. Unlike 2010, these tickets were a little easier to secure. In a rare moment, there was no guilt associated with enjoying myself this way; usually I would have my thoughts on the next performance, questioning whether my actions now would affect my skiing in the future. This had probably served me well in many circumstances, but here, watching Team Canada defeat Sweden for hockey gold, it felt nice to let go of this burden.

Walking to the stadium for the closing ceremonies, we intermingled with the rest of Team Canada and some international friends we'd met along the way. A collection of us skiers stood at the top of the steps before heading in for the official march. It was Marie-Michèle Gagnon, Brad Spence, Morgan Pridy, Phil Brown, Trev Philp, Erin Mielzynski, and me, some leaving satisfied with our results, others not. This was the nature of sport: there were no guarantees. With the setting sun behind us illuminating the sky, the village, and the Black Sea in the background, we stood together, arms draped over each other's shoulders and collectively smiled for a photo.

We walked into the stadium, where I don't remember much of the entertainment, any of the speeches or spectacles of the night, I just remember the smiles and seeing the faces of teammates, staff, my competitors, friends, and athletes from the other sports. We had put in the dedication to get here, been supported, and had ridden the highs and lows along the way.

Everyone had gone to their respective starts.

CHAPTER 29
THE OTHER SIDE

AFTER SOCHI, I HAD ONE more World Cup to go, the slalom in Kranjska Gora. I wanted to rush towards this finish line, to be done, head home, and escape from the pressure cooker of emotions I was feeling, but there were still a couple of weeks between now and then. I spent some days alone in Cinque Terre, Italy, exploring the towns and reflecting on my decision. These towns are normally bustling with tourists in the summer months, but this being the end of February, they were virtually deserted. I walked the rocky shoreline trails, passing groves of fruit trees, brush, and vines, the rolling greenery to one side and the vast Ligurian Sea on the other. As I wandered the old churches, narrow streets, and markets, I wondered if this was the right call, thinking about the ways I could still be a ski racer, to still live this dream. Every time energy would build, though, the feeling would soon go flat. These were just fleeting cries, with no realness behind them. Plus, the wheels were already set in motion in the other direction.

By the time I rejoined my team, Keith, our now-infamous team media manager had sent out a press release and a small press conference would take place over the phone. The mood in the press conference was celebratory, it was special to recap my career and put everything out there and be ok with it. In the world of professional sports, to retire on one's own terms, not due to injury or lack of performance, is rare and the privilege was not lost on me.

With the excitement of the Olympics and the little media attention settled, I was back into life on the road, the life I'd known for half my years.

Small rooms, teammates, tight quarters, schedules, restaurant mealtimes, routines of breakfast, training, lunch, rest, dryland, video, shower, dinner, rest, sleep, repeat. Dustin Cook was my last roommate, an athlete on the rise to the peak of his career and me at the end of mine. I did my best to not let my fatigue with the lifestyle spill over to his relationship with it.

Our pre-race training camp was up in the northeast corner of Italy, Sella Nevea, only a thirty-minute drive from Kranjska Gora. Dustin and I shared a classic Italian hotel room, small, with two single beds, hardwood floors, and a cozy bathroom with a shower just big enough to stand in and hose not long enough to reach your head. Between the two of us, our four duffel bags of gear left little room to walk, let alone stretch out. For most of my life this had been enough, but the morning of my last week, I was over it.

I woke up a bit before Dustin, wanting to keep up with a morning routine of yoga, while not wanting to disturb him. As soon as I sat up, the bed creaked loudly, I was already making too much noise. I moved to turn off my alarm. *Bang! Thud!*

I had knocked a few things from the bedside table, a clumsy start. I got up, grabbed my bags from the floor, stacked them on the bed to clear some floor space and rolled out a mat to go through some sun salutations. I kept it as quiet as possible and was out the door for breakfast just before Dustin's alarm went off. Coming back later, I quickly opened our room door, grabbed the bathroom handle, and pushed to go in. *Bang.* The door didn't move, and my shoulder slammed into it.

"I'm in here," Dustin called out.

"Yeah, alright," I groaned and took my place in line, sitting on the edge of my bed. *I'm definitely getting too old for this,* I thought to myself while chuckling.

While each day at the hotel felt like an exercise in patience and tolerance, out on the hill was absolute freedom. We were training with the Swedes and the Swiss, a few runs a day, nothing too much, just keeping our pace and playing around with last-minute equipment setup adjustments. As soon as I stepped on the snow and clicked in, I instantly felt so much confidence, like coming back to an old friend. I was smiling, making jokes with the other racers, and in no rush to do my runs.

The Swiss had their timing system set up, optional for whoever wanted to use it, and I felt like timing. I exploded from the start gate, feeling so good on my skis and about everything in these conditions: the snow, the way my skis picked up early in the turn. I felt like a kid playing in the school yard. One run, two, three runs down, and I was either the fastest or in the top three of each run.

I could do this forever.

This thought came to me halfway down my fourth run.

Any distinction between self and hill had gone; I was moving with it and it with me.

On the Friday before the weekend of racing, we made the drive across the border and settled into Kranjska Gora, and this time I got my own room. I pulled my bags out of the van and wheeled them across the parking lot and through the hotel's sliding-glass doors. I'd stayed here a dozen times or so, and the familiar sharp scent of cleaning agents and body odour hit my nose.

"Ahh, home sweet home." I took a breath in with a smile.

The room keys were waiting for us on the front desk, the clerk requiring our passports in exchange for them. I practised the little Slovenian I knew during this transaction, the same thing I try to do with the language of every country we visit.

I opened the door to my room and made an audible exhale to the rare and treasured opportunity of having one's own room while on the road. Two beds, a little sofa, some good floor space, a bathroom and closet. The food and smells are not the best, but the rooms are big—each stop on tour has its own charm. I put my bags in the closet, threw my jacket and backpack on the free bed, and sat on the edge of the other. The blinds were open and the tilt and turn windows were set on tilt, letting a breeze come in. I listened to the sounds coming from the street below, the only one that ran through the village. A few cars drove by, people walked and talked, birds chirped, and everyone was enjoying the early-spring warmth and sunshine. I sat on the edge of the bed and looked around the room; everything in here was unmoving, still, ordinary.

Soon thereafter, the familiar pain in my stomach returned. I was uncomfortable and wanted to get up and run. Instead, I slid off the bed and onto the floor with my knees bent up and into my chest, back against the bed frame.

"I'm going to be with this pain if it kills me," I committed to myself.

Over the next thirty minutes, the valley we were in slowly lost its light. I watched the sun set behind the mountain across the way. It was so peaceful outside, while inside, my mind was racing and my body was screaming. "Be with it," I said. "What's the worst that can happen?"

The next morning there wasn't much to do but watch the GS first run on TV from the comfort of my room. For the slalom specialists, we only had to head out after the GS race was over for the traditional free runs on the race hill. I was there to watch the end of the race in person, enjoying being around my fellow competitors, old friends, and sharing stories with the few who'd been a part of this last decade. There was nothing special in my skiing that day, nothing I was looking for as I normally would have; it was more of a social outing, one of the last chances to savour the atmosphere of the circuit. When I got back to the hotel, my mood had changed. I knew it was time to start preparing in some formal capacity. I changed my ski gear for running attire and took off down the road for my pre-race routine, heading in the same direction I'd gone over the last nine years.

The sun was still out as I ran through town, past the pizzeria, the casino, and beyond the last hotel before passing the village limit. The road took a slight incline, and a walk felt more appropriate at this time. Just before the small bridge, I turned right, off the pavement and onto the hiking path that ran along the river. I continued walking, listening to the water running under the melting ice, the snow collapsing under my feet, and I watched the trees catch the final sunlight of the day. As the trail turned to the right again, I went straight and out onto the open snow field. My body walked from memory; there was no need to tell it where to go.

I stood in the same spot I'd been year after year, in the middle of this drainage with hills on either side of me and the biggest mountain up ahead. Facing west with the sun just off my right shoulder, I had come back here looking for another sign. The first time I'd stood here in 2005, I had left feeling filled with motivation, with permission to go for it the next day. Everywhere I went, I found places like this. No matter where I was, I looked for the same thing and it routinely appeared as if to say, *It's ok, you can free yourself and go for it.*

On this day in March 2014, though, I stood there for some time and nothing came. There was no extra feeling, no voice to say, *You'll win, you'll have the race of your life, you'll be able to do it. Go for it one more time.*

It was just the birds, the water, the snow, and the unmoving mountains, void of any assurance. There was nothing left for me out here: all my time on the road had come to an end. The silence was my confirmation that it was ok to go home. As I turned, I sensed an agreement behind me, and there was peace in it.

I didn't sleep much this night either; my stomach pains had grown throughout the day, and I found myself going back and forth between the bed and bathroom. It was just like when I had started the season back home in Whistler when I'd passed out from the pain, but this time I stayed conscious through the knots grabbing and clenching my insides. I felt like they'd gotten worse. "Just be with the sensation," I told myself. "You said you didn't want to run from the nerves any more. You said you could face them. Here's your chance."

The pain was intense.

I lay there in bed, tossing around, hoping to fall asleep. Eventually it was too much, and I started to play the "remember when" game with myself.

"Remember the first trip to Europe with Dusan. We came here to train, he told us to go free skiing and Ben, Scott, and I just sat at the top for an hour, feeling too tired to ski.

"Remember when we raced here that same trip and I was having the run of the year, I made it through the last gate and somehow missed the finish line for a DNF.

"Remember when Morgan came to watch me race here and I was sixth!

"Remember the Europa Cup, Thomas's podiums, my great performances."

A career of experiences ran through my mind, it soothed me and sleep eventually came.

• • •

It was soon the morning of my last World Cup race. I ran through my warmup and got dressed in my gear for one last time. First my long johns, the base layers, socks, always the same thin black socks, then my down-hill suit and slalom shorts. Each layer was part of the armour, a layer of protection, a layer of comfort. Finally putting on my jacket, now covering my armour, I stood staring at the mostly empty, slightly dishevelled room. How many hotel rooms had I left over the years, to return in elation or disappointment? I didn't want to go. Before, I would leave to find myself, now it felt like I was leaving myself behind.

"Just go to the start," I said. "Go to the start."

Many skiers who announce their retirement race their last World Cup in some ceremonial fashion, wearing traditional or funny outfits, stopping at coaches and officials to say thanks along the way. I thought of this, but I wanted to feel the feeling I had in training. I wanted to use this last opportunity, and there was still a part of me that had something to prove, at least to myself. Warmup was easy. I didn't put too much emphasis on my runs; all I was looking for was this feeling, and it was there. It was so much fun skiing these warmup courses.

In inspection, though, I slid down looking at the course, watching all the athletes around me—their intensity, their commitment, their energy.

I stopped at Paulo, then at Max. I knew what to do, how to run this course, how to ski this hill. I'd done it so many times before. Yet I still asked, "What do you see in this section? Anything special I should be aware of? What's the line?"

In the finish area, I ran the course through in my mind, the routine visualization, but it was all a blur. I couldn't focus enough to see myself skiing, so I gave up and went into the team hospitality area.

Riding up the chair for my first run, I thought, *Do I really need to go up? I want this to be over.* I scolded myself for thinking this, realizing how my younger self would react to this sense of ingratitude towards the opportunity. But I just didn't want to be judged anymore.

"Go to the start," I repeated. "The only way home is through the start."

My pre-race routine was a diminished version of what it once was. With so much energy gone, I did as little as needed to make my way into my skis, get the course report, warm the body a bit, and take my place in line. I clicked my poles twice, planted them, and put my head in between my hands.

"Come on, Mike. One last time."

I pushed out but didn't have the feeling for the skis that I'd had in training all week long.

If I had been standing still, my body language would have had me dropping my head and rounding my shoulders forward in a defeated sulk. This was going to be a laboured run. I had to ski smart and use my brain and experience to make my way over the terrain, through the combinations, and to work with the ruts, not against them. I wasn't going to do anything special with this run and had to ski within myself.

I started with bib-33 and crossed the line into twenty-fifth, with seventy-three people in the race. I thought for sure there would be six racers behind me that would be faster and knock me out of the thirty.

Well, I guess this is it, I thought. *The end of my career, not making the second run.*

I gave a polite wave to the camera and crowd, put my head down, and pushed out of the finish area.

The next racer behind me, the American, Nolan Kasper, came down ahead of me.

Yup, this was going to be over soon.

Bib-37, Akira Sasaki, a long-time competitor and friend, pushed me into twenty-seventh. Bib-39, my World Championship podium-mate, Julien Lizeroux, moved ahead of me, and I sat in twenty-eighth. Shortly behind him, the young Swiss racer with bib-48, Ramon Zenhaeusern, moved me to twenty-ninth. After this, though, no one came down with fast-enough times, I stood watching from the athlete corral area—not moving, just watching. I remained planted in the same spot until racer seventy-three crossed the line and I was assured to be in. Quickly leaving, I made it around for inspection with a renewed sense of confidence.

This time around, I wasn't going to pass up the opportunity to trust myself, to believe in myself the way that my coaches in the past had: Johnny, Mika, Dusan, Igor, Jordan, Maria. I knew what to do.

When I came up to Paulo's section, before he could say anything, I called out, "I got this. I know what to do."

"Are you sure?" he asked.

I'd run this hill over a hundred times, watched hours of video on it, and studied each section: the opening first gates; the gradual, building steepness; the sharp transition to flat; the long, rolling bench where speed can continue to build; and then the gradual falling away of the hill, slowly breaking over to the final, steep pitch that keeps up until the last gate. Before ever seeing it in person, I remembered watching video of this race when I was on the BC team and boasting about how I'd ski it if given the chance. I knew what to do, where to make speed, where I needed a quick switch, a patient transition, or a strong commitment to the outside ski, and when to release into the finish. "Yes, I'm sure," I answered Paolo.

On the chair ride up for this second run, my nerves and the pains in my stomach hadn't changed, and neither had my commitment to be with these sensations. I continued to feel conflicted, wanting to find the energy for one last run, while also not wanting to suck again. I didn't want to go on the course and not be able to ski the way I knew I could.

Go to the start.

I rode the chair with Nolan. We made a few comments back and forth, and I kept it light, not wanting to pass my emotions onto him. He wished me luck as we got off the chair, and I felt his sincerity, as I'd ridden the chair with friends before their last runs too.

"One more run," I said to myself. "One more."

My free ski turns down to the top of the course had felt so good, all I wanted to do was this.

In the start area, I didn't even try to fake a warmup this time. I didn't ask for a course report, I just went over to Juri and Stefania, trying my hardest to not let the emotions take over my mind with stories of what if. Most of my attention was drawn to my nerves, which were spreading beyond the stomach, and any movements I had planned came to a standstill.

All of sudden, as I stood there in the midst of this inner turmoil, everything just went silent. There was no longer any chatter in my mind, and my body was free from its pain. The heavy emotions that had been with me all season, making me more immobilized to perform than ever before, were suddenly gone.

I looked around at the other racers, my friends, my competitors, the technicians, physios, doctors, and officials. I smiled, listening to the clatter of radios, seeing guys visualizing, listening to music, warming up, activating; everyone was getting into their performance zones, reaching for their best. It was so cool. I felt connected to everyone, their warmup was my warmup, their visualizations and efforts; I could feel them too.

I continued to stand in silence for a moment more.

"I'm ready," I told Juri and Stefania, and they nodded back.

I lifted my leg for Juri, who cleaned off the bottom of my boot from snow, whacking it with his screwdriver. I loved this feeling. I clicked into my bindings and heard the sound of my boot snapping into place. So satisfying. I thought back to the Torino Olympics when Mare and I had first developed our start-house routine, and I smiled again.

"Come on, Mikey," Juri called, signalling his job was done. I scanned the start area again and saw Yul preparing skis for his new racer.

He looked over with a gesture. "*Allez*, Mike."

I moved into the start tunnel and did some leg activations, not because I felt the need, but just because when I did, it felt right. I grabbed a handful of the early Spring snow and rubbed on the back of my neck, the cold and granular crystals gently scratched and melted over my skin. A pre run ritual performed so many times before, signaling to my body that its time to go. Done out of habit, out of enjoyment.

My friend, American Will Brandenburg, was at the gate in front of me. We fist bumped and wished each other luck. He went on course, and the start was empty. I slowly made my way between the posts and timing wand as I'd done so many times before, looked out at the course, and said with a smile, "I got this."

There were no doubts, no what ifs. There was no battle between negative and positive thoughts; I didn't have to fight with anything. I just looked out and could see myself skiing the course the way I wanted. I was on. I clicked my poles together, planted them firmly again, and rested my head between my hands for one last time.

"This is it." And I pushed.

I knew right away from the first gate, the second, and third that I was connected to the snow and could do anything I wanted from here on out.

Through the first hairpin I moved quickly, switched early, and got on my new ski to carry speed onto the flats. I worked over all the terrain. I was dancing.

This lovely thought returned: *I could do this forever.*

Around halfway down, I was no longer in my body. I could feel everything that was happening, the inherent joy in the movement, yet I was watching it all from above. I was free from the mind and connected to the body. This was absolutely liberating. I didn't have to do anything but observe some of the best skiing of my life.

On the last pitch, I felt like I deliberately let off the gas a bit. I didn't question it or want to keep going full out, I just marvelled at the control I had to do whatever was needed, to be this precise.

I crossed the finish line with the green light, in the lead by two-tenths of a second, and I put my hands up in celebration. I waved at the crowd and savoured the moment, back in my body now, still feeling the joy it was to ski down that run. I spent some time in the leaders' box, one last visit to this coveted space, and when I got beat, moved into the athlete zone of the finish corral. I kept smiling.

I had spent the last four years wondering what was on the other side of the nerves, and here was my answer. Passing through the fear, judgements, worries, and negative stories I didn't want to believe and the positive ones I so desperately did. All the emotions that had routinely held me back were gone, and I was set free. Free to move the way I'd trained, to ski the way I was capable of, to let go of it all and move as if one with the run. There was no one to take credit for the success or pain for a loss, I was just an audience member with a love for the dance.

I finished fifteenth overall on the day. After some media, hugs, and mini celebrations with friends from other nations, I walked into the team hospitality and ran into Max.

"Hey Cico, are you sure you want to stop now?" he asked with a big smile, almost laughing.

I nodded to assure him the answer was still yes.

"Ok, good to know because you know you won that second run! *Che cazzo,* you had the fastest time."

"Really?!" Now I was laughing. I answered my own question to him without surprise and with a shoulder shrug. "Makes sense."

Max shook his head, laughing.

My response was genuine, though; the run itself was my satisfaction, and the fastest time on the second run, this was just icing on a cake.

Back in my hotel room, I sat once again, still in my bib and race suit. In the morning I had been hesitant to put it on, but now I didn't want to take it off. I sat on the edge of the bed and looked through the items in the room; their stillness persisted.

"I did it," I said to myself.

I had made it through, committed to the process, gone through the pain, lived out my dream, and had come to a place where I could say goodbye.

"You're free to go." I looked carefully at all the items in the room again, each one given their own attention, feeling a warm sense of appreciation.

"I can go home now." I closed my eyes. "I can say goodbye."

The End

EPILOGUE

I NEVER WON A WORLD Cup in my career. When I was a kid, I used to dream of standing on top of the podium, beaming out above the crowd, my family, and friends. It was like these victories would be my saviour. When I did reach the height of my career, a World Championship Bronze medal, I never found the true fulfilment that I thought would come from such a result. The pursuit of this dream had given me so much, it had saved me in a way, but it ultimately didn't offer the wholeness that I thought it would bring.

After the 2010 Games, when I tried to retire with my letter to Kirsten, the main reason I found to continue was for self-discovery. Who was I if I was not fulfilled as a ski racer, as an athlete, as an Olympian? Was the answer more results, ownership, or autonomy in my day-to-day life?

In the last run of my last World Cup race, I was given the answer. Before this, I had never felt this powerful sense of peace in the start, a sense of calm, the original feeling of potential and the joy that came from knowing I could go play. Like a kid in a sandbox, everything I had in front of me was to mould in partnership with the mountain, the course, and the run. I had finally found fulfilment before pushing out of the gate, and in this, I was no longer looking to find myself in the result. I was already complete.

I now work in the development levels of the sport, and as much fun as it is to help an athlete learn how to roll up a ski, carve, and generate speed, what is more rewarding is to help connect them with who they are. Because of the inherent nature of competition and the ever-present opportunity to fail, sport has an incredible potential for self-discovery. In each failure there is an opening to sense who you really are and let go of who you are not. When I spend my time with someone in these moments, my hope is that they are able to sense that I'm seeing them for who they are in their greatest form, for all their potential and everything they want to become. This is the way I remember Mom would look at me as a kid. I could see the recognition and support in her eyes, and even though I got lost along the way, it gave me a place to come home to, a place uninhibited by the external pressures of results, qualifications, contracts, and status. Where competition itself is a joy.

First days on snow

My grandfather, Peter Vajda (back skier) skiing with friend

Britt and I helping Stephanie first ski

First summer camp in Mt. Hood at 13 years old

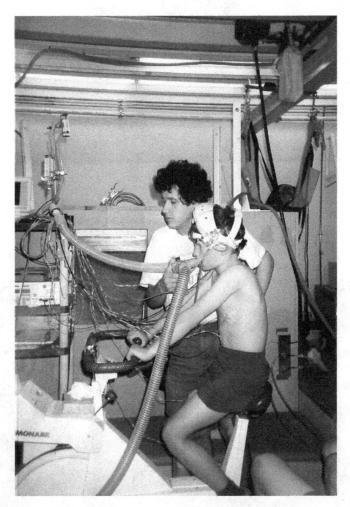

Helping with some research at Simon Fraser University

World Championships, Val d'Isère 2009

Kitzbühel Slalom 2011

On hill with Johnny and Mika

Team shot after a day of skiing in Ushuaia: Back row, left to right - Dave (Physio), Kurt Kothbauer, Paul Stutz, Scott Barrett, JP Roy, Ryan Semple, Marc Gagnon, Mika Gustafsson. Front row, left to right - Johnny Crichton, Patrick Biggs, me, Thomas Grandi

Thomas and Mike, 8th and 7th in Levi, Finland

Putting on the red leader bib in Beaver Creek

Taking a seat minutes before my second run

My service man Yul and I in the Kitzbühel start house

Val d'Isère World Championships podium, Julien Lizeroux, Manfred Pranger, Mike Janyk

Val d'Isère World Championships finish area celebration with coaches, Kip, Mike, Dusan, Johnny

Sochi Olympic Slalom inspection

Team shot in the Sochi Olympic rings in Rosa Khutor. Left to right – Morgan Pridy, Brad Spence, Mike Janyk, Stefania Rizzo, Trevor Philp, Phil Brown

Olympic closing ceremonies Sochi: Trev Philp, Phil Brown, Stefania Rizzo, Mike Janyk, Morgan Pridy

One last finish area inspection – Kranjska Gora, last World Cup race

Schladming World Championships, finish area

Mom and I in my last national championships at home in Whistler 2014. Dressed in ceremonial lederhosen

ACKNOWLEDGEMENTS

WRITING THIS BOOK WAS A cathartic, challenging and incredible process and just like my athletic career, it was supported by many people along the way.

Thank you to my wife, Sarah, who encouraged me and listened to me while I read her the raw and unedited chapters at 3:00 a.m. Thank you to my amazing parents, Bill and Andrée, who provided a life for me to make my dreams come true, and to my sisters, Britt and Stephanie, who put up with me, gave me targets to chase, and helped shape me into the person I've become.

Thank you to my book coach, Les Kletke, who provided structure and kept me going with a chapter a week until it was complete. Thank you to all my unbelievable coaches, from when I was ten years old to my last race, and to my lifelong teammates, ever-encouraging friends, and the community who supported me along the way. I would not have reached these heights and lived out this dream without you. Finally, thank you to my daughter, Poppy, whose arrival into this world helped push this project across the finish line.

ABOUT THE AUTHOR

RAISED IN A FAMILY OF ski racers, Mike Janyk competed on the Canadian Alpine Ski Team for fourteen years, performed in three Olympics, won a World Championship bronze medal, and reached the World Cup podium. He lives in Whistler, BC with his wife, daughter and dog where he enjoys biking, skiing, walking the trails and when life allows for it, doing nothing at all.

Printed in the USA
CPSIA information can be obtained
at www.ICGtesting.com
LVHW092114021123
762799LV00003B/59